Hands-On Healthcare Data
Taming the Complexity of Real-World Data

Andrew Nguyen

Beijing · Boston · Farnham · Sebastopol · Tokyo

Hands-On Healthcare Data

by Andrew Nguyen

Published by O'Reilly Media, Inc., 1005 Gravenstein Highway North, Sebastopol, CA 95472.

O'Reilly books may be purchased for educational, business, or sales promotional use. Online editions are also available for most titles (*http://oreilly.com*). For more information, contact our corporate/institutional sales department: 800-998-9938 or *corporate@oreilly.com*.

Acquisitions Editor: Michelle Smith	**Indexer:** nSight, Inc.
Development Editor: Melissa Potter	**Interior Designer:** David Futato
Production Editor: Christopher Faucher	**Cover Designer:** Karen Montgomery
Copyeditor: Kim Wimpsett	**Illustrator:** Kate Dullea
Proofreader: James Fraleigh	

August 2022:   First Edition

Revision History for the First Edition

2022-08-10:   First Release

See *http://oreilly.com/catalog/errata.csp?isbn=9781098112929* for release details.

978-1-098-11292-9

[LSI]

Table of Contents

Foreword

It is an exciting time to get involved in healthcare data. There is an emergence of advanced technologies, from MLOps to Cloud Computing, that enable new ways to harness machine learning and AI to improve the human condition.

For example, a recent JAMA study (*https://oreil.ly/OjRsv*) showed that neurocognitive decline is associated with a person's decrease in walking speed at age forty-five compared to their pace when they were younger. Imagine being able to send guidance to a 25, 35, or 45-year-old that would improve their future self through the use of machine learning for healthcare. This scenario isn't science fiction; it is possible today.

Similarly, radiology could benefit from advanced computer vision technologies that guide the expert practitioner to look at specific imaging results more closely and automatically identify rare conditions. Primary care physicians could link all available health records automatically to find a complete lineage of medical treatment and improve patient outcomes. These exciting possibilities are on the horizon, but require new ways to work.

The guidance in Andrew's book will get us started on the path to this new world. Healthcare organizations can standardize the creation and processing of healthcare records, thus streamlining the processing of existing and new data, and driving down costs due to efficiency improvements and better treatment outcomes. Several chapters discuss the intricate details of electronic health records data and the associated vocabularies, terminologies, and ontologies. These detailed resources are invaluable for healthcare professionals working to improve how they work with their organization's data.

Further chapters dive into sophisticated technical approaches to solving challenging problems in healthcare. These solutions include coverage of topics like graph-based deep learning, commercial clinical NLP solutions, and data harmonization. Andrew covers these topics from a theoretical standpoint, as well as with hands-on examples with working code.

Andrew's experience with healthcare data and medical informatics makes him the perfect person to propel these discussions. With this book, Andrew gives the reader an excellent opportunity to be part of the drive to revolutionize healthcare and turn what seems like science fiction into our new reality.

— Noah Gift
Executive in Residence, Duke
Master in Interdisciplinary Data Science (MIDS)

Preface

A few years ago, I was at the Google Faculty Institute, where I met Noah Gift during one of the lunch breaks. We got to talking about academia and education, and many of the challenges and opportunities we saw when it came to empowering people to become experts in data. Whether this was data engineering, data science, or even the more basic aspects of programming, we both saw the potential for fundamentally changing how knowledge is disseminated.

It was shortly after this conversation that Noah floated the idea of writing a book. While I had considered this previously, it was a fleeting thought and not something I had seriously considered. I filed the conversation away in the back of my mind and figured it could be the focus of my sabbatical (I was still in academia at the time).

A year later, everything was flipped upside down by COVID-19 and the world's response. Despite having just received tenure and promotion, I decided to leave academia and return to industry—rolling up my sleeves and getting back into the thick of it.

I was a few months into my first project (building a clinicogenomic database that pulled data from a handful of hospitals) when I started to see opportunities to help educate our teams on how we could improve our approach to dealing with the complexities of electronic health record (EHR) data.

By then, we were deep into the pandemic and all riding the roller-coaster of repeated loosening and tightening of the many COVID restrictions. Every day, I saw news articles and reports that were making a desperate attempt to draw conclusions from all of the data and anecdotes about the number of infections, mortality rates, false positives/negatives, and so forth.

As someone who had been working with healthcare data for years, I found it very challenging to listen to data scientists, epidemiologists, public health professionals, and even lay people draw conclusions and make serious decisions based on what I knew was very dirty and faulty data.

It also did not help that COVID-19 became a highly charged and political topic, with people trying to fit the data to preconceived notions, embodying the quote:

> [People] use statistics as a drunken man uses lamp-posts, for support rather than for illumination.[1]

I saw a tremendous opportunity to help people better understand the nuances and complexities of working with data that were collected outside of clinical studies and trials. Healthcare data reflects the underlying complexity of the delivery of care as well as our ever-evolving understanding of biology, physiology, pathophysiology, and interventions.

Whether you are a data scientist or healthcare professional, this book will provide you with a data-centric perspective of various facets of healthcare. It can be difficult to develop the appropriate skills, knowledge, and experience for tackling healthcare data, particularly for those not embedded within medical centers/health systems, public and private payers, or other organizations handling deep patient-level data.

My goal in writing this book is to help bridge this gap, particularly for those who are new to healthcare data. This includes data scientists from other industries and even healthcare professionals who are not familiar with analyzing EHR data. This book also will be useful for epidemiologists, biostatisticians, and data scientists/analysts who have worked with cleaned and processed data, but have not been a part of the data-wrangling process itself.

If you're reading this book, you are interested in working with data and passionate about solving problems in healthcare. However, you might be coming from a more technical, computer science, or data science background. Or, you might be an epidemiologist, researcher, or clinician with domain expertise and training but who is relatively new to working with data at this level.

If you have a technical background, this book will give you a crash course on many of the key learnings from the field of medical informatics over the past several decades. The intent is to help you get up and running more quickly and effectively than if you were to figure it out on your own. I have seen many excellent data engineers and data scientists work their way through one challenge after another, only to have reinvented something that hospital informatics teams have refined over the years. Not only did they reinvent the wheel, they reinvented a square wheel.

If you have a healthcare background, you are used to working with healthcare data but typically from narrow and specific perspectives. As a clinician, you interact with EHRs and other clinical information systems transactionally while caring for patients. As an epidemiologist or clinical researcher, you may have relied on your data and

---

1 For detailed discussion on the attribution of this quote, please see *https://oreil.ly/sqMGO*.

informatics teams to clean and process your data. This book will help you take a step back so you can see the bigger picture and how we can and need to incorporate your knowledge and experience into the data-wrangling process.

The topics we will discuss in this book truly span both technical and domain topics. To be successful with healthcare data, particularly "real-world data" (as we call it in biotech and pharma), you need to have a foundational understanding of both sets of topics.

This book bounces between qualitative discussions of healthcare data and technical walkthroughs. Depending on your background and interest, you might be drawn to some chapters more than others. However, my hope is that you come away from this book with a new perspective and common understanding of the challenges and potential solutions, regardless of your professional background.

As you will see, I also have a deep interest in graphs and graph databases and firmly believe that they are a necessary (but not sufficient) part of our overall solution to leveraging healthcare data at scale. I've taken the liberty of highlighting how many of our challenges can be mitigated or solved using graph databases (versus SQL).

I debated how deep to go into the code examples—too deep and I might lose those with less computer or data science experience; too shallow and you might be left wondering, "That's it?" I tried to strike a balance by walking through a narrow use case, followed by examples of several different approaches. It is impossible to give you a recipe that is universally applicable. There are far too many nuances from one use case to the next. So, my goal was to provide explanations in the context of a use case with the hope and intention that you might adapt this to your own situations and scenarios.

The associated GitLab repository contains examples with more depth. I find examples are always good to get the creative juices flowing. As you think about the ideas in the book or review the code examples, I urge you to always ask yourself:

- How might I adapt this to my use case?
- How is my use case similar or different?
- What would I need to adapt or change in order to make this work for me?

Success with healthcare (real-world) data requires that we be creative with how we frame our use case and how we apply different processes and technology. There is simply no one-size-fits-all solution. So, if you build upon the approaches in this book, please contribute examples back to the repository to help other readers.

I hope you enjoy the journey!

Conventions Used in This Book

The following typographical conventions are used in this book:

Italic

> Indicates new terms, URLs, email addresses, filenames, and file extensions.

`Constant width`

> Used for program listings, as well as within paragraphs to refer to program elements such as variable or function names, databases, data types, environment variables, statements, and keywords.

`Constant width bold`

> Shows commands or other text that should be typed literally by the user.

`Constant width italic`

> Shows text that should be replaced with user-supplied values or by values determined by context.

 This element signifies a tip or suggestion.

 This element signifies a general note.

 This element indicates a warning or caution.

Using Code Examples

Supplemental material (code examples, exercises, etc.) is available for download at *https://gitlab.com/hands-on-healthcare-data*.

If you have a technical question or a problem using the code examples, please send an email to *bookquestions@oreilly.com*.

This book is here to help you get your job done. In general, if example code is offered with this book, you may use it in your programs and documentation. You do not need to contact us for permission unless you're reproducing a significant portion of the code. For example, writing a program that uses several chunks of code from this book does not require permission. Selling or distributing examples from O'Reilly books does require permission. Answering a question by citing this book and quoting example code does not require permission. Incorporating a significant amount of example code from this book into your product's documentation does require permission.

We appreciate, but generally do not require, attribution. An attribution usually includes the title, author, publisher, and ISBN. For example: "*Hands-On Healthcare Data* by Andrew Nguyen (O'Reilly). Copyright 2022 Andrew Nguyen, 978-1-098-11292-9."

If you feel your use of code examples falls outside fair use or the permission given above, feel free to contact us at *permissions@oreilly.com*.

O'Reilly Online Learning

 For more than 40 years, *O'Reilly Media* has provided technology and business training, knowledge, and insight to help companies succeed.

Our unique network of experts and innovators share their knowledge and expertise through books, articles, and our online learning platform. O'Reilly's online learning platform gives you on-demand access to live training courses, in-depth learning paths, interactive coding environments, and a vast collection of text and video from O'Reilly and 200+ other publishers. For more information, visit *https://oreilly.com*.

How to Contact Us

Please address comments and questions concerning this book to the publisher:

O'Reilly Media, Inc.
1005 Gravenstein Highway North
Sebastopol, CA 95472
800-998-9938 (in the United States or Canada)
707-829-0515 (international or local)
707-829-0104 (fax)

We have a web page for this book, where we list errata, examples, and any additional information. You can access this page at *https://oreil.ly/healthcare-data*.

Email *bookquestions@oreilly.com* to comment or ask technical questions about this book.

For news and information about our books and courses, visit *https://oreilly.com*.

Find us on LinkedIn: *https://linkedin.com/company/oreilly-media*.

Follow us on Twitter: *https://twitter.com/oreillymedia*.

Watch us on YouTube: *https://youtube.com/oreillymedia*.

Acknowledgments

Bố, Mẹ
> First and foremost, I want to acknowledge all of the sacrifices you have made over the years as you prioritized our education above all else. In doing so, you helped nurture a certain curiosity that has made today possible. From Stuart Hall to Urban to UCSD to UCSF, you made sure that I never had to worry about anything other than learning what I wanted to. This freedom allowed me to challenge myself and explore my passions (namely, computers and medicine) and carve out my niche in the world.

Day
> You have always helped me remember that life is about balance—too much or too little of anything can be detrimental. I know I don't say it enough but I am grateful for your perspective and influence, without which I would not have been able to enjoy the process of writing as much as I have.

Of course, there are many others who have been instrumental along the way, without whom I would not have gotten to this point:

Brenna Rowe
> As I think back to the late nights writing my dissertation, you always supported my intellectual curiosity and constant thirst for learning and experimenting, helping lay the foundation that led to this book.

David Avrin
> Thank you for introducing me to medical informatics and spending the time to help a young high school student discover an entirely new world. And, most importantly, thank you for pulling me back into medical informatics after a brief foray into the world of software engineering.

Lukasz Kaczmarek
> Thank you for tolerating my monologues and squirrel brain, and for helping me refine my thinking around medical informatics, IT, software, databases, architecture, and how best to communicate complex ideas.

Noah Gift

I remember our first conversation about rethinking the idea of teaching and academia. What started as a random lunch conversation has blossomed into my first book and I am forever grateful. Looking forward to more fun in the future!

Yao Sun

I always enjoyed our weekly conversations because I knew you would understand my crazy ideas enough to ask challenging and thought-provoking questions. I wouldn't be where I am without your support and guidance along the way.

Of course, thank you to all those who reviewed my drafts and provided helpful comments and feedback—Ed Mitchell, Huanmei Wu, and Tim McLerran.

And finally, thank you, Melissa Potter and Chris Faucher for your support, guidance, and tolerance as I stumbled my way through my first book!

## CHAPTER 1

Introduction to Healthcare Data

Healthcare data is an exciting vertical for data science, and there are many opportunities to have real impact, whether from a clinical or technical perspective. For patients and clinicians, there is the alluring promise of truly personalized care where patients get the right treatment at the right time, tailored to their genetics, environment, beliefs, and lifestyle—each requiring effective integration, harmonization, and analysis of highly complex data. For data scientists and computer scientists, there are many open problems for natural language processing, graphs, semantic web, and databases, among many others.

Additionally, there are "frontier" problems that arise given the specific combination of a specific technology and the nuances and complexities of healthcare. For example, there is nothing about healthcare data itself nor data science that requires "regulatory-grade" reproducibility. Data scientists know how to use version control tools such as Git, and IT people know how to create database snapshots and use Docker containers. However, with regulatory bodies such as the US Food and Drug Administration (FDA) or the European Medicines Agency (EMA), there are specific requirements to track and store metadata and other artifacts to "prove" the results of the analysis, including reproducibility. Similarly, there is increasing desire and pressure to ensure reproducibility of studies or the sharing of negative results among academics. How we can address these challenges at scale is still unsolved.

Despite the excitement for working with various types of healthcare data, there are still many misconceptions. Those with extensive experience working in enterprise environments tend to underestimate the complexity, often comparing real-world healthcare data projects to enterprise integrations. This is not to say that a typical enterprise data project is simple or easy. One of the major differences is the relation of how and why the data was captured relative to the actual work being done.

In nearly every industry, the use of data today is a function of engineered systems. In other words, most data is generated by software systems versus collected and entered by a human. For example, in advertising/marketing analytics, the data is generated by websites that track clicks and impressions.

In this chapter, we will walk through some of the nuances and complexities of healthcare data. Much of this complexity is a reflection of the delivery of healthcare itself—it is just really complicated!

For those with a traditional IT background or who have worked in large companies dealing with complex data issues, we will start with a little discussion of the enterprise mindset and how you might frame healthcare data. After this, we will dive into a broader view of the complexities of healthcare data. Once this foundation has been set, you will get a broad overview of common sources of healthcare data.

The Enterprise Mindset

The data science industry has had many successes—from companies using data science, as well as creating new data science methods. When leveraging and using data science, most organizations have the benefit of following the traditional enterprise mindset. Information and data architects within the organization can sit down together, discuss the various sources of data and intended use cases, and then craft an overarching information model and architecture.

Part of this process typically involves getting various stakeholders together into a single room to agree on how best to define individual nuggets of data or information. Until recently, this has been the approach that most companies have taken when trying to build data warehouses. The challenge in healthcare is that the sources of data operate in disconnected silos. When a patient enters the healthcare system, they typically do so via their primary care physician, urgent care, or the emergency department.

Naturally, one might say we should start here in order to create the information model that will be used to represent healthcare data. After all, nearly everything else flows downstream from the moment a patient makes an appointment or shows up at urgent care. Insurance companies or governments will need to reimburse hospitals for providing care; physicians will prescribe medications and companion diagnostics from the biopharma industry.

So, information architects can start by defining the idea of a *patient* and all of the associated data elements, such as demographics, medical history, and medication prescription history. However, as we start to look at the healthcare industry overall, there are already potential issues even when defining the "simple" idea of a patient. How does an insurance company think of patients? At least in the United States, insurance companies typically think of people as *covered lives*, not *patients*. While some may be quick to say that insurance companies are dehumanizing people and thinking only of statistics, it largely comes down to the operational aspects of tracking benefits.

While the person who seeks care is the patient, they may be a beneficiary of someone else who is not the patient. For example, if a child goes to urgent care for some stitches after falling at the playground, they are the patient as far as the clinic is concerned. However, to the insurance company, there are two people who need to be tracked—the child as well as the parent or guardian who is the insurance policy holder. The insurance company must track these two individuals as different people for the claim, though they are obviously related.

The Potential of Graphs

The previous example highlights how graphs can be particularly useful when dealing with complex data. A single claim can be created as a node that is connected to two other nodes, one each for the child and their parent/guardian.

Even this relatively "simple" example can get complicated quickly, and we will discuss similar examples throughout this book, highlighting the hidden complexities of data.

Those who are veterans in the data space will likely see the parallels between the previous discussion and challenges in setting up data warehouses. While an organization may be united in its overall product, each business unit or department within the organization may have very different views of a *customer* or *user*. Anecdotally, it can take upward of 18 months to get all of the stakeholders to agree on a common understanding of concepts that make up an organization's enterprise information architecture. It is important for us to find ways to narrow this window, though it is less about getting everyone to agree and more about getting the right people, process, and tools in place to help us iterate more effectively.

That said, we must keep in mind that there are inherent complexities when delivering healthcare, and those complexities creep into the data that is captured. Instead of chasing the new shiny object (whether that's a new database, orchestration framework, or other technology), we need to consider the core challenge and how to best and most cost-effectively address it.

To start us on our journey, we will spend a bit of time talking about the inherent complexity of healthcare data, particularly real-world data (RWD).

The Complexity of Healthcare Data

Data meshes are one example of the changing landscape when it comes to data—there have already been evolutions from databases to data warehouses to data lakes—and the evolution will continue. This is, however, an example of the shifting thinking around data, highlighting a key aspect of healthcare data.

Organizations and their leadership are starting to realize that there is a lot of potentially useful data that lives outside of traditional systems such as the databases and applications that support sales or manufacturing. As organizations are struggling to keep up with an increasingly heterogenous data landscape, ideas such as the data mesh are invented to try to address shortcomings of existing approaches.

In healthcare, however, these complexities have always been a rate-limiting factor. Administrators are not just starting to see value in data and, as a result, trying to find scalable and repeatable ways to link data from the various service lines within a hospital. Nor are pharmaceutical companies just realizing that there is a tremendous amount of value in claims data from a medical affairs perspective.

Consequently, healthcare has been struggling to find ways to bring disparate data sources together, while still balancing critical issues such as security and privacy, governance, and (most importantly from the perspective of data scientists) normalization and harmonization of the data. Chapter 3 will go into more detail, but data scientists often think of normalization in the context of statistics or machine learning algorithms (e.g., min-max scaling, zero mean and unit variance, etc.). While that definition is certainly true and applicable to healthcare data, there is an additional element of normalization, often referred to as *harmonization*.

Harmonization requires some domain knowledge and is not purely a function of only data. For example, we may need to find all of the ways the dataset might represent the idea of "Tylenol" or "Acetaminophen" and replace them with a single representation; the dataset may even have an internal, hospital-specific code of "M458239." Whether we are attempting descriptive statistics, machine learning, or any other type of analysis, we must first *harmonize* the data to reduce this noise.

Epidemiologists, biostatisticians, clinical researchers, and medical informaticists are well aware of these issues, though I have seen a variety of approaches. Most often, I see people embed any necessary harmonization directly into their code, particularly using SQL at query time. From an engineering standpoint, this makes it quite difficult to maintain over time since you would need to alter the query should you need to change anything. Of course, this means that your dataframes would also be different and may affect your downstream code. As an alternative, many scientists will extract the data with as minimal processing as possible in SQL and do any harmonization in R, Python, SAS, or other environment. While this improves maintainability of the code, it is not easily reusable. As we will discuss throughout this book, there are other ways to handle this that improve the overall engineering. But, as with any technology decision, there will be trade-offs!

Now that we have some high-level exposure to the complexity of healthcare data, let's discuss some specific types and sources of healthcare data.

Sources of Healthcare Data

There are many different sources and types of healthcare data. This book focuses on real-world data, data that are collected during the course of delivering healthcare. This can come in many different forms, though the most common is data from electronic health records (EHRs).

By definition and given the constant innovation, nearly anything can be considered RWD if it's used to help improve the quality and efficiency of care or to help improve patient outcomes. We have seen this a bit with COVID where all sorts of data is being used to help combat the spread of COVID. This might include something as common as your GPS/location data or something more specific such as data from contact tracing apps.

We will review a few common sources of healthcare data so that you have a sense of the landscape. This is by no means an exhaustive list and is simply to help orient you for the rest of this book.

Electronic Health Records

When people think about healthcare data, one of the most common sources that comes to mind is the EHR. You have probably heard of Epic (*https://www.epic.com*) or Cerner (*https://www.cerner.com*), two of the most common EHRs used in the United States. There are many other commercial EHR vendors as well as open source projects, some focused on the United States and others more internationally. While I will list a few common ones, the main focus of this section is to provide you with an introduction to the data typically captured in an EHR and how we need to approach it as data engineers and data scientists.

Electronic health record versus electronic medical record

You may be wondering—what is the difference between an EHR and an electronic medical record (EMR)? NextGen (*https://oreil.ly/TrcOj*), an ambulatory EHR,[1] differentiates an EMR as a patient's record in a single institution and an EHR as a comprehensive record across multiple sources. The Office of the National Coordinator of Health IT (ONCHIT) (*https://oreil.ly/YNg5t*) provides a slightly more specific definition: an EHR is a comprehensive record from *all* the clinicians involved in a patient's care.

Competing Definitions

You may find various definitions of EHRs and EMRs out there. One common distinction is that an EMR is primarily used by clinicians as a replacement for the paper chart *within a single institution*; an EHR is a more comprehensive record of a patient and may include data from multiple sources.

In practice, the industry often uses these terms interchangeably, so be sure to clarify what someone means when they use the term EHR versus EMR.

Despite this distinction, it has been my experience that the terms are used interchangeably to mean the same thing. As I will continue to mention over and over (especially in Chapter 3), it is important to make sure that everyone is using the same definition. In this case, when you are discussing EHRs or EMRs, be sure to clarify if you are discussing records from a single institution or from multiple institutions. Throughout this book, I will use the term EHR to mean a patient's clinical record from one or more sources but will also highlight situations where more specificity is necessary.

EHRs and data harmonization

If I had to choose a single theme to describe this book, it would be this idea of *data harmonization*. Data harmonization and interoperability are closely related and often used interchangeably. In this book, I use *interoperability* to describe the sharing of healthcare data from a transactional perspective. In other words, how can we share data about a patient as part of the patient journey or care process? For example, when a patient is admitted to the emergency department, how do we transfer information about their visit to their primary care physician? Or, if the patient is referred to a specialist, how is their data sent to their new physician?

---

1 *Ambulatory* is being used to mean *outpatient*, distinguishing this type of EHR from an inpatient or hospital EHR.

On the other hand, I use *data harmonization* to refer to the process of integrating data from multiple sources in such a way that as much of the underlying context is preserved and the meaning of the data is normalized across different datasets. For example, as a pharmaceutical company, I may want to combine a claims dataset from a payer with a dataset from a hospital EHR. How can I ensure that the medications in both datasets are normalized such that a simple query such as "I want all patients who received a platinum-based chemotherapy" returns the correct patients from the EHR dataset and the correct claims from the payer dataset?

Both interoperability and data harmonization are big challenges in healthcare. There is also a lot of overlap in the underlying issues and associated solutions as highlighted in Figure 1-1. For example, whether one is transmitting a list of a patient's medication history from one hospital to the next or trying to combine two datasets, the solution may be to link the medications to a standard coding system such as RxNorm (*https:// oreil.ly/4jMHV*) or National Drug Codes (*https://oreil.ly/Fedn2*).

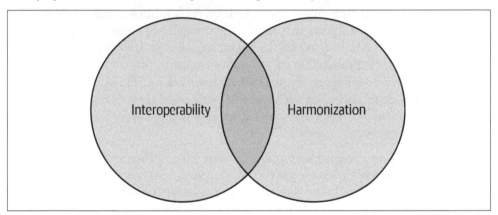

Figure 1-1. Interoperability versus harmonization

For the purpose of this book, the key issue is that how you interpret the data largely depends on why the data was collected, who collected the data, and any workflow or user experience limitations during the collection process—what I collectively refer to as *context*. As data engineers and data scientists, we do not always have access to all of the necessary context, and we oftentimes need to make a best guess. However, it is important that we at least ask ourselves how the data might have been affected.

One of the most commonly highlighted examples of the challenges with data harmonization of EHR data is the use of International Classification of Diseases (ICD) codes within a patient's clinical record. ICD codes (*https://oreil.ly/TRMn3*) are a common method for tracking diagnoses with a patient's clinical record—at least this is the high-level intention and assumption.

However, to dig a little deeper, we need to ask a few questions:

- How are the ICD codes actually used?
- Why ICD codes (versus any other type of code or coding system)?
- Who assigns the codes to a patient's clinical record?

These may seem obvious, but remember that not every organization approaches data the same way. In the United States, ICD codes in an EHR are typically used as part of the billing process and entered into the system by medical billing specialists, not physicians or nurses. This impacts our analyses because we need to keep in mind that the codes may be used to justify other parts of an insurance claim or to satisfy internal reporting requirements, and not intended at all to accurately document a patient's medical history. Let's walk through an example that dives into some of the potential complexities when dealing with something as seemingly simple as diagnosis codes.

A patient may go to their primary care physician for a routine checkup. During the encounter, a physician suspects that their patient may have diabetes and decides to order a hemoglobin A1c test. When the billing specialist reviews this encounter and prepares a claim for submission to the insurance company, they add the ICD-10 code of Z13.1, "Encounter for screening for diabetes mellitus." At the same time, there is an internal policy to also code such patients with the code R73.03, "Prediabetes," which is used to feed a dashboard for subsequent follow-up with educational and other patient engagement materials.

As data scientists, we come along months or years later and are attempting to generate a cohort of *patients who are prediabetic (but not yet diabetic) and subsequently diagnosed as diabetic*. We know that there is the perfect ICD-10 code (R73.03) and proceed to write a SQL query to find all patients who have that code. However, what if our patient had an A1c result of 5.5% (completely within normal limits) and the physician was just being overly cautious? In this scenario, our SQL query would erroneously return this patient as part of our prediabetic cohort.

To further highlight the potential complexity, let's say our clinic is currently participating in a local program with the county's department of public health on a diabetes screening campaign. The physicians in our clinic are now ordering prediabetes screenings at a much higher rate than other counties in the state. If we continue to rely on this "perfect" ICD-10 code of R73.03, it will appear as if this particular county has an extremely high rate of prediabetics who are never subsequently diagnosed with diabetes. This could be interpreted that the campaign is extremely successful in preventing diabetes.

Given this example, what is the solution? Typically, in this sort of a situation where we have an objective definition of "prediabetes," we can just add a threshold to our SQL query, triggering off the A1c result. For example, the threshold for prediabetes may be 5.7–6.4%, so we can update the WHERE clause of our SQL query accordingly.

However, the threshold at which point a person is diagnosed as diabetic is not uniform across all hospitals, clinics, or health systems. For example, while our clinic uses 6.4%, another clinic in the county or state may use a threshold of 6.7%. As data scientists and data engineers, we must then query for the raw lab result and apply additional filtering later in our process.

While the previous example may seem unnecessarily complex, it is actually simpler than many other situations involving diagnoses, especially those in specialties such as oncology or neurology where the diseases themselves are not as well understood. Things also get quite complicated when you start factoring in complexities of specific disease areas. For example, "line of therapy" is quite nuanced and a challenge for researchers and data scientists.[2] I will continue to share similar examples and show how the use of graph databases can make our job as data engineers and data scientists easier and more efficient, particularly through the lens of reproducibility.

That concludes our overview of electronic health record data, but we will spend a bit more time with EHR data in Chapter 4. While EHR data is usually one of the first data sources to come to mind when someone mentions real-world data, another very common type of data is reimbursement claims, which we will cover in the next section.

Claims Data

Claims data captures the financial side of healthcare delivery. While this is commonly associated with the US healthcare system given our reliance on private insurers, countries with national health systems also track similar data (essentially treating the government as the payer). You may hear the term *payer* used to describe insurance companies, and I will also use that term throughout this book.

On the surface, we might assume that the data contained in a claim (e.g., diagnoses, medications, procedures, etc.) corresponds to the data contained in the patient's record in an electronic health record. For example, if you go to your doctor's office for a routine checkup and they do a blood draw and order a panel of lab tests, we should expect the records of these in both the EHR and the claim to correspond to one another.

---

2 Kamal S. Saini and Chris Twelves, "Determining Lines of Therapy in Patients with Solid Cancers: A Proposed New Systematic and Comprehensive Framework," *British Journal of Cancer* 125, (2021): 155–163, *https://doi.org/10.1038/s41416-021-01319-8*.

For simple situations, this may be true. However, there is usually a serious discrepancy between claims and EHR data. You may have heard of the term *upcoding*, which is often used to describe the process by which clinics and hospitals (collectively referred to as *providers*) submit codes fraudulently to increase payments.

For example, a provider may have seen a patient for a short visit where only routine screening services were performed, which should have been coded using 99212 (the evaluation of an established patient with at least two of the following: a problem-focused history, a problem-focused examination, and straightforward medical decision-making). However, the clinic knows that it would get reimbursed more if it submits code 99215 (an evaluation requiring at least two of the following: a comprehensive history, a detailed examination, and medical decision-making of high complexity). While this is a very clear example of fraudulent upcoding, not all situations where codes *appear* to be inflated are fraudulent.

Another example may be when a provider adds a particular diagnosis code that appears to increase the complexity of a patient (as discussed in our diabetes example in the previous section). In this situation, a code was attached to the claim to justify associated lab tests. From the perspective of retrospective analysis, this may initially appear to be upcoding since the patient was not actually diabetic.

Either way, this highlights that claims data may be inaccurate in a clinical sense given the processes behind claims adjudication and reimbursement or may even be fraudulent upcoding. The key takeaway is that we, as data engineers and data scientists, must really understand the nuances underlying the claims data and not assume that it is accurate for our particular use case.

Self-Insured Employers

Most larger companies in the United States are *self-insured* or *self-funded*—this means they take on the financial risk instead of an insurance company. They typically contract with *third-party administrators* (e.g., United HealthCare, Anthem, etc.) to handle the claims processing. In these situations, there is yet another source of influence on how/why data is collected, which then directly impacts any downstream analyses.

Despite the challenges with data quality in both EHR and claims data, they are still the most popular sources of data from the real world. Since the data are collected during the delivery of care, the data collection process itself is not the main focus. This results in many of the data quality issues we see. One way to mitigate this is to set up a registry where data is collected, abstracted, and curated to answer specific research or scientific questions. So, let's quickly talk about clinical registries and disease registries.

Clinical/Disease Registries

Clinical and disease registries are typically used to collect data prospectively given a specific set of criteria (often referred to as a *study protocol*). Many of the same data harmonization challenges exist in registries as they do with EHR data. However, one of the key differences is that the primary intention behind a disease registry is to collect data for later analysis (e.g., clinical research, population health, public health surveillance).

We discuss this notion of *intention* in a bit of detail in Chapters 3 and 4, but this highlights the biggest difference between EHR/claims data and most other data collected in healthcare—whether the data was collected for the purpose of later analysis or not. EHR and claims data are collected primarily to transact the business of healthcare. When a physician captures data in the EHR, they are trying to document so that they (or another clinician) can provide the patient with the appropriate care. When a medical coding specialist assigns ICD-10 codes, they are helping the clinic submit reimbursement claims. The intention is not to collect data for data science.

Registries, on the other hand, are collected so that analysts and scientists can use the data to derive insights about populations of patients. Instead of needing to do a deep dive into a particular hospital's workflow to understand the context and nuance of the data, you would refer to the study protocol instead. This becomes particularly beneficial for us when working with data from multiple institutions or data collection points. In a registry, all sites for data collection use the same study protocol and attempt to collect data as uniformly as possible. In contrast, the local influences on EHR and claims data will vary among clinics, insurance companies, and even employers as discussed previously.

The process of setting up a registry and then executing the data collection, abstraction, and curation is itself a specialty within the healthcare industry. For example, the National Cancer Registrars Association provides a Certified Tumor Registrar credential for those working on cancer registries.

So, EHR, claims, and registry data make up the "big three" of RWD. There are pros and cons to each, and it would be foolish to think that there is a "best" source for RWD. It ultimately comes down to your intended use cases and finding the most cost-effective source of data to help you extract the insights you need. In the next section, we give a brief nod to clinical trials data. While the pharma industry puts clinical trials data into an entirely separate bucket, I am including it here because there is increasing interest across the entire industry to bring all of these sources of data together—EHR, claims, registries, and clinical trials.

Clinical Trials Data

Clinical trials data is likely the "cleanest" of all healthcare data since there are significantly more financial and regulatory incentives in place. The success of a clinical trial and approval by regulatory authorities hinges on having clean data and robust analyses. As a result, pharmaceutical companies and clinical/contract research organizations (CROs) dedicate significant resources to the data collection, cleaning, processing, and analysis.

Additionally, there are clearly defined standards (e.g., CDISC) around clinical trials data since regulatory agencies have clearly defined submission requirements. While such standards help decrease some of the challenges when harmonizing trials data, they do not solve all of the challenges.

Now that we've added clinical trials data to the list, we have covered the biggest sources of data about patients to date. This is already starting to change as we see wearables, mobile devices, and apps becoming part of the fabric of healthcare. Oftentimes, these solutions all get lumped under the term *digital health*, and it is certainly something we should keep our eyes on!

We will now switch gears a little and focus on the data collection process itself, regardless of whether it is for the electronic health record or a clinical registry. Understanding how and why the data was collected is critical to effectively extracting actionable insights from real-world data.

Data Collection and How That Affects Data Scientists

As data scientists, we love to get our hands on data and start playing with it. In most companies and with most data, we know exactly why and how the data was collected. They were collected to facilitate the operation of the business, and analytics are also in service of the business. In other words, the alignment between why the data was collected and how they will be used are quite aligned. For example, in a streaming service, you might see data collected on which songs someone is listening to, how often they skip, how long they might spend on the song's information page, or other songs they are listening to. In retail, you track which items a customer views and revisits, their purchase history, and what they ultimately purchase. The analytics are also closely aligned—recommending new content to consume or items to purchase.

In healthcare, there are many analytics projects that have a close alignment between why the data were collected and the goals of the analysis project. For example, clinical trials collect and analyze data for the purpose of measuring a treatment's safety and efficacy; clinical research studies collect and analyze data to answer specific research questions.

However, when working with real-world data in healthcare, there is usually a big disconnect between why the data was collected and how it is analyzed. Data from EHRs is collected to facilitate the care of patients; clinical research data was collected by following a specific study protocol; claims data was collected to facilitate reimbursement; and the list goes on. Then, we come along and want to use the data to identify digital biomarkers, create risk prediction machine learning models, do population-level analytics, etc.

This forces us to reconcile our current use case and data needs against the data. This section walks you through different ways data is collected in healthcare. While these will help you begin to think about RWD differently, they are not the only considerations. We still need to think about other contexts such as the type of medical center, disease area or indication, and the platform used for data collection, among others.

Our first stop involves looking at two common distinctions of healthcare studies. Understanding the nuance between prospective and retrospective studies will help you better understand the context in which data is collected and analyzed.

We will start with a focus on the distinction between *prospective* and *retrospective* studies, from the perspective of the types of analysis typically performed. Alongside this distinction, we will also discuss a bit the notions of *primary* and *secondary* data. Most RWD use cases I have come across involve retrospective analysis of secondary data.

Prospective studies

The term *prospective* is adapted from descriptions of clinical research studies—highlighting the relationship between when the study starts and when the final outcome is measured. In prospective studies, a study protocol is put in place, and data is collected. Data continues to be collected per the study protocol until the end of the study. Analysis of the data may start immediately (even while the study is ongoing) or may start after the data has been locked and no additional data is collected.

One of the key points to consider with prospective studies is that the criteria for data collection and how the data is collected are explicit and influenced by the purpose of the study. For example, take a study that seeks to identify clinical signs associated with impending death in patients with advanced cancer. This was set up as a prospective study, and the protocol dictated that 52 physical signs were documented every 12 hours, starting with the patient's admission.

In this study, and as with most prospective studies, decisions about the underlying format/data types and the meaning (often referred to as *semantics*) of each data element are determined up front. Those involved with the collection, management, and analysis of the data can all refer to the study protocol for the intended semantics.

The concepts of prospective studies and primary data are often conflated given their frequent association. Data collected in the context of prospective studies is typically considered primary data because it is collected for the purpose of the study. However, though data may have been collected in a prospective study, it could be used as secondary data in a follow-up study. Continuing with the cancer study referenced earlier, if researchers took that data and wanted to look for correlations between various bedside clinical signs and various medications, this would be considered secondary use of the data. That is, the data is being used and analyzed for reasons other than why they were originally collected.

While data from prospective studies is usually considered primary data, it may also be considered secondary data for other analyses—this distinction between primary and secondary use depends entirely on the question(s) being asked of the data, relative to how and why the data was initially collected.

So, prospective studies are those looking forward. Let's look at those studies that look backward.

Retrospective studies

Historically, prospective studies were the major mechanism for gathering healthcare data for analysis, often in the form of clinical research. However, as with most industries, data is being collected more and more frequently—in a variety of forms whether through electronic health records, digital health tools, or even clinical and disease registries. Consequently, people are looking to these data to find insights and are essentially conducting retrospective studies.

Retrospective studies are those where the outcome is already known (e.g., we already know the overall survival of all patients in the dataset) and data is collected from existing sources or memory. As a result, retrospective studies typically involve secondary use of data. This is where things can get confusing between prospective studies and retrospective studies, and primary data and secondary data.

One common example of a retrospective study involving secondary use of data is the extraction of data from electronic health records—a researcher may want to look at the relative overall survival of cancer patients on a particular medication (e.g., bevacizumab) relative to standard chemotherapy alone. Instead of constructing a prospective study, the researcher decides they will extract data on a subset of patients who match the inclusion/exclusion criteria. Though the data has already been collected in the EHR, the researcher is retrospectively analyzing previously collected data for their study.

The previous example also highlights secondary use of data. The data was originally collected in the EHR for the purposes of patient care or billing but are now being used to compare the efficacy of traditional chemotherapy regimens and those that include the addition of bevacizumab.

Generally speaking, from the perspective of the data, whether a study is prospective or retrospective is less important than whether it is a primary or secondary use (and collection) of data. As data engineers or data scientists, we must consider how and why the data were collected since this directly impacts the wrangling (cleaning, processing, normalization, and harmonization) of data.

It is usually easier to wrangle data that have been collected for the specific study being conducted. Data types and formats have been decided; there is an established common understanding of the data elements and how they are supposed to be collected. This does not ensure that the data is in fact clean, but it does decrease the data wrangling challenges.

In the case of secondary use of data, the data was collected for a variety of different (and sometimes conflicting) reasons, so it is not always clear how the data should be cleaned and processed. For example, one common misconception is that a list of ICD-10 codes within a patient's record in the EHR is a good source of identifying patients with a particular diagnosis. While ICD-10 codes are commonly used to track diagnoses in a variety of datasets, it is important to understand the context of the use of ICD-10 codes in many (though not all) EHRs.

Take a patient who comes into their primary care provider's office for a routine checkup and the physician orders a hemoglobin A1c (HbA1c) test to rule out diabetes. That is, the physician feels their patient may have diabetes and is attempting to validate this hypothesis. They will put in the order for the test and continue with the visit. However, somewhere behind the scenes, someone responsible for medical billing also tags the patient's record with the ICD-10 code of E13, indicating "other specified diabetes mellitus."

Why did they do this? Perhaps this allows the hospital administration to track why particular tests are being ordered, or this allows insurance companies to identify erroneous test orders. The insurance company may have a policy that says, "HbA1c tests are approved only for patients having or suspected of having diabetes." To validate incoming claims, the insurance company has pushed the burden onto hospitals. Existing diabetic patients will already have a corresponding ICD-10 code and will pass the validation. However, a patient who has not been diagnosed with diabetes will fail this test, and the claim will be kicked back to the hospital. So, to pass the validation, the hospital codes the patient as having diabetes.

In this example, is the patient diabetic? Perhaps. Perhaps not. Until the result of the HbA1c test is examined, there is no way for a data scientist to know if this is a diabetic patient (and whether to include this patient in the cohort).

Conclusion

We spent most of this chapter talking about healthcare data at a high level. Though we mentioned studies such as clinical trials and clinical research, the majority of the focus of this book will be on what many refer to as *real-world data*. Of course, if you are a medical center simply trying to make sense of your electronic health record data, it's simply *data*. In the biotech and pharma industry, we use RWD to differentiate from interventional and noninterventional study data—basically, data collected for specific study purposes following strict protocols versus data collected during the delivery of healthcare without any clear standards.

As we started the journey on RWD, we discussed some of the inherent complexities between why the data was collected in contrast to the types of analysis we want to perform. Much of this book is dedicated to some of the approaches we use to mitigate this complexity.

I have spent the better part of my professional life dedicated to working with healthcare RWD, and yet there is still so much to learn. This book won't make you an expert overnight, but the goal is to give you the right vocabulary while highlighting many lessons learned so that you can hit the ground running. While we don't often have a choice in what type of data we get, having a basic understanding of the type of data and how/why it was collected makes us better data engineers and scientists. We can begin to factor these into our overall data pipelines and analyses.

If there is one thing to keep in mind as you read this book (or any other book, blog post, library readme/documentation, research paper, etc.), it would be that healthcare is inherently complex, the data is complex, and there is no silver bullet to address all of these complexities. The delivery of healthcare captures and represents the diversity of the human condition—seeking a one-size-fits-all solution is simply impossible.

As a medical informaticist, I always have one foot firmly planted in healthcare data and another in technology and software. This chapter provided us with a basic introduction to healthcare data. In the next chapter, we focus on technology, particularly databases. While our discussion will be in the context of healthcare data, the focus of the chapter is to help level the field for those with a less technical background.

## CHAPTER 2

Technical Introduction

We spent Chapter 1 starting our journey with a discussion about healthcare data. Now, we will shift gears a bit and spend some time discussing purely technical topics such as Docker and databases. The goal of this chapter is to get everyone up to speed with the basics of launching containers and interacting with databases.

The first section contains a basic review of Docker. If you already have Docker installed and running on your system, this will be familiar.

The second section spends a bit of time discussing the basic concepts of databases. We will review both Structured Query Language (SQL) and NoSQL (anything not using SQL) databases, including document and graph databases. The intent is not to go into all of the details of deploying and administering databases; it is simply to provide a basic introduction.

For those with software and IT backgrounds, this is likely also familiar. For those with clinical backgrounds or for data scientists who routinely work with data in CSV files, this section will provide some basic introductions that will help with subsequent chapters. That said, this book generally assumes that you have some proficiency with SQL though there may be many of you who are coming from the healthcare side of the world and may not have a lot of experience with databases. The overview is not intended to provide a deep dive into SQL databases. Instead, it sets the stage, providing a basic introduction to vocabulary concepts with which we can compare and contrast graph databases.

In the first section, we will review Docker, a series of tools that makes it easy to quickly deploy servers and other software without dealing with finicky dependencies between the application and the underlying operating system.

Basic Introduction to Docker and Containers

If you have ever tried to install server-side software such as a web server, application server, or database server, you know how painful it can be to make sure that your environment aligns with the documentation. Your directory structure might be slightly different, your operating system might be a different version, or you have a different version of Java installed.

One solution to this is to use virtual machines and something like VMware or Parallels. However, they both require that you still install a guest operating system and incur significant overhead, particularly RAM and disk space. The modern solution to this problem is to use containers (*https://oreil.ly/L1w3V*).

Containers are a form of virtualization that focus on the application layer. In other words, they allow us to deploy software in a particular environment (called a *container*) where we control the version of the software and all of the dependencies, just as we would in a virtual machine. However, unlike a traditional virtual machine, we do not virtualize the operating system, saving RAM and disk space in the process.

Of course, some magic needs to happen to allow for disk access, networking, security, etc. This is where projects such as Docker come in. There are other container engines such as rkt and LXC/LXD. We focus on Docker given its widespread adoption and support for macOS, MS Windows, and Linux operating systems.

Additionally, containers also allow application developers, data scientists, and others at the top of the stack to create repeatable and reproducible deployments regardless of the underlying operating system. This becomes especially important where there are a mix of Mac, Windows, and Linux workstations and servers.

Docker has many options that are beyond the scope of this book. For additional information and to learn more about Docker, check out Docker's educational resources (*https://oreil.ly/aLF26*). In the meantime, we will walk you through the basics of getting Docker up and running.

Installing and Testing Docker

If you do not have Docker installed, please follow the instructions on Docker's website (*https://oreil.ly/bABVR*). The process is pretty straightforward, and you should be up and running in no time.

The examples throughout this book assume that you have Docker installed and running properly. You should be able to run `docker run hello-world` and get something similar to the following output (specifically, the "Hello from Docker!" and subsequent output):

```
Unable to find image 'hello-world:latest' locally
latest: Pulling from library/hello-world
0e03bdcc26d7: Pull complete
Digest: sha256:d58e752213a51785838f9eed2b7a498ffa1cb3aa7f946dda11af39286c3db9a9
Status: Downloaded newer image for hello-world:latest

Hello from Docker!
This message shows that your installation appears to be working correctly.

To generate this message, Docker took the following steps:
 1. The Docker client contacted the Docker daemon.
 2. The Docker daemon pulled the "hello-world" image from the Docker Hub.
    (amd64)
 3. The Docker daemon created a new container from that image which runs the
    executable that produces the output you are currently reading.
 4. The Docker daemon streamed that output to the Docker client, which sent it
    to your terminal.

To try something more ambitious, you can run an Ubuntu container with:
 $ docker run -it ubuntu bash

Share images, automate workflows, and more with a free Docker ID:
 https://hub.docker.com/

For more examples and ideas, visit:
 https://docs.docker.com/get-started/
```

Now that you have a running version of Docker on your system and we've tested to make sure it works, we can continue our journey on to databases. The remainder of this chapter starts with a high-level introduction to databases and continues with a survey of a variety of database functions and features.

Conceptual Introduction to Databases

There are many aspects to choosing what type of database to use for a particular project. Typically, you would make your choice based on write requirements or read requirements. Write requirements revolve around the data collection and what the system needs to be able to handle so that data is not lost. On the other hand, read requirements consider the needs of the system as you query the data from the database.

In this section, we discuss a few of these considerations, starting with atomicity, consistency, isolation, and durability (ACID) compliance and then focusing on the difference between transactional (for reading and writing data to facilitate a business transaction) and analytical databases (for reading data to power all levels of analytics). After this, we launch right into the specifics of relational/SQL, document, and graph databases with examples of common query languages.

ACID Compliance

A common set of properties of databases (from the perspective of writing to databases) are referred to as ACID. ACID compliance ensures that a database will perform write operations with certain guarantees:

Atomicity

Atomicity is the idea that writes to a database are treated as a single, *atomic* operation such that all components are successful or none are applied to the database. The classic example is a bank database that supports transfers of funds from one account to another. Say Joe wants to transfer $10 to Susie—the database must debit $10 from Joe's account and then credit $10 to Susie's account. What happens if there is a power outage or other glitch in the system after the money is debited from Joe's account and before the money is credited to Susie? The money would be essentially lost forever in that case. If a database supports *atomicity*, both the debit and credit must succeed; otherwise, the debit is rolled back as if nothing happened. A group of writes that must execute together are grouped into a *transaction*.

Consistency

Consistency ensures that the database is always in a valid state. In other words, as software systems interact with the database, queries will either execute successfully or not at all. This may sound similar to *atomicity* but is more basic. The idea of *consistency* applies regardless of the number of queries within a transaction and focuses on whether a write is successful. To continue the previous example, what if Joe simply wanted to withdraw money from his own account? There is really only a single step to the transaction (the debit of $10 from Joe's account), so atomicity doesn't apply. However, if the power outage hits right in the middle of logging Joe's debit, the database needs to ensure that Joe's account and the database as a whole are not corrupted as a result. In a sense, consistency is a building block of atomicity—the database uses consistency to ensure that each step of a transaction is successful, and if all steps are successful, the transaction is completed, thus providing atomicity.

Isolation

Isolation ensures that individual transactions executed against a database are isolated from one another. In other words, whether a transaction consists of a single query or multiple queries, the success or failure of a particular transaction does not affect any other transactions. Isolation is mainly a consideration of concurrent systems, systems that may run particular operations in parallel. So, if two transactions are sent to the database server at the same exact moment, the failure of one should not affect the database.

Durability

Durability ensures that once a transaction is completed and written to the database, the completion of the transaction will not be lost due to a system failure.

I know these all sound very similar, so you're probably wondering why we needed to discuss each of them individually. From the perspective of a data engineer or data scientist, we may not care too much about the nitty-gritty details, but they end up affecting our data pipelines and the options we have. Sometimes the "perfect" solution from the perspective of your data pipeline simply isn't something that can be deployed given these other considerations.

That said, they are important to database engineers, administrators, and system/network administrators. Durability ensures that a successful transaction will never be lost; consistency ensures that successful transactions cannot corrupt the database; isolation ensures that one transaction's success or failure will not affect others; atomicity ensures that all parts of a transaction must succeed for the transaction to succeed. The underlying engineering to make these guarantees becomes especially complex when considering distributed databases that live across multiple servers, data centers, or cloud providers.

ACID considerations apply to all databases, but we often organize databases into two groups—those that apply to transactional workloads and those that apply to analytical workloads. As data scientists, we focus almost exclusively on analytical databases. As data engineers, we may be pulling data from transactional systems and putting them into analytics ones. So, let's quickly discuss online transactional processing (OLTP) and online analytical processing (OLAP) systems.

OLTP Systems

ACID compliance is typically discussed in the context of OLTP systems—online transactional processing. The majority of database usage was focused around OLTP systems that were designed to facilitate business transactions. Whether it's a bank logging money transfers between accounts or a medical center trying to send medication requests from the ICU to the pharmacy, there is a need for database systems to log the request, push it to other systems, and update the database accordingly.

OLTP systems are designed around reliably and quickly reading and writing small chunks of data, especially as the database grows in size. Whether a medical center has 100 patients or 1 million patients, the electronic health record (as an OLTP system) should allow physicians to update or look up a single patient's clinical record within seconds. The New York Stock Exchange should be able to log a single stock trade within milliseconds. There is rarely a need to quickly look up clinical records of all patients or to pull all of the stock trades for the entire stock exchange. These differing requirements allow engineers to design the system accordingly. However, with the focus on small, discrete chunks of data, OLTP systems perform quite poorly when trying to scan the entire database for specific data.

On the other hand, data scientists often want to scan the entire database for a specific set of fields. For example, say we want to run an analysis of adverse reactions to medications that result in anaphylaxis (a life-threatening, systemic allergic reaction). We want to pull known allergies, prescribed medications, and hospital admissions for all patients in our electronic health record. If you are at an organization as large as Kaiser Permanente, you would be running this query against 12.5 million people. Running such a query against an OLTP system would likely take a very long time to return the results and could even take down the system similar to a denial-of-service (DoS) attack. Either way, your database administrators would likely not be very happy with you! Of course, this is a bit of a contrived example. We know that our database and IT administrators are already ensuring that mission-critical systems are insulated from such situations (we hope!).

So, we know we shouldn't be running analytical workloads against OLTP systems, and they simply aren't designed for such workloads. Instead, we should be using OLAP systems, which we will discuss next.

OLAP Systems

Online analytical processing (OLAP) systems were introduced to handle analytics workloads similar to the previous example. These databases may not perform well for transactional use cases but excel at large scans across a subset of the data. You will likely hear discussions of OLAP systems in the context of data warehouses, data marts, and other centralized data storage systems designed around aggregating data for the purpose of analytics.

OLAP systems are built around the *read requirements*—those considerations on how we want to query and extract the data. Unlike with OLTP systems, data architects will consider the anticipated analytical workloads and then design the system accordingly. To continue our EHR-based example, will we want to routinely scan all patients or a subset of patients? Or, will we scan each encounter a patient has (which could be orders of magnitude higher than the number of patients)?

Large scans of a single column/field of data is a common use case and one of the reasons why column-oriented databases have become so popular. We could model the database such that each row is a patient and each column reflects a particular field (e.g., medications, lab values, vital signs, etc.). In a columnar database, asking for "all medications across all patients" becomes a very efficient query.

The topic of OLAP systems and the underlying database options, such as SQL, column-oriented, document-oriented, or graph databases, is a very complex one. This book focuses on graph databases given their ability to model many of the complexities of healthcare data. However, they are not necessarily the best or only solution for healthcare data. Ultimately, the specific type of database depends on a multitude of factors.

Next, we will look at SQL versus NoSQL databases at a high level. After this, we will discuss several different types of graph databases.

SQL Versus NoSQL

When discussing OLAP systems, people often look to NoSQL solutions (compared to SQL systems when considering OLTP systems). However, both SQL and NoSQL databases can be used for either OLAP or OLTP systems. The underlying decision for which type of database to use is a complex topic and beyond the scope of this book. As data engineers and data scientists, we often get involved with projects well after the databases have been deployed.

The key thing to remember is that SQL databases are a fairly homogeneous group of databases. While there are certainly differences from one vendor to the next, they are all conceptually the same. There are tables of rows and columns, and they are connected via primary-foreign key relationships.

NoSQL databases, on the other hand, are an extremely heterogeneous group of databases. By definition, they are all databases that do not follow the relational paradigm. As a result, they are all conceptually very different. The most common are column-oriented databases (e.g., Cassandra), key-value stores (e.g., Redis), document-oriented databases (e.g., MongoDB), and graph databases (e.g., Neo4j). Within each class, there are many options and vendors, each with a particular focus. Also, many database vendors are beginning to support multiple paradigms. For example, ArangoDB is a document-oriented database that also provides graph functionality; RedisGraph is a graph add-on for the Redis key-value store; Datastax also provides a graph database on top of the Cassandra column-oriented database. This is not intended to be an exhaustive list but simply to illustrate that the NoSQL landscape is wide and diverse with the only common characteristic of simply being something other than relational databases.

As a result, the query languages and underlying philosophies differ from database to database. For example, MongoDB and CouchBase are both document-oriented databases but have entirely different approaches to querying the data. MongoDB (*https:// oreil.ly/ikh29*) uses a JavaScript-based query language, whereas CouchBase (*https:// oreil.ly/bQVQ9*) provides a query language that is inspired by SQL itself.

On the graph database front, there are several different philosophical approaches, and the remainder of this chapter will cover three particular approaches. But first, let's look at the tried and true SQL database.

SQL Databases

This section provides a brief overview/review of SQL databases. It is intended for those who may have learned about databases years ago and need a quick review or those who may have heard of SQL databases but lack a little more detail. The main intent for this section is to baseline the vocabulary and basic concepts. I will refer to these concepts as we review the different types of graph databases.

As I mentioned earlier, SQL databases are the gold standard when it comes to database technology. While they are often referred to as SQL databases, they are also often referred to as relational database management systems (RDBMSs) or *relational databases.*

It is a little confusing, but *relations* in a relational database refer to the tables themselves, not the relationships between tables. That said, the power in a relational database is the ability to connect tables to one another and then query these connections. Figure 2-1 highlights how a patient might be connected to medications and diagnoses in a relational database.

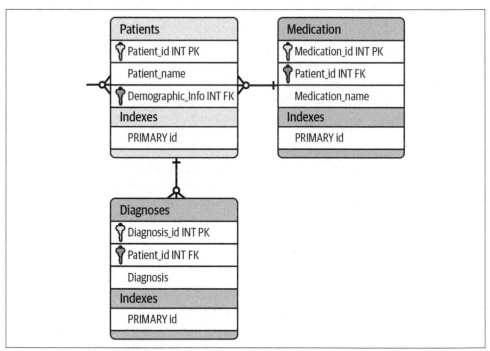

Figure 2-1. Relational database example

As you can see, the `Patients` table is intended to track individual patients, each with a name (`Patient_name`) and a link to `Demographic_Info` (not shown). Additionally, there are two other tables, `Medication` and `Diagnoses`, that each have a link back to `Patients`. The *PK* and *FK* that you see correspond to *primary key* and *foreign key*.

These keys are one of the fundamental building blocks of relational databases and are what allow tables to be linked together. A primary key (PK) is used to uniquely identify rows within a particular table. Sometimes, these keys represent attributes in real life (e.g., medical record number, Social Security number, insurance subscriber ID); other times, they are entirely artificial and do not have any meaning or semantic relevance to the underlying data. The latter are often sequentially generated integers (as in the example in Figure 2-1).

Foreign keys are used in tables to refer to rows in another table. In the previous example, the PK of the `Patients` table is `Patient_id`, presumably a patient identifier assigned by the clinic or hospital. Each patient is likely to be on one or more medications. So, the database architect decided to create a second table to store medications. To link these medications to particular patients, they have set up a primary-foreign key relationship between the `Patients` and `Medication` tables. There is a column in the `Medication` table that will always store `Patient_id`. In this particular setup, a single patient can be linked to multiple entries in the `Medication` table since any number of rows in `Medication` can refer to the same patient. On the other hand, each medication entry can refer only to a single patient. This is what we call a one-to-many relationship between `Patients` and `Medication`.

When linking two tables such as `Patients` and `Medication`, you will typically see one-to-one, one-to-many, or many-to-one relationships. In one-to-one situations, a single row in one table will correspond to a single row in another table. In one-to-many situations, a single row in a table will link to multiple rows in another table. Many-to-one is the same except when looking from the perspective of the other table.

You can model many things using these relationships. But, what about more complex systems where you need many-to-many relationships? To build out the example, what if we don't want to track multiple entries of "Acetaminophen (Tylenol)" within our system? In other words, regardless of how many patients may have been prescribed acetaminophen, we want to track only a single instance of it. This would clean up our database and prevent thousands of duplicate rows where we might need to rename the medication or change some other attribute of it. Figure 2-2 is an example of one way to link patients to medications such that we have a many-to-many relationship. A single patient can be linked to any number of medications, and a particular medication can be linked to any number of patients.

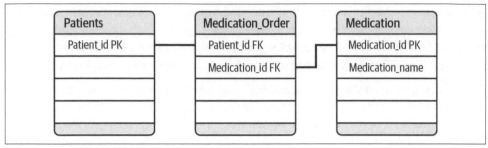

Figure 2-2. Basic join table example

This is what we call a *join table*. As it stands, the join table addresses the basic requirement of having a single entry for a particular medication name, so we don't have multiple entries for "Acetaminophen (Tylenol)." However, you may have noticed that I labeled the join table `Medication_Order`. Figure 2-3 expands on the basic join example with several more columns for the `Medication_Order` table such as `order_date` and `ordered_by`.

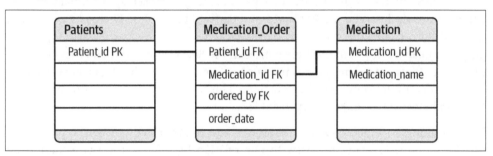

Figure 2-3. Expanded medication order join table example

The `ordered_by` column is a foreign key relation and points back to another table (not shown) of physicians and nurse practitioners who can place medication orders. The column `order_date` is when the medication order was actually entered into the system. This highlights the power of join tables and how they can be used to model complex systems such as the ordering or administration of medications.

For the latter, we may create another table called `Medication_Administration` that has a one-to-one relationship with `Medication_Order`. You may be wondering, why create something with a one-to-one relationship when we can just add additional columns? In this case, the two tables capture very different parts of the workflow, so it makes sense to also separate them in the database. This could make it easier when trying to load this data into a data warehouse but also simplifies the engineering and database administration since updates to the medication ordering versus administration processes can be tested independently.

To continue the example on patients, medications, and medication orders, let's see how they might look from the perspective of SQL queries in Examples 2-1 and 2-2.

Example 2-1. Medication orders in SQL

```
# Get the medication ID for acetaminophen
SELECT Medication_id
FROM Medication
WHERE Medication_name = "Acetaminophen (Tylenol)";

# Get all patients on acetaminophen without a join table
SELECT P.Patient_id FROM Patients P
INNER JOIN Medication M
ON P.Patient_id = M.Patient_id
WHERE M.Medication_name = "Acetaminophen (Tylenol)";

# Get all patients on acetaminophen with a join table
SELECT Patient_id FROM Medication_Order MO
INNER JOIN Medication M
ON MO.Medication_id = M.Medication_id
WHERE M.Medication_name = "Acetaminophen (Tylenol)";
```

Example 2-2. Medication orders with patient date of birth in SQL

```
# Get patient IDs and date of birth on acetaminophen without a join table
SELECT P.Patient_id, P.DOB FROM Patients P
INNER JOIN Medication M
ON P.Patient_id = M.Patient_id
WHERE M.Medication_name = "Acetaminophen (Tylenol)";

# Get patient IDs and date of birth on acetaminophen with a join table
SELECT P.Patient_id, P.DOB FROM Patient P
INNER JOIN Medication_Order MO
ON P.Patient_id = MO.Patient_id
INNER JOIN Medication M
ON MO.Medication_id = M.Medication_id
WHERE M.Medication_name = "Acetaminophen (Tylenol)";
```

Example 2-1 shows some basic SQL queries corresponding to the schema in Figure 2-1 where no join table exists between patients and their medications. This is the simplest schema, and the *INNER JOIN* is the key aspect of SQL that enables this. Joins are the mechanism by which we can query relational databases and extract data that is spread across multiple tables. If you have worked with SQL in the past, this is intended as a review. If you are new to SQL, my main intent here is to give you a high-level overview and help you develop a basic understanding of how to query relational databases.

Example 2-2 expands on the SQL queries and assumes the schema that is provided in Figure 2-3. Here, you can see the query becomes a little bit more complex since we need to join across three different tables. The last query in Example 2-2 also high-lights how the queries can get more complex when trying to query additional proper-ties such as a patient's date of birth.

These examples and the idea of join tables in particular are critical to thinking about graph-based representations of the data, and graph databases. So, let's check out our first type of graph database, the property graph database.

(Labeled) Property Graph Databases

Labeled property graph (LPG) databases, often referred to as just *property graph data-bases*, are probably one of the most common graph databases in use today. They are certainly not the only type of graph database and not even the first. However, compa-nies such as Neo4j have popularized them in recent years. At their core, property graphs are essentially a collection of *nodes* (sometimes referred to as *vertices*) and *relationships* (sometimes referred to as *edges*), as shown in Figure 2-4.

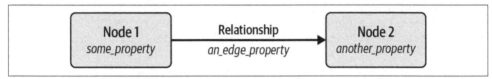

Figure 2-4. Property graph nodes and relationships

Relationships are directional and always point from one node to another. However, graph query languages usually allow you to query relationships while ignoring their directionality. In labeled property graphs, nodes also have *labels*, which provide a higher-level organization of all the nodes that might be in the database. These labels are somewhat analogous to tables in a relational database. To continue the example from earlier, we would have a couple of labels or types of nodes: Patient and Medica-tion. Each node can also have properties that are analogous to columns of a table. One possible graph-based representation of the schema in Figure 2-3 is shown in Figure 2-5.

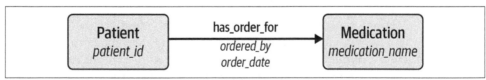

Figure 2-5. Medication order example as a property graph

As you can see, we still have the ability to represent patients, medications, and orders of medications while tracking the relevant columns. When used this way, property graphs and relational databases have many similarities and generally provide the same functionality. You may be wondering, what's the difference and why bother with graph databases (especially if you already have a relational database deployed)?

In relational databases, the relationships focus on connecting tables together as part of the underlying schema of the database. The semantics of how two data points are connected get baked into the design and administration of the underlying database. This needs to be documented well; otherwise, this knowledge will disappear once the responsible engineers leave the organization. This may be especially problematic if the underlying reason has nothing to do with the meaning of the data but is a result of a technical issue. Also, if a data engineer or data scientist wants to add a new type of relationship between tables, they must work with the database administrators and engineers to update the database schema accordingly.

On the other hand, within a property graph database, all aspects of the data (labels, properties, and relationship types) are considered data in the sense that they can be updated on the fly and there is no need to redesign the database schema. As such, property graph databases fall under the umbrella of *schemaless databases*. This is a bit of a misnomer since the databases certainly have a schema. However, the schemas can be changed on the fly and not set/managed by the database administrator. Perhaps a better description would be that they have dynamic schemas.

Schemaless Versus NoSQL

Terms like *schemaless* and *NoSQL* are used often when describing many databases. Despite having some overlap, they capture different ideas. NoSQL databases are all databases that are not relational, SQL databases. Schemaless databases are ones that do not require a strict schema to be defined prior to persisting data.

TypeDB is an example of a NoSQL database that is *not* schemaless since it requires a schema to be loaded before any data can be persisted.

To further confuse things, we are also seeing schema-on-read where data can be persisted without a schema. But, one can create a schema afterward and then use SQL to query the data.

So, you may now be wondering, are these just schemaless versions of relational databases? What are the benefits and trade-offs?

Much of the benefit of property graph databases may lie in their query languages, not in how they represent and store the data. At some level, this is true for almost anything in computer science. Most tools can be used to solve most problems—the specific decision to use one or another largely depends on a variety of tangential factors. In the context of labeled property graphs versus relational databases, some key considerations are:

- Are the types of relationships between various concepts set in stone?
- How likely are new relationships going to be added? By whom?
- Relative importance of requirements around:
  — ACID compliance
  — Read/write latency
  — OLTP versus OLAP
  — Ease of writing/maintaining queries
  — Existing tools in your ecosystem (e.g., reporting tools such as Tableau) and expertise available in your organization
  — Similarity to SQL? Developer friendly?

We will discuss some common query languages and frameworks for working with graphs and graph databases. Unlike SQL databases, there is no single standard for working with graph databases. While we will discuss SPARQL and RDF as standards, they capture only a subset of graph databases. As with other NoSQL databases, each vendor has come up with a query language tailored to the nuances of their underlying technology.

Two of the most common query languages for property graphs are Cypher (and its open sourced counterpart openCypher) and Gremlin. A few vendors (e.g., Redis-Graph) have adopted openCypher, and some have adopted Gremlin (e.g., Janus-Graph, AWS Neptune, OrientDB), while many have support via third-party libraries (e.g., Neo4j). The challenge with third-party libraries, as evident with Neo4j support, is that they may not support the latest versions of a particular database, and support is likely to come and go depending on the needs of the underlying maintainer.

Query languages such as Cypher, Arango Query Language, and GSQL (from Tiger-Graph) are structurally similar to SQL. This decreases the learning curve for those who are accustomed to working with SQL. On the other hand, approaches such as Gremlin are much more programmer-oriented and less of a traditional query language. These are neither pros nor cons in an absolute sense. It does, however, become a consideration when you are considering the demographic of your team and how effective a particular set of tools might be. If no one on your team can use a tool, it doesn't matter if it is a theoretically superior solution or not, because it will not have any measurable impact.

Let's look at some examples of how the SQL queries from Examples 2-1 and 2-2 might look in graph query languages while assuming the graph schema provided in Figure 2-5. First up is Cypher, which is the primary query language for Neo4j.

Cypher

Example 2-3 contains a basic Cypher query that looks for a medication by name, then for all of the patients for which the medication has been ordered, and then for some information on the patient. As you can see, it's similar in many ways to SQL, making it easier to learn for those who have been working in the relational world.

Example 2-3. Medication orders in Cypher

```
# Get the medication ID for acetaminophen
MATCH (m:Medication {Medication_name: "Acetaminophen (Tylenol)"})
RETURN m.Medication_id

# Get all patients on acetaminophen via the has_order_for relationship
MATCH (p:Patient)-[:has_order_for]->
    (m:Medication {Medication_name: "Acetaminophen (Tylenol)"})
RETURN p

# Get patient IDs and date of birth on acetaminophen via
# the has_order_for relationship
MATCH (p:Patient)-[:has_order_for]->
    (m:Medication {Medication_name: "Acetaminophen (Tylenol)"})
RETURN p.Patient_id, p.DOB
```

As you can see, the queries are similar to one another and are not too different from their SQL counterparts. However, the syntax is much more compact. While it is certainly possible to use SQL to model this particular use case, the Cypher-based approach feels much simpler and easier. This simplicity is particularly highlighted by the additional query for the patient's date of birth. In the SQL example, it required an additional INNER JOIN clause, while the Cypher version simply required an additional p.DOB.

Cypher appears to have been designed for those who are comfortable (and maybe prefer) working with SQL. As an alternative, the Tinkerpop graph framework created Gremlin, which is much more similar to writing code. Many developers prefer Gremlin since it is more natural than wrapping a query language with code. So, let's see how our example looks in Gremlin.

Gremlin

As you can see in Example 2-4, the syntax is quite different from Cypher. This looks more like Python or Groovy code rather than a query language. Given this fundamental design difference, Gremlin could be challenging for those data analysts or data scientists who are familiar with SQL or who lack experience writing code.

Example 2-4. Medication orders in Gremlin

```
# Get the medication ID for acetaminophen
g.V()
 .has("Medication_name", "Acetaminophen (Tylenol)")
 .property("Medication_id")

# Get all patients on acetaminophen via the has_order_for relationship
g.V()
 .has("Medication_name", "Acetaminophen (Tylenol)")
 .in("has_order_for")

# Get patient IDs and date of birth on acetaminophen via the has_order_for
# relationship
 g.V()
  .has("Medication_name", "Acetaminophen (Tylenol)")
  .in("has_order_for")
  .values("Patient_id", "DOB")
```

Again, we can see that the traversal of relationships within the graph add a minimal amount of syntax to the overall query. In the early days, using Gremlin meant building your stack on the Java ecosystem using either Java or Groovy as your primary programming language. However, drivers now exist for Python, making it easier to integrate into the increasingly ubiquitous Python data ecosystem.

Now, we shift to a less popular query language that is specific to a single database. Though Neo4j is a much more popular database, ArangoDB has a unique approach in that it natively supports both documents (e.g., JSON) and graphs. This could be particularly useful when working with data coming in JSON-based formats such as Fast Health Interoperability Resources (FHIR).

ArangoDB query language

ArangoDB came across my radar because it is a document-oriented database that seamlessly integrates into a JSON-based ecosystem. On top of that, its query language also supports graphs. As a multimodal database, ArangoDB potentially pairs the best of document-oriented and graph databases. In Example 2-5, we adapt the same queries to AQL.

Example 2-5. Medication orders in the ArangoDB query language

```
# Get the medication ID for acetaminophen
FOR m IN Medication
  FILTER m.Medication_name == "Acetaminophen (Tylenol)"
  RETURN m.Medication_id

# Get all patients on acetaminophen via the has_order_for relationship
FOR m IN Medication
  FILTER m.Medication_name == "Acetaminophen (Tylenol)"
  FOR p in 1..1 INBOUND m has_order_for
    RETURN p

# Get patient IDs and date of birth on acetaminophen via the has_order_for
# relationship
FOR m IN Medication
  FILTER m.Medication_name == "Acetaminophen (Tylenol)"
  FOR p in 1..1 INBOUND m has_order_for
    RETURN {id: p.Patient_id, dob: p.DOB}
```

AQL feels a bit like the combination of a query language as well as a traversal language. That said, we can see that the queries increase in syntactic complexity as compared to Cypher and Gremlin.

This concludes our introduction to property graph databases; next up are hypergraphs. They are a slightly more generalized approach to graph databases. They support the same abilities to create properties for nodes and relationships, but they have the added ability to represent multiple nodes in a single relationship or to have relationships linked to one another.

Hypergraph Databases

Hypergraphs are not nearly as common when considering the landscape of graph databases. When someone mentions "graph database," nearly everyone will assume they are talking about a property graph or RDF database. In a property graph, an edge connects exactly two vertices (or, a relationship connects two nodes). A hypergraph, on the other hand, contains *hyperedges* that can connect any number of vertices. In Figure 2-6, I compare a property graph representation and a hypergraph representation of the same information.

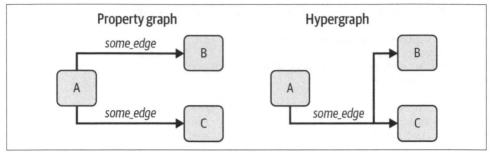

Figure 2-6. Property graph versus hypergraph

As you can see, node A is connected to nodes B and C via the relationship some_edge. In a property graph database, two separate relationships are stored, A→B and A→C. In the hypergraph representation, a single edge is stored, but that edge connects A to *both* B and C. Additionally, the hypergraph database I will be covering in this book also treats hyperedges as a vertex. This means that an edge can itself be part of another edge.

You may be scratching your head a bit and wondering why would we want to treat an edge as a vertex, and wouldn't that confuse things? Yes, this can be a difficult concept to wrap your head around and may feel very "meta." In the example we have been using around patients and medication orders, the hypergraph idea does not provide any benefit. After all, our relationship is connecting only two nodes anyway (a patient and a medication via the has_order_for relationship). The hypergraph representation is the same. But, what about the situation for combination therapies where multiple medications are ordered for a single patient? Figure 2-7 illustrates an example where a patient may be on multiple medications, A, B, and C.

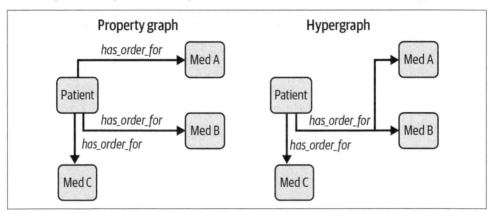

Figure 2-7. Property graph versus hypergraph with multiple medications

The additional context, however, is that medications A and B must be taken together as a combination therapy—the patient should not take one without the other. Additionally, the patient is also on medication C. In the property graph representation, it is unclear if the patient just happens to be on three separate medications at the same time or if A and B are ordered together. In the hypergraph representation, this is made very clear since A and B are connected via the same has_order_for relationship. Of course, we can solve this by adding additional properties or nodes to the property graph representation, but we are now changing the representation of the data to account for shortcomings in the underlying graph representation.

In the next section, we spend a little time with TypeDB (formerly Grakn) and its query language, TypeQL, as a particular implementation of hypergraphs.

TypeDB and TypeQL

TypeDB is a strongly typed database that is an abstraction over an underlying graph database. This allows it to provide a reasoning engine that can leverage strongly typed schemas to provide powerful inferencing functionality not immediately available within graph databases.[1] When I started this book, it was known as Grakn Labs, and the database was called Grakn. The company has since rebranded, but its technical approach remains the same, and its functionality is unique and a potentially good fit for many use cases in healthcare.

In Example 2-6, we continue with the same example of querying the system for acetaminophen and building up our query to extract patient-level data of those for whom it was prescribed.

Example 2-6. Medication orders in TypeQL

```
# Get the medication ID for acetaminophen
match
    $medication isa Medication,
              has Medication_name "Acetaminophen (Tylenol)",
              has Medication_id $id;
get $id;

# Get all patients on acetaminophen via the has_order_for relationship
match
    $medication isa Medication,
              has Medication_name "Acetaminophen (Tylenol)";

    $patient isa Patient;

    (patient: $patient, medication: $medication) isa order;
```

---

1 "Comparing TypeDB to Property Graph Databases" (*https://oreil.ly/Qc4p5*), Vaticle.

```
get $patient

# Get patient IDs and date of birth on acetaminophen via the has_order_for
# relationship
match
    $medication isa Medication,
                has Medication_name "Acetaminophen (Tylenol)";

    $patient isa Patient, has dob $dob, has Patient_id $id;

    (patient: $patient, medication: $medication) isa order;
get $dob, $id;
```

As you can see, TypeQL has a structure similar to the other query languages and makes it pretty clear and easy to query across relationships or properties.

Last on our list are RDF databases, sometimes referred to as *triple stores*. They have been around quite a while and are flexible and expressive. However, that comes with added complexity that makes the learning curve quite steep. They are also the most generalized graph database—anything we can do with property graphs or hypergraphs, we can do with an RDF database.

Resource Description Framework Databases

Resource description framework (RDF) graphs have been around for a long time and are part of the World Wide Web Consortium (W3C) and of the Semantic Web. RDF graphs are extremely flexible and quite powerful given the trade-off that they have a fairly steep learning curve and, as a result, often carry the stigma that they are "too academic."

You may often hear RDF graph databases referred to as *triple stores*. This comes from the idea that RDF graphs are a collection of triples of the form *subject-predicate-object* (referred to as an *RDF triple*), as shown in Figure 2-8.

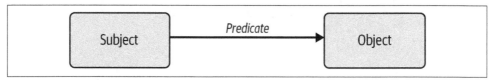

Figure 2-8. RDF triple

While Figure 2-8 shows a diagram similar to what we saw with property graphs, they are a bit more abstract in the sense that everything in an RDF graph is stored as a triple. In other words, what would be a column in a relational database or a property in a property graph database is itself an RDF triple. Figure 2-9 shows how a property graph would store and represent a particular patient with an ID of 1234 and a date of birth of 2020-01-01.

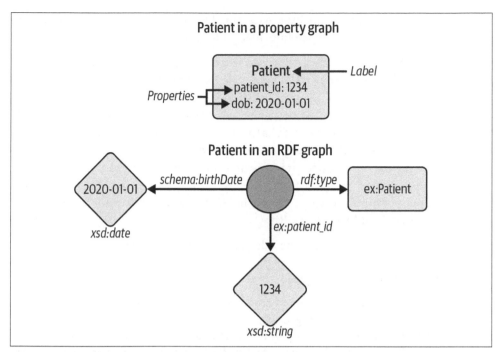

Figure 2-9. Property versus RDF graph patient example

In the RDF representation of a patient, the circle is the *subject* in three different tri-ples—one each for the birth date, patient ID, and type of node. The *predicate* provides the context of how the *object* should be interpreted. In this case, the predicate is what tells us that 2020-01-01 is actually a birth date and 1234 is a patient identifier.

The power behind this approach is that nearly anything can be modeled using this basic schema. You may have also noticed that a particular notation is used throughout the example, consisting of two strings separated by a colon. This is an adaptation of XML namespacing where a *namespace* can be defined that corresponds to the base of a URI, to which an identifier can be appended. The key point here is that RDF relies heavily on uniform resource identifiers (URIs). Because URIs for a particular seman-tic context often have the same base, the use of namespaces allows us to simplify the representation, making it more compact and easier to read.

Because RDF was created as a standard to represent data and information on the web, URIs are baked into the underlying standard. The intent is that any particular idea or notion is backed by a clearly defined concept that is accessible at the specified URI. This allows anything represented as RDF to be *self-describing*. This is particularly important in the context of the semantic web because anyone should be able to pub-lish and link information to anything else on the web. Unlike with most database systems (where information models are designed to support very specific use cases), RDF was designed to support open information models.

In Figure 2-9, the schema namespace (used in `schema:birthDate`) is used to shorten the URI `https://schema.org/birthDate`. The base `https://schema.org/` is shortened to `schema` so that we don't need to list the entire URI. Similarly, the ex namespace is a completely fictional namespace made up for this example. It could easily refer to something like `https://mydomain.com/example/` or anything else. The one requirement is that the URI be resolvable and provide specific details of the underlying resource. As you may notice, `https` is used in the previous examples—there is a general discussion over the use of `http` versus `https` (*https://oreil.ly/bTJ5V*) though that is generally beyond the scope of this book. The key point to remember is that resources are identified by unique URIs.

Let's take a look at the underlying query language for RDF triple stores.

SPARQL protocol and RDF query language

SPARQL stands for SPARQL protocol and RDF query language—pronounced "sparkle"—and is an is the underlying query language for RDF graphs. As part of the semantic web standard, it is fully open and implemented by many different vendors. Of course, RDF triple stores implement SPARQL, but many property graphs also have SPARQL implementations as well. For example, there is a SPARQL-gremlin (*https://oreil.ly/JMMSR*) connector such that SPARQL could be run against any database supporting gremlin.

SPARQL looks similar to SQL in many ways but integrates concepts such as namespaces and URIs. One thing you will notice in Example 2-7 is the addition of `PREFIX`—this allows query authors to shorten their queries by taking advantage of namespacing. Otherwise, the query should be similar to SQL. However, you will likely notice that the `WHERE` clause is a bit more verbose and reflects the subject-predicate-object nature of RDF. Every clause in the `WHERE` block is itself a triple.

Example 2-7. Medication orders with patient date of birth in SQL

```
# Get the medication ID for acetaminophen
PREFIX schema: <http://schema.org/>
PREFIX ex: <http://mydomain.com/some_example/>

SELECT ?medication_id
WHERE {
  ?medication ex:medication_name "Acetaminophen (Tylenol)" .
  ?medication ex:medication_id ?medication_id .
}

# Get all patients on acetaminophen via the has_order_for relationship
```

```
SELECT ?patient_id
WHERE {
  ?medication ex:medication_name "Acetaminophen (Tylenol)" .
  ?patient ex:has_order_for ?medication .
  ?patient ex:patient_id ?patient_id .
}

# Get patient IDs and date of birth on acetaminophen via the has_order_for
# relationship
SELECT ?patient_id ?dob
WHERE {
  ?medication ex:medication_name "Acetaminophen (Tylenol)" .
  ?patient ex:has_order_for ?medication .
  ?patient ex:patient_id ?patient_id .
  ?patient schema:birthDate ?dob .
}
```

This syntax may take you a bit of getting used to but is extremely flexible and power-ful. The RDF approach allows for a lot of flexibility in representing different data and information models. However, this flexibility comes with a common trade-off—per-formance. Because the data is stored as a series of triples, queries of large graphs can incur significant latency. Depending on your use case, this may be acceptable, or the flexibility is worth the cost of servers with significant CPU and RAM resources.

We have covered quite a bit about databases in general and graph databases in partic-ular. Let's do a quick recap before we jump into how we can use databases to manage healthcare vocabularies and terminologies in Chapter 4.

Conclusion

The intent of this chapter was not to make you an expert in the different types of graph databases. My goal was simply to give you a high-level overview of each and how their query languages compare to one another. I will dive much more deeply into each of these types of databases throughout the remainder of this book, particularly in the context of analyzing electronic health record and claims data.

The choice of which database to use depends on many factors and is generally beyond the scope of this book. As with any data project, the decision rests between a set of functional and nonfunctional requirements. Of course, the query language and underlying representation of the data are important considerations. But, as with nearly any software project, you can use any database to accomplish the task at hand —it may just require additional engineering on your part.

When looking at graph databases specifically, you may hear the term *graph-native* used quite a bit. Given the growing popularity of graph-based representations of data, many database vendors are starting to support graphs. Whether the database was originally a SQL database, document store, or even key-value store, you can find one that also supports graphs in some capacity. While any database can be used to represent a graph, graph-native refers to how the underlying data is stored. Particularly, graph-native databases provide *index-free adjacency*. That is, nodes that are connected by relationships are stored such that the retrieval of related nodes/edges does not require additional indexing.

This may or may not be a concern for you. After all, does it matter if the underlying database requires additional indexing to provide graph functionality? For small graphs, this may not matter. For large graphs, the indexes themselves could become very large and nonperformant. This is one example of the types of additional considerations when considering graph databases.

Now that you have a bit of a technical introduction to graph databases, we will switch gears a bit in the next chapter and focus on vocabularies, terminologies, and ontologies. If you have worked with the semantic web in the past, you have worked with ontologies before. The next chapter is not a general introduction to ontologies or semantic web principles—instead, it is focused on specific applications and examples of these approaches within healthcare. Within this context, we will cover some basic ideas when it comes to semantics but only in support of healthcare-specific examples.

## CHAPTER 3

Standardized Vocabularies in Healthcare

In this chapter, we cover *standardized vocabularies, controlled vocabularies, terminologies*, and *ontologies*. Some use these terms quite interchangeably, while others adhere to fairly precise definitions that may be confusing at first. We will start with a short introduction to these ideas, how they are similar, where they overlap, and also how they differ. You will see me use the term *terminology* as a nebulous reference to a particular source of content that spans the spectrum of vocabulary to ontology. For example, International Classification of Diseases, Revision 10 (ICD-10), ICD-9, and Systematized Nomenclature of Medicine—Clinical Terms (SNOMED-CT) would all be referred to as terminologies. Some are simply a collection of terms and definitions (e.g., vocabularies), while others capture hierarchies or even richer relationships (e.g., ontologies).

In addition to the content, there are also associated tools and processes that build on top of the *semantic web*. For example, many ontologies come in Web Ontology Language (OWL) and build on top of Resource Description Framework (RDF). These technologies are not specific to healthcare or medicine, but this is one area where we have seen a larger adoption of these technologies.

If there is a single technical chapter in this book that differentiates it from books about data (especially in other industries), it would be this one. Many of the challenges when working with healthcare data are mitigated by the use of semantic technologies—both the tools as well as the content. For example, ICD codes are often used to track diagnoses within EHRs. This is intended to simplify our approach to data and to standardize how we code diseases. This allows clinics and hospitals throughout the country to submit claims for reimbursement from the government and insurance companies. On the other hand, maintaining and managing such controlled vocabularies becomes a core informatics function that can often feel distracting and unwieldy.

In addition to a high-level introduction of these vocabularies, terminologies, and ontologies, we will also spend some time with the Unified Medical Language System (UMLS), a suite of datafiles and associated software that makes it easier to work with the multitude of sources available (the *UMLS Metathesaurus*). It also provides some linkages between many of the sources, facilitating some semantic interoperability between different vocabularies (the *UMLS Semantic Network*).

Before we get too much into the details of working with different sources of vocabularies, terminologies, and ontologies, this next section will give you a basic foundation to these concepts as well as orient you to how we use them when working with healthcare data.

Controlled Vocabularies, Terminologies, and Ontologies

In healthcare, there is a varying degree of adoption of ideas from the semantic web and the field of information science. As such, you may hear informatics folks talk about ontologies or vocabularies. In most cases, adoption of these ideas attempts to remain true to the W3C standards. However, there is one big difference between the goals of the semantic web and how we use these ideas in healthcare—the semantic web sets the foundation for connecting data, information, and knowledge across the open web; in healthcare, we often have a much narrower and highly curated view of the world, focusing on very nuanced interpretations. Consequently, we see varied adoption of semantic web ideas and standards, some more rigorous than others.

Whenever you hear someone talk about semantic web concepts such as *ontologies* or *vocabularies*, it would be prudent to find out how that term is being used. For example, if someone says, "I built an ontology for Parkinson's disease," you should be wondering if they had collected a handful of concepts pertaining to Parkinson's disease (PD) or if they had developed a formal definition of PD and its symptoms and medications in the OWL (*https://www.w3.org/OWL*), or anything in between.

Per the W3C (*https://oreil.ly/Euswg*), the distinction between *vocabulary* and *ontology* is not very clear—"The trend is to use the word *ontology* for more complex, and possibly quite formal, collections of terms, whereas *vocabulary* is used when such strict formalism is not necessarily used or only in a very loose sense."

In any case, it is generally accepted that *vocabularies* are a collection of terms and their definitions, representing a set of concepts used in a particular context. For example, the set of ICD-10 codes could be considered a vocabulary. Other examples include the drop-down list of medications that were hand-coded within a home-grown electronic health record and the list of COVID symptoms in your employer's health screening app. In some cases (e.g., ICD-10 or SNOMED CT), the vocabularies are explicitly developed and maintained by subject-matter and domain experts to serve as industry standards. In other cases (as with many desktop and mobile apps), they are developed implicitly by software developers and IT professionals. Though there was likely input from subject-matter experts, the intent was to provide certain app functionality and not necessarily to create a rigorous set of terms and their definitions.

Coding Systems

You may also see the term *coding system* used, mostly in the context of medical coding (*https://oreil.ly/LymFz*). We often use medical codes and coding systems as vocabularies and terminologies (as we will discuss later in this chapter). The challenge is that medical coding is focused on documentation for reimbursement, not to capture and preserve data for analytics. As a result, coding systems are not necessarily exhaustive nor rigorous in what terms/concepts are defined.

On the other end of the spectrum, most people think of ontologies as a collection of terms and their definitions but with a specific focus on the underlying concept (not necessarily its name or textual representation) *and* formal relationships between concepts. If a single concept might have different names or labels, they would be attached to the concept as synonyms with one being specified as the *preferred name/label*. Ontologies can become quite complex quickly because everything becomes formally defined. For example, what does "preferred name" even mean? How do we standardize the definition of this attribute? Many ontologies leverage SKOS, the Simple Knowledge Organization System, allowing ontologies to be developed with the same foundational approach to things like labels (*https://oreil.ly/DGOWF*).

As with any software library, there is a wide spectrum of how ontologies are developed. Some focus on implementation details, adhering rigidly to semantic web standards and approaches, while others are more philosophical and may be just a diagram. Yet, authors of both may refer to their products as ontologies. As data engineers and scientists, you generally need to ask two questions when considering a particular ontology:

1. Is the content aligned with my data and use case?

2. What would it take to integrate this ontology into my data pipeline?

Somewhere between ontologies and vocabularies are the more nebulous *terminologies*. I have seen people refer to everything from vocabularies to ontologies simply as "terminologies." I tend to use the term when referring to something that is a collection of terms (and their definitions) that are concept oriented, have nonsemantic unique identifiers, and may have some relationships between the concepts.[1] Typically, these relationships capture some sort of hierarchy or how one concept directly relates to another.

There are many different ways to manage terminologies, often depending on where they lie on the spectrum. For example, if you are working only with ICD codes and performing lookups, the deployment of a full-blown RDF triple store would be over-kill. However, trying to distill a complex ontology into a single table within your data model would likely create many headaches. That said, we often hear the term *terminology service* used to describe the underlying system used to manage and maintain (and sometimes link) the spectrum of terminologies. There is no standard definition of what functionality a terminology service is required to provide, though the HL7 FHIR standard does have a specification (*https://oreil.ly/BoNrU*) for a terminology service. We will go into a little more detail about FHIR in Chapter 4. There are a range of tools available from open source to commercial products, and I am still encountering new solutions all the time.

As you look at both terminologies themselves or tools to help manage them, there are a few things to keep in mind. Next, we will look at some key things for you to con-sider and discuss across your entire team (from domain experts to IT) as you decide how best to proceed.

Key Considerations

As I briefly mentioned previously, there are two levels in which we need to think about how we can integrate terminologies into our data projects and pipelines. We need to consider the tools themselves and the plumbing needed to connect it all together. On the other hand, we need to consider the terminologies themselves and the quality and alignment of the content to our particular use case. For large organi-zations that have many different projects, you may also need to consider your infra-structure such that you can support multiple different (and possibly conflicting) needs.

From a tooling standpoint, the biggest questions are:

What does a terminology service even look like for your project?
    If you just need a simple lookup, you might be able to get away with loading the terminologies you need into a SQL database and using the built-in free-text matching. Or, perhaps a simple setup of ElasticSearch or Solr would suffice.

---

[1] Though it was published a while ago, there is a paper by Jim Cimino, titled *Desiderata for Controlled Medical Vocabularies in the Twenty-First Century* (*https://oreil.ly/bMrmR*) that highlights many of the common themes when working with vocabularies, terminologies, and ontologies. It is a must-read for anyone working on cre-ating or maintaining them, and a really-should-read for anyone consuming them.

However, if you are planning on interacting with any other system using FHIR, then you might need a terminology service that supports the FHIR spec. These are not trivial questions and something that requires understanding your use case, your data sources, and having the necessary medical informatics experts on hand to help navigate the many options and decision points.

How do you integrate terminologies with your data?

This highlights the fact that it is as much a data challenge as it is a tooling challenge. If you are working with data in a SQL or property graph database and you find the perfect ontology for your use case but it's only available in OWL, you will need to decide how best to connect your data to the ontology. There are libraries such as neosemantics (*https://oreil.ly/wETe0*) that attempt to bridge the gap between RDF and property graphs. If you're working in SQL, perhaps it is enough to add a new column to your table that contains the unique identifier of the concept from your ontology. Or, you have decided to go all in with RDF and convert your data from SQL to an RDF triple store using something like OntoRefine (*https://oreil.ly/keuTq*). Again, this requires having the necessary experts on hand and also people who understand both the technical requirements as well as the data side of things.

So, after consulting with our experts, we have decided on integrating a commercial terminology service that supports FHIR, such as Ontoserver (*https://oreil.ly/B2phE*). We have also decided to use SNOMED codes as our main approach for representing semantic concepts. However, our source data consists primarily of ICD-10 codes. There are still some key things to consider, particularly as we move away from the tooling and toward the actual semantic harmonization.

Different organizations use terms/concepts differently

While ICD is intended to be a standard, the nuances around choosing one code over another similar code are dependent on local context. For example, is the code being chosen as part of a reimbursement claim, is it being used for reporting cause of death, or is it being entered by a clinician or billing specialist? This sort of context (as we discussed a bit in Chapter 1) plays a major role in how codes are interpreted and normalized. Despite the use of standardized coding systems such as ICD-9 or ICD-10, we still need to answer these sorts of questions when working with healthcare data.

Different releases and versions of ICD (e.g., ICD-9 versus ICD-10)

While ICD is sometimes thought of as a single standard, there are several different versions of ICD. Most data being generated today that is coded using ICD will use ICD-10. The majority of the world has been using ICD-10 for decades. The United States made the decision in 2009 to adopt ICD-10 (*https://oreil.ly/fWvaC*), but the final implementation was not until 2015.

As a result, you are likely to encounter data coded in both ICD-9 as well as ICD-10, depending on when and where it was collected. To make it more challenging, ICD-11 has been released, though not yet formally adopted by most countries and organizations (*https://oreil.ly/U8P1R*).

Even within a particular version of ICD-9 or ICD-10, there are different "releases." There releases occur on multiple levels, making it very difficult for data producers/collectors and data scientists alike. The WHO publishes official releases (*https://oreil.ly/CMa1I*). Additionally, local health agencies (e.g., Centers for Medicare and Medicaid Services (*https://oreil.ly/fWvaC*)) also modify and publish updates to the coding systems.

As if managing these different levels of releases weren't complex enough, there are also guidelines on *how* the codes should be used. So, as shown in Figure 3-1, in addition to knowing which release of ICD (e.g., ICD-10), you would need to know which updates have been applied to the data, what local modifications there may be, and then which version of guidelines was used to choose the appropriate code.

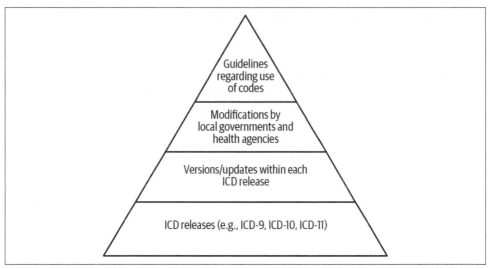

Figure 3-1. Layers of ICD complexity

Sometimes, it is impossible to get clarity at all levels, but it is important to realize that each of these layers has some effect on the data and how they should be interpreted. For example, if one hospital is using the 2005 update of ICD-10 and another hospital is using 2010, this may have a direct impact on the comparability of codes between the two hospitals.

Understanding these nuances and the underlying context of coding systems and terminologies and how they are applied to data may seem like venturing off into the weeds. However, it is important because it provides us with context. This context is helpful in determining what, if anything, we need to address during the data harmonization process. If you're lucky enough to work only with datasets that have been cleaned and curated, this may be less of a concern. The more raw the data source, the more someone needs to be asking these questions.

One common misunderstanding I've seen among those who are new to terminologies is making too many assumptions about the coding systems, the data, or the mapping process. For example, I often hear data scientists who lack RWD experience assume that if a code is chosen, it is the most appropriate code. There are many levels of challenges with this one assumption.

First, it assumes that the notion of choosing the "appropriate" code is absolute. What is appropriate for one use case (e.g., billing) may be different for another (e.g., tracking outcomes), and it is difficult for this statement to be evaluated with a deeper understanding of why the data was collected and who was responsible for choosing or mapping the codes that are ultimately captured.

Second, different disease areas will have different levels of granularity, especially as we move from one terminology to the next. This is usually a function of two inputs—the purpose of the terminology, as well as our understanding of the disease and its treatment. For example, SNOMED is much more granular and detailed than ICD-10, but it addresses both scientific and clinical practice perspectives. ICD-10 was created to track diagnoses at a much higher level. Additionally, if you look into cancer codes, we will see differing levels of granularity as we move from one cancer to another.

Sometimes this is a function of how much understanding we have about a cancer's subtype. Other times, it is a function of pre-coordination versus post-coordination of terms. In the next section, we will explore the differences between pre- and post-coordination and see how this impacts coded data.

Pre-coordination Versus Post-coordination

Controlled vocabularies can be useful when dealing with data as complex as RWD. We want to minimize ambiguity as much as possible and capture the meaning and context as precisely as possible. However, the concepts we frequently encounter in biology and medicine are quite complex and are often a combination of more fundamental concepts. For example, if someone suffers a fracture of their right ulna (the forearm bone on the pinky side), how do we capture this within the context of a controlled vocabulary?

We could create separate concepts for laterality (right), type of injury (fracture), and bone (ulna), and combine them as necessary. This is called *post-coordination*. The challenge with this approach is that we would need to combine them to capture any specific injury. Additionally, we may end up in situations where the combination does not make any clinical sense. Take the oversimplified example of laterality, type of injury, and bones within the body, as captured in Table 3-1. Using the post-coordination approach, we would choose one value from each column. This would cover our previous example of a "fracture of the right ulna," but it could also allow someone to code the "fracture of the right coccyx." Also known as the tailbone, the coccyx is at the base of the spinal column and thus does not have a laterality. So, "fracture of the right coccyx" would be confusing.

Table 3-1. Post-coordinating concepts

Laterality	Injury	Body part
Left	Fracture	Ulna
Right	Sprain	Radius
	...	Coccyx
		...

Our solution to this could be to make laterality optional. So, one could just leave that particular value blank, allowing for "fracture of the coccyx" to be a valid combination. However, this then sets us up for potential data quality issues—would we also accept "fracture of the ulna" as a valid concept? In this case, laterality is applicable but absent.

The other approach would be to use pre-coordination. Instead of providing three separate lists to choose from, we could pre-specify all of the possible combinations: fracture of the left ulna, fracture of the right ulna, fracture of the coccyx, etc. In this situation, we could specify all valid combinations and prevent invalid combinations. The trade-off, however, is that we could have very long lists of combinations that may be possible but seldom observed in real patients. Also, if we were to use these pre-coordinated terms as part of a list of options, the user interface would need to display hundreds to thousands of options, even after an initial filter.

You might be wondering which is the "better" option—pre-coordination or post-coordination. As with most things when it comes to healthcare RWD, the answer is *it depends*. If you are mapping data such that invalid combinations are unacceptable, then a pre-coordinated approach might be best. On the other hand, if a pre-coordinated approach creates an intractable number of options, a post-coordinated approach may be better. Also, you may be restricted based on other aspects of your stack. For example, if you're working with data that needs to be stored in OMOP (a data model from the Observational Health Data Sciences and Informatics program), you will need to use pre-coordination. As we will discuss more in Chapters 4 and 5, the OMOP common data model assumes pre-coordinated concepts.

It would be impossible to provide a comprehensive checklist on all of the different considerations you would need to make when working with terminologies. However, I've tried to highlight the most common issues that I've seen over the years, and this is intended simply as a starting point. Now, let's dive into a case study as we start getting into the nitty-gritty details of electronic health record data. In addition to this case study, we will spend Chapter 4 with a much deeper discussion of EHRs.

Case Study Example: EHR Data

As discussed in Chapter 1, data from electronic health records is highly fragmented and complex. In this section, I will introduce the Medical Information Mart for Intensive Care (MIMIC) dataset (*https://oreil.ly/ElJov*), a publicly available research dataset released by Harvard and MIT. The dataset originally started with intensive-care patients from the Beth Israel Deaconess Medical Center in Boston, Massachusetts. Generally, it is an extract of data from the hospital electronic health record system and associated modules (imaging, claims). The current release of the MIMIC data is MIMIC-IV.

However, the MIMIC-IV dataset does not have a version of the data in the native schema that is accessible without a data use agreement (DUA). The only public data for MIMIC-IV is currently in the OMOP format. While we will discuss the OMOP data structure a bit in this book, one of the key points of focus is the comparison of the native data model with the OMOP data model.

Complexity of MIMIC Data

MIMIC is an extremely valuable dataset and provides good insights into the data contained within an electronic health record. However, it is also important to note that it is the product of an entire biomedical informatics team. The data has been cleaned, curated, and de-identified using both automated and manual techniques. As a result, while you will get firsthand experience with many of the complexities when working with EHR data, you are also getting the benefit of this expert team's help in cleaning and curating the data to some degree.

Although the MIMIC data has been cleaned and curated a bit, it still suffers from many of the data quality challenges you would typically encounter when working with electronic health record data. In the context of ICD codes, as you can see in the MIMIC documentation (*https://oreil.ly/Api5s*), the schema for the table d_icd_diag noses (containing data on diagnosis codes) has a column named icd9_code. This tells us that all of the codes in this particular database are using ICD-9 codes, despite that we are currently using ICD-10 codes throughout the industry.

In the context of the pyramid in Figure 3-1, we would document that ICD-9 codes are the only codes being used in this dataset for the bottommost layer. For the next two layers, we would need to query the documentation or talk to the project team to see which particular updates and modifications of ICD-9 were used by the medical center. Since this is a medical center in the United States, we know that they are using the clinical modification, known as ICD-9-CM. For the topmost layer of the pyramid, we want to find out who generated these codes and what guidelines were used. For example, were these captured as part of the billing process, assigned by a medical billing expert or clinician, or via some automated system?

If we look at the MIMIC-III documentation for the `diagnoses_icd` table (*https://oreil.ly/rAiXT*), we see a few key statements:

- The ICD codes are generated for billing purposes at the end of the hospital stay.
- All ICD codes in MIMIC-III are ICD-9 based. The Beth Israel Deaconess Medical Center will begin using ICD-10 codes in 2015.
- The code field for the ICD-9-CM Principal and Other Diagnosis Codes is six characters in length, with the decimal point implied between the third and fourth digits for all diagnosis codes other than the V codes. The decimal is implied for V codes between the second and third digits.

Based on this, we know that the codes were generated for billing purposes, so they may not accurately reflect the patient's true clinical status (as we discussed in Chapter 1). Additionally, we have confirmed that this dataset contains only ICD-9 codes since ICD-10 codes were not integrated into the medical center's systems until 2015. While the documentation does not go into any detail about which guidelines were used or whether an autocoder was used or not, we have a much better understanding of this particular set of codes. Therefore, if we were trying to identify certain cohorts of patients, we know that we can start with these ICD codes but will also have many false negatives (e.g., patients may have cancer, but because their stay at Beth Israel may have been for a completely unrelated condition, they may not show up in the dataset because they were not billed for any cancer services) and false positives (e.g., a particular ICD code was assigned for billing purposes but may not reflect a patient's current clinical status).

We will go into much more detail about electronic health record data in Chapter 4 but, ideally, this case study highlighted how we need to be thinking about terminologies and specific terms/codes within the context of EHRs. Now, let's take a step back and look at some common terminologies that are used in healthcare.

Common Terminologies

Since the UMLS is a collection of industry-standard controlled vocabularies and terminologies, we will cover a few commonly used ones at a high level. This will give you a bit of necessary background as we dive into electronic health record and claims data in the next couple of chapters.

The systems discussed in this section are the ones that I have encountered most often, but the following list is not exhaustive—there are definitely others! The explanations I provide are mainly to guide the interpretation of data as data engineers and data scientists. They do not necessarily capture the full nuance and complexity of the delivery of healthcare services. For example, there are additional code systems used in US healthcare reimbursement such as Healthcare Common Procedure Coding System (HCPCS) (*https://oreil.ly/cMR1P*) and Diagnosis Related Group (DRG) (*https://oreil.ly/MvoEA*) codes.

In this section, we will cover Current Procedural Terminology (CPT), International Classification of Diseases (ICD-9/10), Logical Observation Identifiers, Names, and Codes (LOINC), RxNorm, and SNOMED CT.

CPT

Another controlled vocabulary that is focused on procedures is the Current Procedural Terminology (*https://oreil.ly/8ghrH*), managed by the American Medical Association. Generally, CPT codes are used to bill for physician and outpatient services, while ICD codes are ultimately used to bill for inpatient hospital procedures.

Procedure codes (similar to medications) give us a peek into the interventions that a patient received outside of medications. For example, we can look to procedure codes to see if a cancer patient underwent debulking surgery (the removal of as much tumor tissue as possible). Sometimes, knowing what procedure was performed can give us a sense of the underlying condition or diagnoses. Let's continue our debulking surgery example—if the specific code is 58575 (*https://oreil.ly/eqvnt*) ("The provider removes the uterus, cervix, ovaries, and fallopian tubes and then removes the entire omentum through the laparoscope, via the trocar ports or through the vaginal canal. The provider performs the procedure because of cancer."), then we can infer that the patient has cancer. However, we would not know specific details such as the subtype of cancer, whether it was found on just the ovaries, or if it had metastasized, among other details.

When we talk about such inferences, rule engines are a powerful (and often underutilized) tool. While systems like TypeDB have a built-in reasoning engine that will infer new nodes and relationships based on predefined rules, it is also possible to integrate rule engines (e.g., Drools, clara-rules) into your overall solution.

ICD-9 and ICD-10

Some of the most common codes you will encounter when working with RWD are ICD codes. Since 2015, the United States has transitioned entirely over to ICD-10. Prior to 2015, we were using ICD-9 codes. The majority of the world has been using ICD-10 codes for much longer!

As with most things in healthcare, things can get pretty complicated pretty quickly. "ICD-10" in its purest sense should refer to the World Health Organization's (WHO's) release of ICD-10 since it is the official maintainer of the ICD coding system. The WHO version contains only diagnosis codes.

However, if you are working with US healthcare organizations, most of the time, people mean ICD-10-CM even if they just call it "ICD-10." The -CM stands for "clinical modification" and includes modifications that are specific to the US healthcare system. In addition to ICD-10-CM, there is also the ICD-10-PCS, an extension to ICD-10 focused on procedure codes. Again, this is a US-specific modification and not part of the official WHO release.

Historically, ICD codes were originally created to track mortality statistics. However, they have since become embedded in the reimbursement process as well as EHRs for tracking diagnoses in general. However, given the initial focus on mortality statistics, there are certain nuances with ICD codes that may not be intuitive to clinicians and data scientists. For example, each code in ICD can belong to only a single hierarchy (preventing double counting), but this is problematic for diseases such as uterine cancer that are both an OB/GYN consideration as well as cancer.

LOINC

Another common set of codes are known as LOINC—Logical Observation Identifiers Names and Codes, pronounced "loink" (*https://loinc.org*)—codes. We often think of LOINC codes in terms of lab tests (e.g., blood tests), but they help capture many different types of observations. For example, surveys and questionnaires and even imaging codes are available within LOINC.

LOINC codes provide quite a bit of knowledge about the underlying test or observation. For example, take the LOINC code 57698-3 (*https://loinc.org/57698-3*) (Lipid panel with direct LDL, Serum or Plasma)—we know that it is a part of a chemistry panel, that it is a point-in-time test (versus over a time interval), and that it is something that is explicitly ordered.

RxNorm

RxNorm is a US-specific terminology that captures medications that are available in the United States. It is maintained by the National Library of Medicine and made available as part of the UMLS but also accessible via a dedicated API (*https://oreil.ly/vYuKr*).

RxNorm contains both generic and trade names as well as other information such as drug-drug interactions, drug classes, and links to National Drug Codes (NDC). Since RxNorm is entirely focused on medications and related data, it has specific properties/attributes such as the strength of a medication and its unit of measure (including support for concentrations such as 5mg/mL). Since RxNorm is also linked to the UMLS, there are associated concept unique identifiers (CUIs) and the ability to link RxNorm terms and concepts to other sources within the UMLS.

Unlike diagnosis or procedure codes, medication codes are closely tied to the countries or regions in which they are used. This is a result of the drug approval process— a drug approved in one country may not be approved in another country. RxNorm is specific to the United States, so you may see codes from other standards and terminologies if you work with data from other countries. Two other standards that I have encountered in the past are the Anatomic Therapeutic Chemical (ATC) classification system (*https://oreil.ly/3n1CF*) and the Identification of Medicinal Products (IDMP) (*https://oreil.ly/tjNll*).

SNOMED CT

SNOMED CT (though often referred to as just SNOMED, pronounced "snow med") is the Systematized Nomenclature of Medicine (*https://www.snomed.org*). It is much more comprehensive than other commonly used terminologies and covers both the delivery of healthcare and medicine (e.g., diagnoses, procedures) as well as more generalized biomedical knowledge (e.g., anatomy, chemistry, microorganisms). One of the most powerful features is that these concepts are all connected by semantic relationships, making SNOMED more of an ontology than a simple controlled vocabulary.

These relationships connect the many different types of concepts allowing for queries such as "all diseases related to the heart." While extremely powerful and certainly helpful for us as data scientists, it is important to remember that the "knowledge" contained within SNOMED is curated by committees of experts that are always playing catch-up. The field of medicine, from our understanding of biological processes to the practice of medicine itself, is constantly evolving. As a result, the content of SNOMED (both the concepts as well as the relationships) may not be fully aligned with the data that you are working with. Avoid the trap of thinking that "Oh, we have SNOMED, so we no longer need additional domain expert curation" of either the data or the mappings of your data to various coding systems.

Additionally, keep in mind that SNOMED has hundreds of thousands of terms! One thing that I have noticed in many projects and datasets is that sometimes the choice of codes appears inconsistent or confusing. There are many reasons for this—ranging from annoyed clinicians choosing any code so that they can proceed to the next screen, to many codes that sound similar and no obvious sign which code is optimal. In addition, when you have this many terms and a diversity of professional backgrounds and experience, it is almost guaranteed that you will have inconsistencies in the data.

SNOMED Code Example

One example of how the "wrong" code might get chosen can be found when looking at myocardial infarctions (heart attacks). Say we have two patients who are admitted with a diagnoses of "acute posterior myocardial infarction" and someone chooses SNOMED code 233838001 ("acute posterior myocardial infarction") for the first patient, while someone else chooses 57054005 ("acute myocardial infarction") for the second patient.

The latter code is not wrong; it is simply not as specific. Perhaps the second person did not have this level of specificity at the time of coding or simply did not think it was necessary to capture this level of specificity. In either case, this can create challenges for us since any trained models will treat these as separate categorical variables.

There are many other coding systems, vocabularies, and terminologies. Many health systems and medical centers have their own internal coding systems as well. We cannot cover them all, but you should have a basic understanding of the most common ones. But, regardless of which specific terminology you might encounter, there are some key takeaways as we'll discuss next.

Key Takeaways

We just did a pretty quick walk-through of several common terminologies and coding systems. Whether you're trying to standardize diagnoses, procedures, or medications and drugs, there is rarely a "best" terminology. Most often, we are working with data where a particular set of terminologies has already been adopted or used. However, if you do find yourself with an opportunity to choose a terminology, it can be a pretty challenging decision. You will need to balance the expressivity of the terminology and how well the conceptual definitions align with your use case and data. Licensing is also a consideration since not all countries and organizations have access. You will also need to factor in available tooling within your organization to host and maintain the terminologies. However, one of the most salient factors may be the level of expertise available in your organization and appetite for the chosen terminology.

One underutilized resource are *clinical terminologists*. These are typically subject-matter experts ranging from biologists to clinicians who have hands-on experience in their domain of practice. With that foundation, they also develop working knowledge of terminologies such as those listed earlier. While the job descriptions vary, these are the two most common bullet points that I have seen. Some terminologists excel at curating concepts and their taxonomies/hierarchies. Others may focus more on mapping data between terminologists. As with other fields of practice in healthcare, while many may have *clinical terminologist* as a job title, their specific expertise and areas of focus may vary.

As a final point, the terminologies listed earlier are not an exhaustive list. There are many other sources and mappings/crosswalks, including commercial ones. Healthcare organizations themselves (e.g., health systems and hospitals) often have internal coding systems and terminologies as well, even if they may not refer to them as such. The same questions and challenges apply when mapping among industry, commercial, or internal terminologies.

Now that we have a sense of different terminologies out there and some of the key things we need to consider when working with them, let's move on to the UMLS (*https://oreil.ly/iD1X8*). It is maintained by the United States National Library of Medicine and brings together many different sources, linking them through unique concept identifiers and providing semantic relationships between many of the concepts. Though it is not a silver bullet to solve all problems, it is quite powerful, and we will spend a bit of time diving into it in the next section.

Using the Unified Medical Language System

The UMLS is a project that is funded and maintained by the United States National Library of Medicine (NLM), one of the institutes within the National Institutes of Health (NIH). You may hear folks refer to the UMLS as an *ontology* or a *terminology*, though this is not really accurate—the UMLS is more of a collection of terminologies and vocabularies of varying complexity. Some sources, such as SNOMED CT, are very close to being ontologies, and many may consider them to be ontologies. However, they are not necessarily defined and maintained using the rigor that one might expect of a formal ontology.

Often, these definitions are within a particular context and not necessarily generalizable to other contexts or use cases. This is a particularly important point to note as we dive deeper and deeper into the complexities of healthcare and healthcare data. For example, take the idea of "therapy"—how would you define this based on your knowledge of healthcare? Most think of sessions with a therapist. However, in cancer, "therapy" most often refers to a particular course of treatment for the cancer itself, such as chemotherapy. So, we may develop or use a controlled vocabulary that includes the term *therapy* in cancer, and its definition and meaning would be very different than if we were using a vocabulary in the field of psychiatry or psychology.

One of the first steps when working with healthcare data is to identify the controlled vocabulary underlying the data. Whether the data is coming from relational databases (which we most often associate with structured data) or is more free text in nature, there is most certainly an underlying vocabulary. Most clinical natural language processing (NLP) techniques are attempts at automatically identifying the concept that is synonymous with a particular string of text.

Unfortunately, depending on use case, a controlled vocabulary may not yet be clearly defined, and you are tasked with (implicitly) defining one. Data scientists do this all the time when given a new dataset. We take a particular column of data and identify that it contains some sort of categorical data. As part of the exploratory data analysis (EDA) phase, we will look at the distinct/unique values contained within the particular column of data. We might look to other columns to add additional context as we decipher the meaning of the data. This process is basically the creation of a controlled vocabulary for this particular dataset.

Sometimes, we are told that the column of data "contains ICD-10 codes" or "contains medications," giving us a starting point. Ideally, the source data used an industry-standard controlled vocabulary. However, don't be lulled into thinking your work is done. Despite industry-standard vocabularies, the surrounding context may have significant impact on how the code is to be interpreted. For example, we may come across a dataset that uses RxNorm (a commonly used source within the UMLS) codes to capture medication information.

Let's take, for example, "ibuprofen 200 mg" (e.g., Advil or Motrin), which has an RXCUI code of 316074. We may have a dataset that clearly says medications use RxNorm as the underlying coding system for medications, and a column named `medi cations`. Are these medications that are part of the patient's medical history, list of currently prescribed medications, or something that the patient is taking over the counter? This sort of context is critical to interpreting and analyzing patient-level data and is not solved by the UMLS.

Before we get too far into the UMLS, there are some key terms and definitions that make it easier to discuss the UMLS, so let's review them quickly.

Some Basic Definitions

Before we dive deeper into the UMLS and how to use it, let's cover some basic definitions. Additional details can be found in the UMLS Glossary (*https://oreil.ly/yJuQz*).

Atom
> Atoms are the most fundamental block of meaning within the UMLS. Each atom represents a concept in the context of a single *source* within the UMLS. Typically,

an atom can be thought of as a tuple of a string label, code, and source. Thus, the same string label (and concept) in different sources (e.g., ICD-9 versus ICD-10) would be treated as different atoms, each with their own *atom unique identifier* (AUI) (see Figure 3-2 for a comparison of concepts and atoms).

Atom unique identifier

An AUI is a numeric identifier prefixed by the letter *A*. Unlike CUIs, the same concept across multiple different sources within the the UMLS will have different AUIs. As a result, there is no inherent meaning when looking at AUIs. Their main function is to provide primary-foreign key relationships across the UMLS.

Concept

Concepts sit at the core of the UMLS and represent a single meaning, regardless of the source of textual representation. The same concept is likely to exist across sources within the UMLS—while the atoms and AUIs will be different across the sources, they will all share the same CUI if the atoms represent the same concept. In the example in Figure 3-2, the two atoms represent the same concept across ICD-9 and ICD-10, so they share a common CUI.

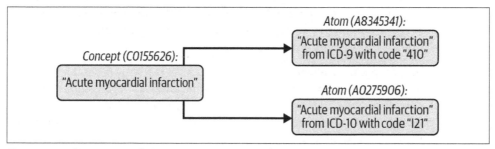

Figure 3-2. Concepts and CUIs versus atoms and AUIs

CUI

A CUI is a numeric identifier prefixed by the letter *C* such that each CUI is unique and synonymous concepts share the same CUI. Regardless of the underlying source or textual representations, two concepts that share a CUI are considered equivalent in meaning.

Source

The UMLS is a collection of vocabularies, terminologies, and ontologies, each referred to as a *source*. So, we can think of the UMLS as a collection of sources and mappings and relationships between them. In addition to mapping at the conceptual level, the UMLS has additional tools such as the lexical variant generator (*https://oreil.ly/7yBuK*) that operate on the level of text/words.

These ideas and definitions capture only a small part of the features contained within the UMLS. It is powerful but, as a result, quite complex and can be overwhelming if this is your first exposure to the UMLS. These should help you get started and provide you with the basic vocabulary as we explore the UMLS in a bit more detail.

Two of these ideas, *concepts* and the *concept unique identifier (CUI)*, are central to working with the UMLS. Next up is a deeper dive into this idea of "concept orientation"—focusing on the underlying concepts and not just the codes or terms that we use to communicate.

Concept Orientation

Whether we are working with a controlled vocabulary, terminology, or ontology, one of the common themes is that we try to focus on the underlying concepts, not the labels or terms used to describe them. For example, whether we call it a "heart attack" or a "myocardial infarction" or the ICD-10 code "I21," we are referring to the medical condition where a coronary artery in the heart is occluded, thus resulting in the death of the heart muscle and tissue.

Within the UMLS, this is captured via the use of *concept unique identifiers*, which are randomly generated numeric codes prefixed with the letter *C*. Each CUI represents a specific concept that may be represented by several different *atoms* (*https://oreil.ly/0CqGt*), each corresponding to an entry of the concept in a particular source within the UMLS.

The key thing to remember when working in the UMLS is that it is centered around the use of CUIs. Equivalent concepts, regardless of the atoms or strings that represent them, will share the same CUI across the different sources. In other words, if two terms or concepts from different source terminologies within the UMLS share the same CUI, they are considered synonymous. That said, it is important to remember that the ideas of "equivalence" or "synonymous" can be highly use case dependent. Two concepts may be considered equivalent from one perspective but not another.

Now that you have a foundational understanding of the UMLS, we need to first cover a few nuts and bolts before you can really start integrating the UMLS into your database of choice.

Working with the UMLS

To get access to the UMLS, you will need to apply for a license (*https://oreil.ly/ZsQkg*). Please visit the link to register and apply.

Given its scale and complexity, there are several different ways people typically use and work with the UMLS.

Download the raw UMLS files and use MetamorphoSys (https://oreil.ly/Q5P1l)
    This is the most flexible but also has a higher learning curve since you will need to decide which sources you want to include and then use the MetamorphoSys

tool to generate the subset of interest. Once you have done this, you will still need to Extract, Transform, and Load (ETL) it into a database of some sort (or access the raw RRF files directly). Depending on which source you choose to include in your subset, the resulting RRF files may be quite large.

We often look to downloading entire sources using this approach when we don't know which concepts we will need to load, so we load them all. For example, the informatics department of an academic medical center that is supporting all research informatics can't predict which concepts may be used by different researchers. In this situation, it may be worth the up-front hassle so that they can support nearly any research question.

Use the UMLS REST API (https://oreil.ly/JHzqY)
If you don't need or want to download entire sources of the UMLS, the REST API becomes a very attractive alternative. Since it is a straightforward REST API, you don't need to learn how to interact with MetamorphoSys and deal with parsing and ETLing RRF files. You would query the appropriate API endpoint and parse the JSON results as you would any other API.

This API approach is great when you know that you are dealing with a con-strained set of concepts. For example, in the next chapter, we will be working with the public subset of the MIMIC-III dataset. Instead of downloading hun-dreds of thousands of concepts from UMLS, we could do some quick processing of the MIMIC-III data to extract a distinct list of codes. We then look these codes up in the API and load the concepts into our database of choice; or we simply export them into a CSV file that we can use later in our project.

When working with the UMLS REST API, you need to first authenticate with the service. There is some sample code (*https://oreil.ly/kaRHg*) available from the United States Department of Health and Human Services on how to authenticate.

To use this code, you would simply create an instance of the `Authentication` class, passing in your API key similar to Example 3-1.

Example 3-1. Authenticating with the UMLS REST API

```
import json
import os
import requests

# Assumes you have an environment variable `UMLS_APIKEY` that contains your key
umls = Authentication(os.environ.get("UMLS_APIKEY"))
tgt = umls.gettgt()
ticket = umls.getst(tgt)

...
```

```
# Endpoint to get properties of an active NDC code
cui = "C123456"
uri = "https://uts-ws.nlm.nih.gov/rest/content-views/current/CUI/{cui}"

# We use the ticket that we got from Authentication.getst()
r = requests.get(uri, params={
  'ticket': ticket
})
r.encoding = "utf-8"

p = json.loads(r.text)
```

Representative Code Snippets

As you first saw in Chapter 2 with the database queries, throughout this book, there are small pieces of code that capture the most salient details related to the topics being discussed. These snippets are representative and are intended to be examples that you can run on your system or adapt to your needs.

Please check out the repository associated with this book (*https://gitlab.com/hands-on-healthcare-data*) for code that you can run on your system alongside the examples covered in this book.

To give you a more concrete example of working with the UMLS, we are going to walk through a small exercise highlighting the key steps to connect real data with RxNorm (one of the sources/terminologies within the UMLS). So, let's get started.

Here's what we're going to do at a high level:

1. Read in the PRESCRIPTIONS.csv file from the MIMIC-III public dataset.
2. Extract a unique list of NDC codes.
3. For each NDC code, we retain the various string labels associated with the NDC code along with the code itself.
4. Query the UMLS REST API for each NDC code and download the RxCUI and concept name per the UMLS. *Note that this step is the most time consuming since we make a separate call to the server for each code. Because of this, I use something like the multiprocess library (https://oreil.ly/G9T4l) to parallelize the job.*

If you are not familiar with the pandas library, it is extremely straightforward to read in a CSV file. Example 3-2 shows a couple lines where we read in the CSV file and then filter the data a little. Specifically, we keep only those rows with a unique NDC code and also keep only a few of the columns. Basically, we are extracting a list of unique NDC codes along with some associated columns.

Example 3-2. Reading PRESCRIPTIONS.csv

```
# Assumes
# import pandas as pd

data = pd.read_csv("mimic_1.4_demo/PRESCRIPTIONS.csv", dtype=str)

unique_rx = data.drop_duplicates(subset=['ndc']).filter(items=[
    'drug',
    'drug_name_poe',
    'drug_name_generic',
    'ndc'
])
```

Now that we have a dataframe that contains a unique list of NDC codes and a few extra columns, let's query the UMLS API for each NDC code. Example 3-3 contains a set of functions that we can use to query the API. We would need to apply this to every row of our unique_rx dataframe. Note that the RxNorm API itself does not require UMLS authentication since it returns data that is provided freely by the National Library of Medicine.

Example 3-3. Function to query the RxNorm API for a single code

```
import requests

def rxcui_from_ndc_status(ndc_resp):
    if ndc_resp[1]:
        return ndc_resp[1]['ndcStatus']['rxcui']
    else:
        return 'MISSING RXCUI'

def conceptName_from_ndc_status(ndc_resp):
    if ndc_resp[1]:
        return ndc_resp[1]['ndcStatus']['conceptName']
    else:
        return 'MISSING NAME'


def get_NDC_status(ndc):
    rxnorm_base = "https://rxnav.nlm.nih.gov/REST"
    uri = rxnorm_base + "/ndcstatus.json"
    query = {
        'ndc': ndc
    }
    r = requests.get(uri, params=query)
    r.encoding = 'utf-8'

    if r.status_code == 200:
        body = json.loads(r.text)
    else:
```

```
        # May want to handle the error some other way
        body = {}

    return r.status_code, body

ndc_code = "00006494300" # Should return rxcui 1658472

status = get_NDC_status(ndc_code)
rxcui = rxcui_from_ndc_status(status)
name = conceptName_from_ndc_status(status)
```

I broke the steps down into separate functions to make the code a bit easier to read, but you can optimize it as necessary. Thehttps://oreil.ly/qKJJD[RxNorm API documentation for getting the NDC status details] is a good resource.

Now that we've seen how we can interact with the UMLS via an API, the other option is to extract a subset and load it into a database. We won't go into detail about creating a subset of the UMLS, though the NLM has very good documentation available (*https://oreil.ly/SXGno*).

MetamorphoSys Directory Structure

When you unpack the UMLS download, there will be a zip file, *mmsys.zip*, that contains the MetamorphoSys tools. Some tools will create a subdirectory called *mmsys* in which the files are unzipped. Make sure that the files are not unzipped in a subdirectory but instead are in the top-level UMLS directory.

In other words, the **.nlm* and *run*_* files should all be in the same directory.

Once you have created a subset, you will end up with a series of Rich Release Format (RRF) files (*https://oreil.ly/PxrKT*) that are delimited by the pipe (|) character. The UMLS provides some basic support for ingesting the UMLS into SQL databases but not others.

In the next few sections, we will walk through ingesting the UMLS RRF files into various databases and look at some of the potential opportunities and trade-offs. For each database, I'll provide a short intro, and then we will walk through how to load and query the database. So, let's start with relational/SQL databases.

UMLS and Relational Databases

The RRF file structure naturally lends itself to relational databases, and the UMLS provides scripts for loading the data into MySQL and Oracle databases. These could easily be adapted to other SQL databases such as PostgreSQL or your database of choice. Depending on the size of the subset and the number of terminology sources that are included, you will likely want to work with your database administration team to make sure that the database is tuned appropriately. Default options are likely to result in performance issues though this would ultimately depend on specific workload details.

So, let's get to loading a MySQL instance with the UMLS subset.

Loading UMLS into MySQL

To keep things simple, we will use MySQL here because the UMLS provides DDL files for creating the tables and indices for us. They also provide support for Oracle databases.

First, we need to create a Docker instance using something similar to Example 3-4.

Example 3-4. Creating a MySQL Docker instance

```
docker run --name umls-mysql \
  -e MYSQL_ROOT_PASSWORD=umls \
  -p3306:3306 \
  -v $PWD/umls-mysql:/var/lib/mysql \
  -d \
  mysql:5.7
```

Connecting to MySQL in Docker

If you are connecting via the command line to a MySQL Docker instance using a command similar to the one in Example 3-4, be sure to use -h 127.0.0.1 instead of -h localhost since that will force the mysql client to use TCP instead of sockets.

Once you have created your MySQL instance, you should be able to call the provided populate_mysql_db.sh script that is in the META directory of the UMLS subset, created by MetamorphoSys. This process might take a while—on my system, it took about 2.5 hours.

After the data has loaded, let's look at how we can query the UMLS. The key is to understand the nuances of the different tables and columns. The UMLS Reference Manual (*https://oreil.ly/5GHrh*) is a great resource.

Querying UMLS in MySQL

Let's say we wanted to query for all concepts that contained the string "heparin." We would start with querying the MRCONSO table, which contains all of the concepts and atoms along with their associated strings. One thing to note is that the MRCONSO table contains all atoms associated with concepts, including those in other languages. So, you will likely want to make sure your query includes LAT =

"ENG". Often, we don't care about the specific terms since we're trying to find the underlying concept. We can do a `GROUP BY CUI` to aggregate all of results by concept unique identifier. Example 3-5 brings this all together.

Example 3-5. Simple UMLS SQL query

```
SELECT c.CUI, MIN(c.STR)
FROM MRCONSO c
WHERE LAT = "ENG"
  AND c.STR LIKE "%heparin%"
GROUP BY CUI;
```

This query would return quite a few entries. So, what if we want to filter our results so that we only get concepts corresponding to a specific semantic type? We will go much deeper into the example in Chapter 4, but let's say we want only those mentions of heparin that are pharmacologic substances (versus clinical drugs, therapies, or other semantic types). We would need to join with another table and filter accordingly, as we see in Example 3-6.

Example 3-6. UMLS SQL query joining concept and semantic type

```
SELECT c.CUI, MIN(c.STR), MIN(s.TUI), MIN(s.STY)
FROM MRCONSO c
LEFT JOIN MRSTY s on c.CUI = s.CUI
WHERE c.LAT = "ENG"
  AND c.STR LIKE "%heparin%"
  AND s.TUI = "T121"
GROUP BY c.CUI;
```

We narrow the query to include only concepts with a semantic-type unique identifier (TUI) of "T121." This will narrow down our results to include only those concepts that are a "pharmacologic substance," which is defined in the UMLS as:

> A substance used in the treatment or prevention of pathologic disorders. This includes substances that occur naturally in the body and are administered therapeutically.

If we didn't specify the semantic type, we would also match other semantic concepts such as "clinical drug" (among other semantic types), which is defined as:

> A pharmaceutical preparation as produced by the manufacturer. The name usually includes the substance, its strength, and the form, but may include the substance and only one of the other two items.

This sounds a lot like the previous one with the nuance being the underlying substance versus the manufactured drug. This is where a clinical terminologist would be a very valuable asset for the team. They are trained and/or have experience in navigating the nuances of various clinical terminologies and how to connect them to the data.

(Clinical) Terminologist

Terminologists are an important resource when working with biomedical data that involves structured codes or terms. They help bridge the gap between domain knowledge and the specific nuances within the terminologies and how the terms and concepts are defined. Some terminologists have a scientific background in biology or physiology, while others have a clinical background. The latter are often referred to as *clinical terminologists* and combine knowledge of the underlying disease processes as well as their treatments and interventions.

So, we've now filtered our results to include only those concepts that contained the string "heparin" but are "pharmacologic substances," excluding all other semantic types.

Though this was a pretty straightforward section to load and query the UMLS subset using a SQL database, we may want to process and manipulate the UMLS data to help us load it into a different type of database, such as Neo4j or TypeDB. In the next section, we'll look at preprocessing the UMLS for import into other databases.

Preprocessing the UMLS

Given the size and complexity of the RRF files in the UMLS subset, working directly with the text files is cumbersome and slow. In this section, we'll look at an open source project that pulls the UMLS into a SQLite database and then runs queries against that database to generate CSV files that can be imported into your database of choice.

I have created a fork (*https://oreil.ly/cvijY*) of the original clinical_informatics_umls repo (*https://oreil.ly/8CFlV*), making some minor changes to make the code slightly more portable and to support more than just Neo4j.

After cloning the repo, you should set up a Python virtual environment (*https://oreil.ly/LUjWK*), though I personally use virtualenvwrapper (*https://oreil.ly/dZ89q*). Virtual environments allow you to manage different (often conflicting) sets of Python modules, so I highly recommend it. Otherwise, you run the risk that the dependencies needed will conflict with those you already have on your system.

Once you have your virtual environment set up, you will want to change into the clinical_informatics_umls repo, install poetry, and then initialize the project, as shown in Example 3-7. You will need to make sure that you are running Python version 3.8.x and that you have mariadb installed (or at least the dependencies), needed by the Python libraries for mariadb, which are part of the clinical_informatics_umls project. On a Mac with Homebrew, this would simply be `brew install mariadb`.

Example 3-7. Setting up the clinical_informatics_umls project

```
# Change into the directory
cd clinical_informatics_umls

# Install poetry into the virtual environment
# Assumes you have already activated the virtual environment
pip install poetry

# Initialize the project
poetry install
```

Now that the project is initialized, we need to make sure that we know the location of our subset directory and then pass that into `create_sqlite_db.py`, the first of many scripts, which will create a new SQLite database and load it with the UMLS RRF files, as shown in Example 3-8.

Example 3-8. Loading SQLite and generating CSV files

```
# From the top-level of the project directory
# <db dir> is the directory to which the sqlite db will be written
poetry run python clinical_informatics_umls/create_sqlite_db.py
    <path to UMLS subset dir> <db dir>

# <db dir> is the directory with the sqlite db
# <csv dir> is where the csv files will be written
poetry run python clinical_informatics_umls/neo4j.py
    <db dir> <csv dir>
```

The previous example uses the `neo4j.py` script, which generates CSV files that are easily imported into Neo4j. Support for other databases is included in the GitLab repo and, if not, please feel free to extend the project! One aspect that we will not discuss are the specific filters one can apply to the RRF files when running the SQL queries that are used to generate the CSV files. The UMLS can be tailored to specific use cases, so please consult the Reference Manual for complete documentation.

Example SQL Queries for UMLS

The SQL queries used to generate the CSV files are not necessarily optimized for any particular use case. Unless we include everything from the UMLS (most of which you are unlikely to ever use), it is impossible to produce a set of SQL queries that would extract exactly the data you would need for your project.

Please don't assume that the CSV files generated in this chapter would be good for your use case. They are simply to highlight how to work with the UMLS.

These preprocessed files can now be imported into your database of choice. In the next section, we will walk through importing the UMLS into the Neo4j property graph database.

UMLS and Property Graph Databases

While the UMLS subset comes as a set of relational datafiles, the information contained within the UMLS is more of a graph than simply a series of tables. This is especially true if you use the Semantic Network and not just the Metathesaurus. As a quick review (following our initial introduction in Chapter 2), property graph databases are one type of graph databases that have become increasingly popular over the past decade or so. While SQL databases connect data at the table level, property graphs allow us to connect data at the node level. Conceptually, labels (using the Neo4j terminology) are similar to SQL tables, and each node of the label would be a row in the table. Relationships function similarly to join tables but connect individual nodes. Properties are equivalent to the columns within each table, and both nodes and relationships can have properties.

Modeling data using graphs is typically done from the perspective of your use case and working back to determine how best to represent the data. In other words, what questions are we trying to answer with the data and how do we represent the data to best answer these questions. For the purpose of this section (as well as the next section involving hypergraphs), I'm keeping the graph schema as close to the UMLS as possible. If you decide to integrate graphs into your use case and you plan on using UMLS, it would be a good idea to spend a little time to see if you can streamline and simplify the graph schema per the needs of your use case.

So, let's get to it and start loading the UMLS into Neo4j. We will be using CSV files generated by following the preprocessing steps of the previous section.

Loading UMLS into Neo4j

If you ran the previous code, your `<csv dir>` should contain a series of CSV files that can now be loaded into Neo4j. First, we'll need to start an instance of Neo4j in Docker, as shown in Example 3-9.

Example 3-9. Starting Neo4j in Docker

```
docker run \
    --name umls-neo4j \
    -p7474:7474 -p7687:7687 \
    -d \
    -v $PWD/neo4j/data:/data \
    -v $PWD/neo4j/logs:/logs \
    -v $PWD/neo4j/import:/var/lib/neo4j/import \
    -v $PWD/neo4j/plugins:/plugins \
    --env=NEO4J_dbms_memory_heap_initial__size=8g \
    --env=NEO4J_dbms_memory_heap_max__size=8g \
    --env=NEO4J_AUTH=neo4j/test \
    --env NEO4J_apoc_import_file_enabled=true \
    --env=NEO4JLABS_PLUGINS='["apoc", "graph-data-science", "n10s"]' \
    neo4j:4.4-community
```

Now that we have our Neo4j instance up and running, one option is to use the `neo4j-admin` tool to import the data, as shown in Example 3-10.

Example 3-10. Importing CSV files into Neo4j

```
./bin/neo4j-admin import \
    --database=neo4j \
    --nodes='import/semanticTypeNode.csv' \
    --nodes='import/conceptNode.csv' \
    --nodes='import/atomNode.csv' \
    --nodes='import/codeNode.csv' \
    --relationships='import/has_sty_rel.csv' \
    --relationships='import/has_aui_rel.csv' \
    --relationships='import/has_cui_rel.csv' \
    --relationships='import/tui_tui_rel.csv' \
    --relationships='import/concept_concept_rel.csv' \
    --relationships='import/child_of_rel.csv' \
    --relationships='import/cui_code_rel.csv' \
    --skip-bad-relationships=true \
    --skip-duplicate-nodes=true \
    --trim-strings=true
```

There are two primary downsides or challenges to this approach:

The database must be stopped during the import
> To mitigate this, you would need to create your own Docker container that runs `neo4j-admin` while pointing to the same Neo4j directories/shared volumes.

The database must be new and unused
> This is the bigger issue since this means we can only load the UMLS into a brand new instance of Neo4j. However, if we have an existing graph that we want to combine with UMLS, we would need to find an alternative.

One alternative is to use the APOC (*https://oreil.ly/APSL3*) add-on for Neo4j, which contains additional functionality, as shown in Example 3-11. The `apoc.import.csv()` function has similar semantics to the admin import function but can be run against a live database.

Example 3-11. Importing CSV files into Neo4j Using APOC

```
CALL apoc.import.csv(
[
    {fileName: 'file:/semanticTypeNode.csv', labels: ['test', 'UMLS']},
    {fileName: 'file:/conceptNode.csv', labels: ['test', 'UMLS']},
    {fileName: 'file:/atomNode.csv', labels: ['test', 'UMLS']},
    {fileName: 'file:/codeNode.csv', labels: ['test', 'UMLS']}
],
[
    {fileName: 'file:/has_sty_rel.csv', type: ''},
    {fileName: 'file:/has_aui_rel.csv', type: ''},
    {fileName: 'file:/has_cui_rel.csv', type: ''},
    {fileName: 'file:/tui_tui_rel.csv', type: ''},
    {fileName: 'file:/concept_concept_rel.csv', type: ''},
    {fileName: 'file:/child_of_rel.csv', type: ''},
    {fileName: 'file:/cui_code_rel.csv', type: ''}
], {})
```

One thing to note is that the CSV files contain the Neo4j *labels* (as introduced in Chapter 2) that are attached to each node. However, the `apoc.import.csv()` function also requires that a label be specified. This label is assigned in addition to the ones specified in the CSV files. I find it helpful to use this additional label to "tag" the nodes that were imported—you can use a timestamp or other identifier that suits your needs.

Now that we have the UMLS loaded into Neo4j, let's try some queries to better understand how we can interact with the UMLS in a property graph.

Querying UMLS in Neo4j

In this section, we'll walk through a few queries. One thing to keep in mind is that the UMLS network is quite complex and it will take a bit of experimentation on your part to effectively integrate it into your use case. There is a lot of nuance as you look at the different semantic types, how concepts are defined, or how the various elements are connected.

In Example 3-12, we have a Cypher query that starts with a search for atoms that contain the string "heparin" and associated concepts, just as we did earlier in the SQL example. To further narrow our results, we again specify that we want those concepts connected to the semantic type with a TUI of "T121."

Example 3-12. UMLS Neo4j query for heparin

```
MATCH (a:AUI)-[:HAS_CUI]->(c:Concept)-[:HAS_STY]->(t:TUI {TUI: "T121"})
WHERE a.STR contains "heparin"
RETURN c, t
```

As you can see, this query is much more compact than the SQL version even though the data model is quite similar. If we change our query to also follow the DIRECT_SUB STANCE_OF relationship, we will find that we're connected to a few more concepts of semantic type "Therapeutic or Preventative Procedure" with the definition of:

> A procedure, method, or technique designed to prevent a disease or a disorder, or to improve physical function, or used in the process of treating a disease or injury.

Though we didn't do this in the previous SQL example, Example 3-13 contains a query that gives us therapeutics that involve our heparin drugs. It was as simple as adding another graph traversal to our query, while the SQL version would involve an additional join with the MRREL table, which contains relationships between atoms.

Example 3-13. UMLS Neo4j query of relationships

```
MATCH (a:AUI)-[:HAS_CUI]->(c:Concept)-[:HAS_STY]->(t:TUI {TUI: "T121"}),
      (c)-[:DIRECT_SUBSTANCE_OF]->(c2)
WHERE a.STR contains "heparin"
RETURN c, c2, t
```

We can start to see the power of the UMLS where we link a specific substance to its use as a therapeutic through a graph traversal. This is captured visually in Figure 3-3.

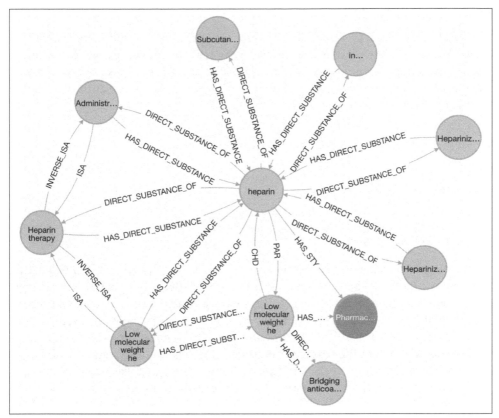

Figure 3-3. Neo4j heparin graph

Now that we have had a short introduction to working with UMLS in Neo4j, let's see how we would do it in TypeDB, a hypergraph database.

UMLS and Hypergraph Databases

Our last consideration is a strongly typed database that also provides the functionality of a hypergraph, TypeDB, which was introduced in Chapter 2. As a quick review, the simplest way to think about hypergraphs is that they are similar to other graphs with the additional ability for edges to connect an arbitrary number of vertices (or, relationships connecting an arbitrary number of nodes). This allows us to model the data with a bit more expressivity.

That said, to keep things conceptually similar to the previous Neo4j example, we will use the same input CSV files and keep the same structure of nodes and relationships, called *entities* and *relations* in TypeDB. So, let's walk through loading the UMLS into TypeDB.

Loading UMLS into TypeDB

As usual, we'll need to start the Docker container using a command similar to Example 3-14. While there is a TypeDB loader tool, it is under active development and requires that you build the tool from Java source. So, for this section, we will load the UMLS via Python scripts that follow the same general structure as the loading we will do in Chapter 4 with the MIMIC data.

Example 3-14. Starting TypeDB in Docker

```
docker run \
    --name umls-typedb \
    -p 1729:1729 \
    -d \
    -v $PWD/typedb:/typedb-all-linux/server/data/ \
    vaticle/typedb:latest
```

Before we get started with loading the actual data, we will spend a little time looking at schemas and how they are used within TypeDB. Because TypeDB is a strongly typed database, there is a bit more up-front work to define the schema and load it into the database. So, let's first take a look at a subset of our schema in Example 3-15 (the complete file is available in the GitLab repo). This schema is tailored to the structure of the CSV output files from our preprocessing step, not the original UMLS RRF schema. I have left out all of the attribute definitions since I am treating everything as a string, and you will see examples of attribute definitions in the next chapter in Example 4-13.

Example 3-15. TypeDB schema for UMLS

```
define

    childof sub relation,
        relates child,
        relates parent;

    atom sub entity,
        plays childof:parent,
        plays childof:child,
        plays atomcui:atom,
        plays auicode:atom,

        owns id,

        owns str,
        owns sab,
        owns code,
        owns tty,
        owns ispref,
```

```
    owns ts;

...

conceptcode sub relation,
    relates concept,
    relates code;

atomcode sub relation,
    relates atom,
    relates code;


...
```

To load this schema, we will use the native Python driver typedb-client. Since the connection and transactions need to be closed, we will use Python's with ... construct. Example 3-16 contains two very simple blocks of code that use the with construct to create the database if it doesn't yet exist and then load the schema within a write transaction.

Example 3-16. Loading the TypeDB Schema

```python
from typedb.client import TypeDB, SessionType, TransactionType

db = "test2"
schema_file = "umls-schema.tql"

with TypeDB.core_client("localhost:1729") as client:
    if not client.databases().contains(db):
        client.databases().create(db)

with TypeDB.core_client("localhost:1729") as client:
    with client.session(db, SessionType.SCHEMA) as session:
        with session.transaction(TransactionType.WRITE) as tx:
            with open(schema_file, "r") as f:
                q = f.read()
                tx.query().define(q)
                tx.commit()
```

Once our schema has been loaded, we now need to load each of our CSV files. The overall skeleton of the loading process is shown in Example 3-17. Most of this code is boilerplate and the necessary minimum for interacting with TypeDB. Given the number of entities that we will be creating for each of the input files, we break up the queries into batches of 10,000 for each transaction (this was not a rigorously tested number, so you may consider doing some experiments to see what batch size might be best for you).

Example 3-17. Loading the UMLS into TypeDB

```
files = [
    "semanticTypeNode.csv",
    "atomNode.csv",
    "codeNode.csv",
    "conceptNode.csv",
    "child_of_rel.csv",
    "cui_code_rel.csv",
    "has_aui_rel.csv",
    "has_cui_rel.csv",
    "has_sty_rel.csv",
    "tui_tui_rel.csv",
    "concept_concept_rel.csv"
]

def chunks(lst, n):
    for i in range(0, len(lst), n):
        yield lst[i:i + n]

with TypeDB.core_client("localhost:1729") as client:
    with client.session(db, SessionType.DATA) as session:
        for f in files:
            print(f"Processing: {f}")
            data = pd.read_csv(os.path.join(csv_path, f), dtype=str)
            data = data.replace(np.nan, "")
            queries = [templaters[f](x) for x in data.itertuples()]
            print(queries[0])

            batches = chunks(queries, 10000)
            counter = 1
            for batch in batches:
                print(f"Batch: {counter}, {len(batch)} items")
                counter = counter + 1
                with session.transaction(TransactionType.WRITE) as tx:
                    for q in batch:
                        tx.query().insert(q)
                    tx.commit()
```

As you can see, the bulk of the work, however, is handled by template functions that take each row of the dataframe as input and return a TypeQL query string. Example 3-18 shows a few templates for entities and relations along with a helper function for cleaning the strings.

Example 3-18. TypeDB template examples

```
def clean_getattr(x, attr):
    return getattr(x, attr).replace("\"", "\\\"")

def code_template(x):
    return f"""
```

```
    insert $x isa sourcecode,
        has id "{clean_getattr(x, '_1')}",
        has sab "{clean_getattr(x, 'SAB')}",
        has code "{clean_getattr(x, 'CODE')}";
    """

def conceptsty_template(x):
    return f"""
    match
        $c isa concept, has id "{clean_getattr(x, '_1')}";
        $sty isa semantictype, has id "{clean_getattr(x, '_2')}";
    insert
        (concept: $c, semantictype: $sty) isa conceptsty;
    """

templaters = {
    "atomNode.csv": atom_template,
    "codeNode.csv": code_template,
    ...
    "tui_tui_rel.csv": tuitui_template,
    "concept_concept_rel.csv": concept_concept_template
}
```

You can see that there is a dictionary that connects the appropriate template to be used to each filename. This is used by our loader to cycle through all of the files and get them loaded. The loading process will take a while, so I look forward to the TypeDB Loader being production-ready.

So, we have the UMLS loaded—let's run some queries.

Querying UMLS in TypeDB

We've walked through this example several times now, so let's cut straight to the query. Example 3-19 contains the TypeQL query that will find all atoms containing "heparin" and associated concepts and then filter them to only include pharmacologic substances. This is basically the same as we did with Neo4j though the syntax is quite different.

Example 3-19. UMLS TypeDB query for heparin

```
match
    # Find all atoms with "heparin"
    $atom isa atom, has str contains "heparin";

    # Get the semantic type entity for "pharmacologic substance"
    $pharmsub isa semantictype, has id "T121";

    # Get all concepts linked to our matched atoms
    (atom: $atom, concept: $drug) isa atomcui;
    $drug isa concept, has str $str;
```

```
    # Filter by semantic type
    (concept: $drug, semantictype: $pharmsub) isa conceptsty;
get $drug, $str;
```

We can expand this even more to find linked therapeutic or preventative procedures
(as we did in Example 3-13) by bringing in more relations. Example 3-20 shows our
expanded query, which you can see is quite a bit more complex than the Neo4j version. If your focus is entirely on brevity or simplicity of the query, Cypher is much
cleaner for such queries. However, we can simplify these queries by implementing
rules that we can preload into the database. Similar to abstracting code via functions,
if we turned the following query into a rule, future queries that rely on connecting
pharmacologic substances and therapeutic/preventative procedures would be significantly simpler. We will go a bit more into rules in Chapter 4 when discussing TypeDB
in the context of electronic health record data.

Example 3-20. UMLS TypeDB query for therapeutics

```
match
    # Get semantictypes for pharmacologic and therapeutic
    $pharmsub_type isa semantictype, has id "T121";

    $therapy_type isa semantictype, has id "T061";

    # Find atoms with "heparin" and associated concepts
    # that are pharmacologic substances
    $atom isa atom, has str contains "heparin";

    $drug isa concept, has str $drug_name;
    (atom: $atom, concept: $drug) isa atomcui;

    $pharmsub_links (concept: $drug, semantictype: $pharmsub_type)
    isa conceptsty;

    # Find all linked therapeutic concepts of which the drug
    # is a DIRECT_SUBSTANCE_OF
    $therapy isa concept, has str $therapy_name;

    $dso (from: $drug, to: $therapy) isa conceptrel, has reltype
    "DIRECT_SUBSTANCE_OF";

    $therapy_links (concept: $therapy, semantictype: $therapy_type)
    isa conceptsty;
get $therapy, $therapy_name;
```

So, this concludes our journey through several different types of databases. I know
this only begins to scratch the surface of working with the UMLS, and we could easily
spend an entire book learning how to effectively integrate the UMLS into a variety of

---

use cases. However, my hope is that this gives you a taste of the UMLS and a basic foundational understanding that you can use to begin your own experiments. Given the overall complexity of both the UMLS and the databases we covered, let's do a quick review of the key points when working with the UMLS.

Review of the UMLS

This chapter was intended to give you a high-level introduction to the UMLS and begin to orient you a bit to working with it in the context of different databases. In the next two chapters, we will see how the UMLS helps us work with EHR and claims data.Some key points to keep in mind:

- The UMLS is concept oriented, and it is easiest to focus on CUIs. Rarely will we, as data scientists, need to worry about details such as atoms and lexical variants.

- The UMLS is a collection of *sources* that are maintained and managed by independent organizations. The UMLS provides some linkages between these various coding systems but is not intended to be exhaustive.

- Interpreting the knowledge that is contained within the UMLS and its sources is highly dependent on the use case. Assuming that the concept and relationship definitions within the UMLS are "good" without manually validating this for your particular data sources *and* use case is a recipe for disaster.

Conclusion

Working with various vocabularies, terminologies, and ontologies is critical to healthcare RWD. They can be quite complex and seem unwieldy at times. However, whether we are trying to track and pay for healthcare services or trying to link rare diseases with genetic variations, terminologies and ontologies have become integral to working with all levels of healthcare data.

Once we get our data linked to various terminologies, we are able to process and analyze the data with shared semantics. In other words, we are able to harmonize the data across different patients, hospital service lines, or health systems. With sources such as SNOMED CT, we are also able to begin to make some inferences based on the knowledge contained within the source itself. For example, if we know that a patient has a history of congestive heart failure, the *has finding site* relationship will allow us to run queries on all patients who have heart diseases.

Beyond more complex sources such as SNOMED CT, the UMLS provides a great framework for starting to integrate multiple different sources through its Metathesaurus as well as the Semantic Network. It allows us to identify synonyms across different vocabularies, terminologies, or ontologies, while also providing semantic relationships between concepts. It can be a powerful resource, particularly for those projects that rely on linkages between different types of concepts (e.g., diagnoses to medications) or between different sources (e.g., ICD-10 to SNOMED CT). Because it is conceptually oriented (focusing on the underlying concept and not necessarily the string or text representation), it is also well suited as part of the underlying data infrastructure when dealing with data across different languages.

However, we also need to be careful that we don't look to these terminologies as a panacea or silver bullet. While they are important and quite useful, they are not perfect. Terminologies are created for specific purposes and then reused for others. This mismatch in intention can create hidden data quality problems. For example, an ontology created by scientists may take a more biological view of a disease, making distinctions that are important to researchers. On the other hand, clinicians may have a different view of the same disease, oriented to treatment and intervention options. Unless you are an expert with that particular terminology or disease, the mismatch may not be evident.

Also, simply having and integrating a terminology (or set of terminologies) is not enough. It is also important to have a clearly documented process that captures why and how you are doing the integration. This includes clearly communicating the assumptions you are making about the data, the terminologies, and the process for bringing them together. This really highlights that success in working with real-world data requires a combination of people, process, and technologies. Simply claiming that you support, integrate, or use the right tools is only a small part of the solution.

In the next chapter, we will dive into working with data from EHRs. There will be a bit of a discussion of EHR data overall, from data models to standards, and how we can represent that data in both relational and graph forms. Within the context of a medication normalization/harmonization problem, we will look at how to approach EHR data as well as the incorporation of RxNorm, one of the "terminologies" that we discussed in this chapter. It is a part of the UMLS though we will be focusing primarily on just RxNorm in the example.

## CHAPTER 4

Deep Dive: Electronic Health Records Data

We have been spending a lot of time on foundational ideas, so I'm sure you are ready to start playing around with some data. In this chapter, we will dive into electronic health record data. As we discussed in Chapter 1, I use *electronic health record* and *electronic medical record* somewhat interchangeably. For the purpose of this book, EHR data is that data collected by hospitals and clinics during the course of transacting healthcare delivery. As such, some of the primary motivations are to capture data for billing, legal compliance, or communication with other caregivers. This is important to keep in mind since it can affect the quality and meaning of the data, depending on the use case.

Now, we'll go back to a dataset that I introduced in Chapter 3 in the EHR case study. The MIMIC dataset is a publicly accessible dataset from a hospital intensive care unit. Though most simply refer to it as "the MIMIC data," it is the Medical Information Mart for Intensive Care dataset. Though this dataset represents a specific subset of EHR data, it is real data and reflects many of the challenges we have as an industry when working with real-world data. I will also discuss the Synthea synthetic dataset though we won't be working with it in any detail.

Before we get too deep into the MIMIC dataset, I'd like to take a step back and look at publicly accessible data in general, particularly in the context of de-identification and anonymization.

Publicly Accessible Data

From regulatory requirements to privacy concerns to complexity of the data, there are many challenges in making data available to the general public. In the United States, one common regulatory hurdle is the Health Insurance Portability and Accountability Act (HIPAA) though many states also have their own requirements in addition to HIPAA (e.g., California Consumer Privacy Act) that may or may not be healthcare specific. In European Union, there is the General Data Protection Regulation (GDPR) in addition to country-specific regulations.

Even if organizations are fully compliant with legal requirements, there is still the risk of privacy breaches and the ensuing political and public relations challenges. For example, in 2006, Netflix released a de-identified dataset with which researchers were able to subsequently re-identify 68% of reviewers.[1] Additionally, there are moral and ethical considerations to protecting the privacy of patients in the healthcare system.

In this section, we will discuss two datasets. One is a real dataset that has undergone de-identification. The other is a synthetic dataset generated in a variety of data models.

De-identification Versus Anonymization

De-identification, anonymization, and pseudononymization are different approaches to mitigating privacy concerns in datasets. While there are generally accepted definitions, these terms are also defined by statute, case law, and regulatory frameworks. So, it is important to be sure that you understand what exactly is required of each.

With that out of the way, let's look at the MIMIC dataset in a bit more detail.

Medical Information Mart for Intensive Care

The MIMIC dataset (*https://oreil.ly/hTiv6*) is an NIH-funded project that started as a collaboration between Harvard and MIT. It began in 2003 as a multiparameter dataset of ICU patient data and was first publicly released in 2011 to the broader community.

Since then, it has gone through several major iterations and is currently available as MIMIC-IV. Each of the high-level releases (MIMIC-II, MIMIC-III, MIMIC-IV) is essentially a different dataset that happens to have overlapping patient populations. Within each release, there is additional versioning—the latest version of MIMIC-III is v1.4, while the latest version of MIMIC-IV is v1.0.

The MIMIC data is a great source of data and contains everything from demographics to medications to lab tests to free-text clinical notes. In some cases, there are associated datasets of electrocardiograms (ECG/EKG) and other bedside monitoring and physiological waveform data. The MIMIC data has been popular with data scientists

---

1 Arvind Narayanan and Vitaly Shmatikov, "Robust De-anonymization of Large Datasets (How To Break Anonymity of the Netflix Prize Dataset)," University of Texas at Austin, 2008. *https://arxiv.org/abs/cs/0610105*.

looking to develop digital biomarkers, create clinical natural language processing algorithms, and even conduct more traditional clinical research.

For this book, we will be working with MIMIC-III since MIMIC-IV was only recently released. I will provide a short overview of the schema and of a few tables we will reference in this book. For more information, there is fairly comprehensive documentation available on the MIMIC website (*https://oreil.ly/ZuJMQ*).

MIMIC-III schema

The MIMIC-III schema is fairly straightforward and reflects the delivery of inpatient care. In this section, we will talk through several tables, noting some key considerations for those who may be less familiar with inpatient patient care.

Patients. The MIMIC-III dataset is a patient-level dataset, and it is easiest to anchor our discussion around the PATIENTS table (*https://oreil.ly/GKSJ5*). Every single unique patient within the dataset contains an entry in PATIENTS, which also contains basic demographics such as date of birth/death and genotypical sex (though referred to as "gender") of the patient. One thing to note is that there are multiple dates of death that are tracked—the date from the hospital system and the date from the Social Security database. There is also a generic date of death column that merges the two dates, giving priority to the hospital system.

Admissions. Next, each patient is connected to rows within the ADMISSIONS table (*https://oreil.ly/jmE3W*), one row per hospital admission. This table is sourced from what is typically referred to as the ADT system, or the admission, discharge, and transfer system. This includes the date/time a patient was admitted to and discharged from the hospital and the location of admission/discharge (e.g., they were admitted via the emergency department but discharged to a skilled nursing facility or to home health). Other information typically considered demographic information is also contained within this table. For example, religion, language, marital status, etc., are also contained within this table. As a result, it is important to note that a patient might be admitted to the hospital multiple times and have differing data for each of these fields.

ICU stays. One thing to note is that while admitted to the hospital, a patient may then be admitted to the intensive care unit multiple times. For example, a patient may be on the medical-surgical floor of the hospital, develop sepsis, and be moved to the ICU, improve and be moved back to their original unit, and then deteriorate and be moved to the ICU again. In this case, there is a single hospital admissions with multiple ICU stays. Each ICU stay is an entry in the ICUSTAYS table (*https://oreil.ly/pA7gV*). Similar to the ADMISSIONS table, there are timestamps indicating when the patient was transferred to/from the ICU.

As with most hospitals, there are multiple different types of ICUs such as the medical ICU, surgical ICU, and coronary care unit. Patients may also be transferred from one type of ICU to another; this table tracks the first and last units with additional details of transfers captured in the TRANSFERS table. Abbreviations and descriptions of the different care units can be found in Table 4-1.

Table 4-1. MIMIC-III care units

Abbreviation	Description
CCU	Coronary care unit
CSRU	Cardiac surgery recovery unit
MICU	Medical intensive care unit
NICU	Neonatal intensive care unit
NWARD	Neonatal ward
SICU	Surgical intensive care unit
TSICU	Trauma/surgical intensive care unit

Transfers.   The TRANSFERS table (*https://oreil.ly/ZBKD9*) sources its data from the ADT system and contains a listing of each transfer of a patient between care units. While the ICUSTAYS table tracks the first and last units, intermediate units can be found within this table. Within the dataset, if a patient is transferred to an ICU within 24 hours of a previous ICU stay, it is considered to be the same stay, thus resulting in only a single entry in the ICUSTAY table.

One point of note is that data for patients from 2001 through 2008 is sourced from the CareVue system, while data from patients from 2008 through 2012 is sourced from the MetaVision system. These are two different systems for tracking ICU patients and may have an impact on the underlying data (e.g., querying data regarding input events).[2]

Prescriptions.   Now that we have a bit of understanding of the tables that contain more general data on patients and their stays in the hospital, let's dive a bit into the more clinically focused tables. Since we will spend some time discussing EHR versus claims data, one obvious point of focus is medication/prescription data.

The PRESCRIPTIONS table (*https://oreil.ly/tGSZg*) contains medication orders that are entered within the hospital's order entry system (also known as the computerized provider order entry, or CPOE, system). Of course, there are typical columns you would expect, such as timestamps for starting or discontinuing the medication, or the ICU stay or hospital admission with which the order is associated.

---

2 See the Open Data Stack Exchange, "MIMIC-III inputevents MV or CV" (*https://oreil.ly/woTBj*).

The more interesting columns, however, are those that capture the medication name, dosage information, and links back to standard coding systems. For example, the PROD_STRENGTH column contains a free-text string that captures information typically seen on product packaging (e.g., "25mcg/0.5mL Vial" or "10mg Suppository"). In addition, there are additional columns DOSE_VAL_RX and DOSE_UNIT_RX that break this information down for easier computation. Another interesting column is ROUTE, which captures the route of administration (e.g., "PO" for oral medications, or "SC" for injections under the skin).

Dose Versus Dosage

Dose is the amount of a medication taken at one time. For example, a common dose for ibuprofen is 200mg though it may be available with a prescription as an 800mg dose.

Dosage contains more information such as the amount, number of pills, frequency, and duration.

One of the challenges we often have working with data such as medications is linking it to other data such as claims. This table also contains NDC and GSN codes to facilitate these linkages. NDC codes are *national drug codes* (*https://oreil.ly/dBThU*) that are used in the United States. One point of note is that the NDC code is a combination of labeler (manufacturer, repacker, relabler, distributor), product information (strength, dosage, and formulation), and package information (size and type of packaging).

As a result, the NDC code often provides too much granularity for many use cases. For example, say we are trying to link our EHR dataset with the FDA's Adverse Event Reporting System (FAERS) (*https://oreil.ly/ZUg0U*) to see if certain combinations of drugs correlate with length of stay or transfers to the ICU, with a particular focus on acetaminophen (Tylenol).

Acetaminophen is found as an active ingredient in many drugs and, consequently, will be buried among many NDC codes. This is where something such as the UMLS can come in handy. While not perfect, it contains many mappings and relationships that can help us find all NDC codes that contain acetaminophen as an active ingredient; then we can link this set of codes against the NDC codes contained within this table.

Procedure events. Similar to the PRESCRIPTIONS table, the dataset also tracks procedures that are ordered for patients. Although there are two different systems (Care-Vue and MetaVision), there is only a single table containing procedure events, the PROCEDUREEVENTS_MV table (*https://oreil.ly/WMn3v*).

This table contains a listing of a variety of procedures that a patient might undergo, ranging from starting an IV to imaging or to dressing changes. It is structured to contain all procedures for all patients across all admissions and ICU stays. As a result, it relies heavily on primary-foreign key relationships with the D_ITEMS table.

There are also quite a few fields to provide additional context and information regarding a specific procedure. While some are generally self-explanatory (e.g., start/end time), most require some knowledge of clinical practice or anatomy and physiology.

D_ITEMS.   There are several tables that begin with *D_*, one of which is D_ITEMS (*https://oreil.ly/4JQf5*). These are known as definition tables and store definitions of sets of codes (though not necessarily standardized codes). D_ITEMS stores definitions for items in either the CareVue or MetaVision databases. The *DBSOURCE* column contains a string that indicates which system.

Because this table is linked to a variety of different event tables, it is a very generic table and contains two columns (*UNITNAME* and *PARAM_TYPE*), which are used to interpret the specific values in the corresponding event table. In some cases, the unit name is also captured in the linked table (e.g., the *VALUEUOM* column in PROCE DUREEVENTS_MV also captures the unit of measure).

One point of note is that while this table may seem like it contains a controlled vocabulary, it most certainly does not! There might be multiple items (i.e., row) within this table that capture the same concept but with spelling mistakes or synonyms. This occurs because the data is sourced from two different systems (CareVue versus MetaVision) and also as a result of free-text entry in CareVue.

This will be one area where graph databases shine as we work to link synonymous or equivalent concepts across the dataset. For example, the items with *ITEMID*s of 211 and 220045 both represent "heart rate" as taken from CareVue and MetaVision. In a SQL-based system, linking these would be done at the level of the SQL query. This requires that the data engineers and scientists track and document this within their queries. In a graph-based system, we can easily link these with an edge that captures synonymy or equivalence so that others can benefit from the mapping as well.

D_CPT, D_ICD_DIAGNOSES, D_ICD_PROCEDURES, and D_LABITEMS.   As with D_ITEMS, the D_CPT, D_ICD_DIAGNOSES, D_ICD_PROCEDURES, and D_LABITEMS tables all contain definitions that are referenced in other tables. However, they all contain definitions that are aligned with controlled vocabularies. The columns within each table are tailored to the nuances that come with the associated controlled vocabulary.

The D_CPT table (*https://oreil.ly/FOi08*) contains definitions for items that are part of the Current Procedural Terminology (CPT) (*https://oreil.ly/XrnQD*), which is a set of codes maintained by the American Medical Association. CPT codes are primarily used as part of the billing and claims process between healthcare providers and payers (both public and private).

The D_ICD_DIAGNOSES table (*https://oreil.ly/JVZfr*) contains ICD-9 (not ICD-10) codes related to patient diagnoses. Given that the MIMIC-III dataset contains data only from 2001–2012, it does not contain any ICD-10 codes since the mandate to move from ICD-9 to ICD-10 did not take effect until 2015 (*https://oreil.ly/1xY3r*).

Similar to D_ICD_DIAGNOSES, the D_ICD_PROCEDURES table (*https://oreil.ly/3g2fG*) contains ICD-9 codes related to hospital procedures pre-2015.

CPT Versus ICD-9 Procedure Codes

While both CPT and ICD-9 (and ICD-10) procedure codes capture medical procedures, you may be wondering what the difference is.

CPT codes are primarily used to bill for physician services, while ICD procedure codes are used to bill for hospital services. While not commonly known, physician services and hospital services are billed separately and use different sets of codes to manage the reimbursement process.

If you've ever dealt with the claims process for a hospital admission, this is one reason it gets so confusing! You get a series of different bills because no one organization is behind all of the services that are provided. One exception to this is the integrated health system where the people (physicians, nurses, pharmacists, etc.) and the hospital itself are all part of the same organization.

As a point of note, while there was an industry shift (in the United States) to move to ICD-10 for billing and reimbursement in 2015, there was a window of time where many institutions were performing "dual coding" as part of the transition. During this time, organizations often used both ICD-9 and ICD-10 codes simultaneously.

However, not all datasets that span the 2015 implementation date contain both sets of codes. When working with datasets that span the implementation date, either all pre-2015 codes need to be mapped to their ICD-10 equivalent or all post-2015 codes need to be mapped to their ICD-9 equivalent. This is often accomplished through the use of "crosswalks," a table of mappings from one coding system to another.

Mapping ICD-9 and ICD-10

There are many more ICD-10 codes than ICD-9 codes, so it's natural to assume that ICD-10 codes are more granular and detailed. For example, there may be two different codes to handle laterality (e.g., left arm versus right arm) of a particular diagnosis. The natural conclusion is that a particular ICD-9 code maps to one or more ICD-10 codes (1:1 or 1:many mappings). However, this isn't always true. Given the intended uses of ICD, there were some codes where multiple ICD-9 codes were compressed into a single ICD-10 code.

For example, both ICD-9 codes 493.00 (Extrinsic asthma, unspecified) and 493.10 (Intrinsic asthma, unspecified) get mapped to a single ICD-10 code J45.50 (Severe persistent asthma, uncomplicated). This is because ICD-9 asthma codes are organized by intrinsic versus extrinsic asthma, while ICD-10 asthma codes are organized by severity.[3,4]

The last table we will cover in this section is D_LABITEMS (*https://oreil.ly/1vMmP*), which contains definitions for laboratory and other observational tests and is linked to LOINC codes. However, while most concepts extracted from the hospital's lab system were mapped to LOINC codes, not all have been.

That was a whirlwind tour of the schema and was intended as more of an orientation than anything. The more time you spend with the data, the more intuitive it will become. Another element of experience is being able to recognize when a dataset will not work for a particular use case. Though it's great to be excited when we get our hands on data, it is important for us to know of any limitations. While the MIMIC datasets are tremendously valuable, let's spend a little bit of time looking at some of the limitations.

Limitations

The biggest limitation to the MIMIC-III dataset is that it is focused on patients who have had an ICU stay during their admission. As a result, there is a huge bias in the dataset toward higher-acuity patients (that is, patients who have more complex medical situations). So, any insights generated from this dataset will likely not apply to the majority of the population.

---

3 ACDIS, "Q&A: Is 'backward mapping' from ICD-10-CM/PCS to ICD-9-CM appropriate?" (*https://oreil.ly/OoJjQ*)

4 "Asthma Data Analysis Guidance: ICD-9-CM to ICD-10-CM Conversion" (*https://oreil.ly/o0Uih*)," US Centers for Disease Control and Prevention.

For example, let's say we wanted to look at diabetics within this dataset and correlate blood sugar levels to hospital readmissions or adverse event reactions involving insulin. It would be difficult to remove confounding factors such as interactions with inpatient medications such as sedatives that are not typically administered outside the hospital. So, as with any dataset, it is important to think through the potential biases; however, the biases within this dataset may be buried deep in the clinical context and not otherwise evident.

For example, this dataset is captured at an academic medical center that is affiliated with a top-tier medical school. Buried deep in the clinical workflow is a direct connection to cutting-edge research that may not make it to community hospitals for years. So, even if you are working on an inpatient analytics project and your patient populations match those within the MIMIC dataset, you need to further consider if your clinical practices are closely aligned enough.

Sometimes, you need a dataset that you can freely share and you are not interested in extracting any actual insights. Synthetic data is an active area of research and has significant potential to help us break through the privacy concerns that often limit researchers and innovators. In this next section, we will discuss Synthea, one of the first synthetic datasets that was made available to the public.

Synthea

Mainly used in the context of data engineering, another common dataset is the Synthea dataset (*https://oreil.ly/TsWdU*). It is a fully synthetic dataset, so it does not contain any actual patient data. This makes it easy to work with the data, especially if you want to include data in a variety of formats or data models as part of unit and integration tests.

As a project, Synthea is an open source data simulator/generator (*https://oreil.ly/YcibE*). That is, it generates realistic healthcare data (as opposed to just creating data that may be syntactically correct but is semantically meaningless). However, there are a few pregenerated datasets that you can download from the Synthea website as well.

Synthea (*https://oreil.ly/5byXa*) is a powerful framework that uses a modular approach for generating different aspects of healthcare data. This allows data engineers and scientists to tune the system to match local patient populations as necessary. Their documentation (*https://oreil.ly/YGjMu*) does a good job of providing examples and guides for creating your own modules.

As with any dataset, one of the first things we need to consider is the schema or data dictionary and how well it aligns with our needs. So, let's take a look at the Synthea schema.

Schema

Unlike the MIMIC dataset, the data from SyntheticMass is available in a variety of data models/formats. This makes SyntheticMass a very rich source of realistic data, especially when testing data engineering and mapping pipelines. However, like any dataset, there are trade-offs between the various pregenerated datasets, so you may find that you need to create a custom dataset to meet your needs and requirements.

Some of the datasets are available in both CSV and FHIR formats, making them great options for testing data engineering pipelines that convert to/from FHIR. However, it is important to note that such tests are more about the technology of your pipeline. Given the synthetic nature, it won't help you validate your data mappings or semantic harmonization tasks.

The CSV version of the dataset is a normalized, relational structure such that each CSV file could be loaded as a separate table in a relational database. Universally unique identifiers (UUIDs) (*https://oreil.ly/l2fZn*) are used to link across files.

There is one CSV file for each of the following:

- Allergies
- Careplans
- Claims
- Claims Transactions
- Conditions
- Devices
- Encounters
- Imaging Studies
- Immunizations
- Medications
- Observations
- Organizations
- Patients
- Payer Transitions
- Payers
- Procedures
- Providers
- Supplies

Within each CSV file, the first line is a header line that identifies each of the columns. For example, the `conditions.csv` file contains the following header:

```
START,STOP,PATIENT,ENCOUNTER,CODE,DESCRIPTION
```

In the FHIR version of the generated dataset, each JSON file corresponds to a single patient and follows the FHIR schema. We will discuss this later in this chapter in the section "Fast Health Interoperability Resources" on page 93.

Though I mentioned some potential limitations of the Synthea data earlier, I wanted to quickly discuss the most obvious limitation when working with Synthea.

Limitations

Obviously, the main limitation to the Synthea dataset is that it's not a real dataset. The modules used to generate different aspects are tunable and often reflect our current understanding (mainly, from observational research studies). However, this assumes that the underlying research used to tune the modules is accurate and reflective of the patient population we are trying to study. Additionally, because these observational studies tend to focus on descriptive statistics of observed variables, they may not reflect higher-order interactions between variables (especially if this higher-order interaction is not yet understood or even evident to researchers).

We have looked at the MIMIC-III and Synthea data, each containing its own data model. When every data source comes with its own data model, we struggle with adapting or rebuilding our data pipelines to account for the new data model. In this next section, we will dive into two commonly discussed data models when working with EHR data. Both of these attempt to work toward a common data model though one is focused on storing data for analytics, while the other is focused on the communication and transport of data.

Data Models

When working with data of any kind, one of the first considerations is the data model. Most of the time, as data scientists, we do not have much say in which data model is used since that decision is made much further upstream. In the case of healthcare data, the data model is often decided upon by the EHR manufacturer or the team that developed the clinical data warehouse. When we get access to datasets in the life sciences, we are often at the mercy of the data vendors and whatever data model they choose to use, frequently a proprietary one. Regardless, it is important that we look at the underlying goals or intention of the data model, which we will discuss next.

Goals

There is a slow but increasing trend to focus on the use of "common" data models. The idea is to create an ecosystem of tools and data sources that all operate on a single data model, minimizing the need to constantly reinvent the wheel. One of the best analogies I have heard is that we are all thirsty for insights, yet we are all digging our own wells to the same sources of data.

We will cover a couple examples of projects that are attempting to do this, but before we do, it's important to note that there will never be a silver bullet. If you talk to most data and information architects (myself included), one of the first points they will make is that the model is dependent on the use case—where did the data come from and what sorts of questions are being asked of the data? Depending on the requirements of the project, sometimes the data model might depend on other requirements such as write latency (as often seen in transactional, relational data models).

The most common challenge when trying to create a common data model for healthcare data (particularly RWD) is the variation in what data need to be collected as we go from one disease area to another. For example, in oncology, we need to track a patient's staging (of which there are already two options, TNM staging and group staging), the morphology and histology of the cancer, and the body part/location.

Cancer staging data is a common source of headache for those working with data in the oncology space. Right off the bat, there is the need to harmonize "group staging" and "TNM staging" (*https://oreil.ly/ttHrf*), two different approaches to determining the stage of a patient's cancer. Group staging is the most generally recognized and is just a single number (e.g., stage 1, 2, 3, …). It captures the presence of cancer, the size of the tumor, and how much it has spread to nearby tissue or other parts of the body.

Given our increasing understanding of cancers, another form of staging is called TNM staging:

T

Primary tumor—the size or extent of the *main* tumor

N

Regional lymph nodes—whether lymph nodes are involved and, if so, the number and location

M

Metastases—whether the cancer has spread to other parts of the body

In addition to the different types of staging, there is the consideration of the AJCC staging guidelines for TNM staging. The AJCC is the American Joint Committee on Cancer and has developed cancer staging guidelines (*https://oreil.ly/6dtm9*) for use by clinicians and scientists. While they have been historically published as editions, the AJCC has recently shifted (as of 2021) to versioning the guidelines.

While the staging guidelines were originally intended for human consumption as a set of guidelines, it is evolving to become more computable, including API access as well as a shift away from publishing "editions" to releasing "versions."

This doesn't even include the latest developments in genetic sequencing and biomarker data! These are all data elements that are specific to solid tumors and not applicable to other disease areas. So, how do we create a common data model that would enable a hospital to work with data across all disease areas and medical specialties?

Despite the (sometimes overwhelming!) quantity of nuances within RWD, why is there still such a push for common data models? For example, we see academics, biopharma companies, and data vendors investing a significant amount of time and money into such efforts.[5]

While there are certainly a lot of nuances between cancer and neurology, or between descriptive statistics for evidence generation and predictive analytics models for decision support, there are also many areas of overlap. For example, regardless of the type of analytics, one of the first steps is to define a cohort of patients and perform some high-level exploratory analysis. Before spending the time and effort diving into a dataset, we first want to know roughly how many patients actually meet our inclusion/exclusion criteria or what the distributions of key variables and data elements might be.

So, perhaps we can use a common data model to help facilitate this early phase of analytics projects. Once the data scientists are happy with the cohort they have defined, they can extract the same subset of patients from the original dataset. This allows us to speed up the identification of the appropriate dataset and patient cohorts while also providing data scientists with the full depth and nuance available within the original dataset.

So, let's take a look at two examples of common data models that are gaining traction across all levels of the healthcare industry.

Examples of Data Models

There are quite a few "common" data models out there, most coming from the academic side of healthcare. However, there is no single, authoritative body, so adoption is organic and bottom-up. We will cover two of the most commonly discussed data models (among many others), ones that are quickly gaining popularity across both academic medicine as well as on the industry side.

Observational Health Data Sciences and Informatics (OHDSI) OMOP Data Model

OHDSI (pronounced "odyssey") is a collaborative that is centrally coordinated through a research group at Columbia University, though it has numerous collaborators and sponsors from industry. In addition to providing a community and forum, concrete artifacts include the specifications for a common data model (OMOP, pronounced "oh mop"), as well as tools for mapping and interacting with the data (*https://ohdsi.org/software-tools*) and a curated set of terminologies (*https://oreil.ly/ZgvSQ*).

---

5 OHDSI OMOP Collaborators (*https://oreil.ly/V8AaX*).

The OHDSI documentation is quite good, including third-party materials such as those provided by the European Health Data Evidence Network (EHDEN) Academy (*https://academy.ehden.eu*). My goal here isn't to make you an expert in OMOP but to give you a basic introduction as we compare and contrast with FHIR and other approaches. Please check out the Book of OHDSI (*https://oreil.ly/FqeQ3*) and other OHDSI resources (*https://ohdsi.org/resources*) if you would like to dive more deeply into the world of OHDSI.

We will discuss the high-level approach that OHDSI has taken with OMOP and considerations from our perspective as data engineers and data scientists, particularly as it relates to the different types of databases we are comparing.

Working with OMOP.   The latest version of the OMOP CDM is v5.4 (*https://oreil.ly/i7Lu0*) and was just released in September 2021. If you poke around the OMOP documentation, you will also see mention of v6.0 (*https://oreil.ly/RCPVg*). Although this is a "released" version, OHDSI specifically recommends that new projects continue to use the 5.x branch of the CDM. Version 6.0 makes some breaking changes, and the current set of released tools (as well as the community overall) have not yet begun to support v6.0.

As you can see in Figure 4-1, the CDM is patient-centric with everything stemming from the `Person` table. Similar to the schema from the MIMIC dataset, patients are immediately associated with visits. Since OMOP is not specific to inpatient data, the idea of a visit can be either in- or outpatient. From there, there are tables to connect the patient to a variety of observational data ranging from conditions (i.e., diagnoses) to medications to procedures, etc.

One thing you will notice is that the tables are grouped into several categories:

- Clinical data
- Health system data
- Health economics data
- Derived elements
- Metadata
- Vocabularies

In addition to the clinical focus that we would expect, OMOP was also designed to integrate data from the broader healthcare ecosystem, particularly claims data as well as data on a single patient from multiple different providers.

Lastly, you will also notice that nearly every clinical table has connections to a `Concept` table. OMOP is closely aligned with the use of controlled vocabularies, particularly industry-standard terminologies such as SNOMED-CT and LOINC. Please see the Athena documentation for a complete list of supported terminologies. Because many terminologies support a richer set of relationships beyond simple hierarchy, the other vocabulary tables allow us to capture these relationships in a SQL format. This makes it extremely convenient for us to work with these relationships, embedding them directly within the SQL query (versus needing to interact with a separate terminology management service). The trade-off, however, is that the SQL queries themselves can become quite complex and difficult to read.

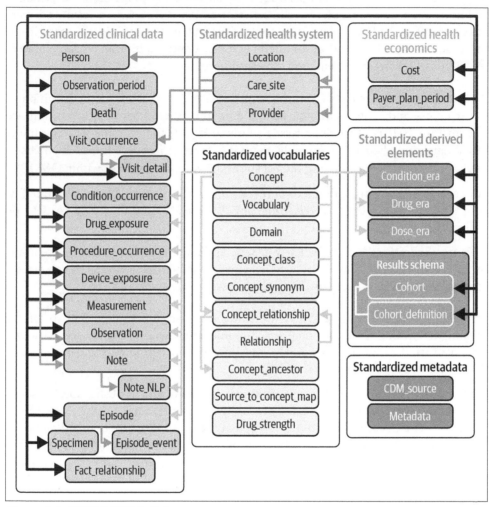

Figure 4-1. OMOP CDM v5.4

Fast Health Interoperability Resources

Another common data model that is gaining traction is FHIR (pronounced "fire"). That said, calling it a "data model" is a bit of a misnomer. Typically, when we talk about data models, we do so in the context of data storage and persistence, namely, in a database. FHIR, however, was not designed to be a storage model. However, since it is available as both JSON and XML, many have started to save the JSON directly into a document-oriented database or any other database that natively supports JSON documents (e.g., PostgreSQL with JSON support).

FHIR was designed as an interoperability standard in order to facilitate the exchange of information between different clinical information systems. As a result, it is verbose and often duplicates data in multiple places rather than efficiently normalizing the data. On the other hand, as an interoperability standard, it provides some powerful features such as implementation guides and profiles.

Resources.   At the core of FHIR is the *resource* (*https://oreil.ly/8doV1*), a definition of the structure and contents of a payload of data to be shared between two healthcare information systems. In many ways, a resource is similar to a table within a traditional database schema. For example, there is a `Patient` resource to which an `Observation` may be linked, similar to the `Person` and `Observation` tables within OMOP.

For each key-value pair within a resource, there is a rigorous definition of cardinality, data type, and flags (*https://oreil.ly/nXVTq*) that dictate how the resource is to be defined and used.

Resource definitions tend to be fairly generic and tend to capture the absolute minimum specificity. This allows FHIR to be a great starting point that users can extend and add additional restrictions. To do this, we will use *profiles*.

Profiles.   So, when we look at FHIR resources, we see something akin to typical schema definitions of a data model. FHIR *profiles* are where we start to see FHIR differentiate itself as an interoperability and information exchange standard versus a data or information model.

Profiles are a way for specific implementations to create and publish a specific set of resource definitions that contains constraints or extensions to the base set of resources. The key feature within FHIR is that these profiles are published and consumable by systems in a computable manner. This allows implementations within electronic health records or other software systems to be able to process and, more importantly, validate data that conforms to particular profiles and resource definitions at runtime.

Implementation guides.   Another key element of the FHIR approach is the *implementation guide*, essentially a set of rules and constraints about how specific resources/ profiles are to be used within a particular context. While creating implementation guides is outside the scope of this book, there are tools to facilitate the creation of implementation guides such as FHIR Shorthand (FSH, pronounced "fish") (*https:// oreil.ly/tx8Zg*) and SUSHI Unshortens Short Hand Inputs (SUSHI) (*https:// github.com/FHIR/sushi*).

Of course, OMOP and FHIR are not the only common data models out there. The following are several other ones that pop up often.

Other data models

There are many other data models that you might encounter as you work with RWD. Here are some that I have encountered or used in the past:

Analysis Data Model (ADaM)
> The ADaM model (*https://oreil.ly/Z9oJs*) comes from the Clinical Data Interchange Standards Consortium (CDISC) and sits downstream of SDTM. ADaM focuses on supporting the analysis process, again with a regulatory perspective. This includes facilitating replication or studies and traceability of results.

Informatics for Integrating Biology and the Bedside (i2b2)
> The i2b2 data model (*https://oreil.ly/Y5HYm*) is another research-focused data model that uses a star schema to represent facts and modifiers of those facts. This makes it an extremely flexible and powerful data model. The trade-off, however, is that it is quite complex and can be challenging for newcomers or organizations that lack the resources to effectively manage data in i2b2, though it is used by more than 200 institutions.

The National Patient Centered Outcomes Research Network (PCORnet)
> As the name implies, the PCORnet data model (*https://pcornet.org/data*) is used to support patient-centered outcomes research. Similar to OMOP, PCORnet is intended to facilitate the consolidation of data within a single institution from a variety of clinical information systems and then enable comparison of queries and analyses across multiple institutions.

Study Data Tabulation Model (SDTM)
> The SDTM (*https://oreil.ly/T9mys*) model is another standard from CDISC and sits upstream of ADaM. It is one of the required data standards for submitting data to the FDA and other regulatory agencies. The intent is to facilitate the aggregation and warehousing of study data that will eventually be used as part of the regulatory submission process.

There are also plenty of proprietary data models that are controlled by vendors that produce datasets. Since those typically require licenses to the data and nondisclosure agreements, we can't really discuss them.

Similar to terminologies or other data standards, the key consideration is what the intended use cases are and how to balance that against operational considerations. For example, it may make sense to adopt a particular data model that isn't perfect, but it is also one that all of your collaborators are already using or one for which you already have tooling and infrastructure in place. No data model is perfect, and there will always be trade-offs. Some may be focused entirely on syntactic and structural considerations, while others attempt to handle some level of semantics.

Some are quick to say that they are using graphs as the data model. While this may be true in a very technical sense, even the use of graph databases require that we clearly define some sort of schema and structure to our data beyond simply "graphs." As we will see later in this chapter, even though we persist the data in a graph database, we are essentially maintaining the MIMIC-III data model.

Regardless of what data model you choose, there are always going to be limitations. The most obvious is that there will be some number of use cases that your data model simply doesn't support or that would be too cumbersome. One common challenge (though not always obvious) is that translation of data from one data model to another naturally results in some amount of information loss or shift. For example, if working with the OMOP data model, it has very strict rules on what data to include or remove (e.g., as a result of missing values). As you consider what data models to use, it is important to engage your data science teams early in the process to conduct feasibility studies. This should generally involve translating a subset of your data (or all of it if you have the time and resources) to the new data model and then conducting the same analysis on both datasets. As you compare the results, you would need to determine what accounts for any differences. This can include the data getting filtered, bugs in the translation process, or variations in structured codes.

Now that we have a sense of data models, some that are closer to EHR data than others, let's start our deep dive into EHR data in the context of a use case around medication data.

Case Study: Medications

As we discussed earlier, a common problem of working with medication data is the variety of coding systems out there, assuming that a coding system was used in the first place. For now, we will ignore the free-text medication problem where the medication names are just free-text strings. Instead, we will focus on the problem of linking data when a coding system such as NDC is being used.

For this case study, we will use the MIMIC-III dataset, focusing on the use of medication data within the PRESCRIPTIONS table. There is a column, ndc, that contains the NDC code corresponding to the string name provided in the column drug. As I discussed earlier, the NDC code is highly specific such that there would be a different code for the tablet form versus the capsule form of a drug. There would even be a different code between the 12-pack versus 100-pill bottle. So, as data scientists, how do we analyze this data such that we can ask broad questions about an active ingredient?

One solution would be to include every possible NDC code within a SQL query as we extract the data. This creates a problem when managing our queries, especially if new data or new mappings are added in the future. This also makes it harder for data scientists and engineers to interact with the queries because they would be dealing with extremely long lists of seemingly random numbers.

Another solution would be to map all of these together during the ETL phase when loading the data into our analytics system. The challenge with this approach is that we assume all requirements are known during the ETL phase. But, what happens if we decide the drugs are equivalent after we have already ETL'ed all the data? We could default back to embedding this in the SQL query, but now we need to manage this knowledge of equivalent drugs in two different places.

The Medication Harmonization Problem

Heparin is a commonly used medication within the inpatient setting since it helps reduce blood clotting in a variety of situations (e.g., following surgery). That said, if the patient is already on another medication that also results in reduced clotting, such as aspirin and other nonsteroidal anti-inflammatory drugs (NSAIDs), this could result in a dangerous situation. Of course, clinicians are aware of this potential interaction between medications. However, we have been tasked to create a decision support tool that will help flag potentially dangerous situations.

From a high level, we will need to do a few things with the data:

1. Find all instances of heparin and determine all of the ways it may be captured or represented within the dataset.
2. Determine all other anticoagulants (or medications that reduce clotting factors).

With the MIMIC dataset, we can do one of two things (or some combination thereof):

1. Search the `drug`, `drug_name_poe`, and `drug_name_generic` columns within PRE SCRIPTIONS table for case-insensitive "heparin."
2. Look up all the NDC codes for formulations that contain heparin.

While these might be the simplest (and even fastest) solution to get to some immediate results, they come with some major trade-offs. If we just search through the few columns that contain free-text strings, we will naturally overfit to the data that we currently have access to. Can we be sure that any future data coming in might conform—what if there are misspellings or abbreviations?

More critically, the string "heparin" might also match "heparin flush," which is used to flush IV catheters to help prevent clots from forming in the tubing and catheter.

Heparin flushes are not used to treat patients and will likely be excluded from most analyses looking at patients being prescribed multiple anticoagulants. To address this, we might consider excluding mentions of "flush" though we are now getting into the realm of increasingly complex (and fragile) data pipelines.

The latter option is the cleaner of the two but, as we discussed earlier, imparts some implicit clinical knowledge into your SQL query and analysis code. For many use cases, this may not be a problem but runs counter to the idea of *separation of concerns.*[6] Do we really want to be in a situation where we need to update our analytics code every time there is an update to the NDC database, or a clarification of the scientific question?

Given the complexity of biomedical data and especially in combination with clinical care, it's important that we build robust data pipelines. However, it also highlights that we need to have a good communication channel between our data teams and our clinical teams.

This whole discussion highlights one of the main differences in perspective when working with data. If a clinician data scientist (i.e., someone with dual training as a clinician and a data scientist) were to approach the previous problem, they would immediately realize the differences between "heparin" and "heparin flush." So, for simple analyses and with the appropriate training, this may be the simplest approach.

However, as organizations scale their approach to data science, it would be very difficult to staff an entire team of clinician data scientists. If we start to integrate data scientists who lack clinical experience, how do we ensure that such nuances are captured during analysis? Additionally, if we are building more complex analytics (e.g., machine learning), how do we ensure that future data pipelines (e.g., in the context of ML ops) can account for these nuances?

This is where proper data engineering at the semantic level is critical! We need ways to scale the organization's approach to such complex problems while also ensuring that we capture the subtle nuance that can make or break a machine learning model. And, more critically, how do we ensure that production deployments of such models account for these nuances?

While we won't answer these questions directly, in the next section, we jump into loading the MIMIC data into a variety of databases and then query that data in the context of our heparin example. The approaches we will discuss are tools for your toolbox, a toolbox that will help you design data pipelines that mitigate many of these concerns.

---

6 Wikipedia, "Separation of Concerns" (*https://oreil.ly/ZuhwY*).

Technical Deep Dive

In this section, we explore the process of:

1. Loading MIMIC data into a database

2. Handling some basic harmonization tasks

3. Extracting/querying the data from the database

We will walk through each of the previous using a variety of databases—SQL, property graph, and hypergraph. The SQL database is a pretty straightforward load using the existing schema of the MIMIC dataset. For the NoSQL databases, we keep the schema fairly simple while focusing on the key opportunities and challenges of the particular database. *The schemas presented have not been optimized for any particular use case. So, while you are free to adapt them to your projects, please keep in mind that your project will likely need a different schema.*

We will be using the MIMIC-III Clinical Database Demo, a subset of the full MIMIC-III database containing 100 patients. Access to the full dataset requires accepting a data use agreement (DUA).

The code in this section assumes that you can run the necessary containers in Docker and that you have configured your environment appropriately. Our first stop is to look at MIMIC-III in a relational database.

Relational database with SQLite

If you are using PostgreSQL, I recommend using the repo available here (*https://oreil.ly/RhRqA*) since we won't be loading the MIMIC data any differently than using the scripts provided by the MIMIC team. My fork contains some very minor changes from the upstream version. Namely, it sets several environment variables given the directory structure used in the book.

To start the containers, you just need to run `./build.sh` from the terminal. The script will start the containers, wait for them to initialize, and then start the process of copying the MIMIC data into its respective tables. This will start both the database server as well as the web interface. There is also a GraphQL implementation.

That said, SQLite is a very lightweight SQL database that uses a single simple file to store and manage the database. It does not require setting up a database server nor fiddling with network settings and IP addresses. Though many developers use SQLite because it is easy to embed within applications, it is also a great for small experiments or working locally on your machine. So, for this section, we will walk through the heparin example by loading the MIMIC data into SQLite.

Importing data into SQLite. Since this is a very small dataset, to keep things simple we will not be dealing with foreign key constraints or indexes. We will simply import each CSV file as a different table using some Python code, as shown in Example 4-1.

Example 4-1. Importing MIMIC-III files into SQLite

```
import os
import pandas as pd
import numpy as np
import sqlite3

mimic_path = "mimic-iii-clinical-database-demo-1.4"
# In case we are using ~ for path
mimic_path = os.path.expanduser(mimic_path)
db_path = "mimic-iii.db"
db_path = os.path.expanduser(db_path)

conn = sqlite3.connect(db_path)

csv_files = [f for f in os.listdir(mimic_path) if f.endswith(".csv")]

# Sort to make it easier to debug since tables are in predictable order
csv_files.sort()

print(f"Found {len(csv_files)} files, expected 26")

for f in csv_files:
    path = os.path.join(mimic_path, f)
    table_name = f.split(".")[0]
    print(f"Importing: {path} into table: {table_name}")
    data = pd.read_csv(path, dtype=str)
    data.to_sql(table_name, conn, if_exists="replace")
```

Querying data in SQLite. Now that we have data loaded, let's go ahead and query the database in the context of our heparin example. Example 4-2 contains a simple SQL query that does a case-insensitive search for drugs that contain "heparin" within the drug, drug_name_generic, or drug_name_poe columns. SQLite defaults to the case-insensitive LIKE, but, if not, simply run the following command in the SQLite command-line utility: PRAGMA case_sensitive_like=OFF;.

Example 4-2. Querying PRESCRIPTIONS for "heparin"

```
SELECT count(*) FROM `PRESCRIPTIONS`
WHERE drug LIKE "%heparin%"
    OR drug_name_generic LIKE "%heparin%"
    OR drug_name_poe LIKE "%heparin%"
```

However, as noted, this will return all drugs containing heparin, both those used therapeutically as well as to maintain IVs and catheters. To investigate this further, Example 4-3 gives us a distinct list.

Example 4-3. Distinct entries for heparin

```
SELECT DISTINCT ndc, drug FROM `PRESCRIPTIONS`
WHERE drug LIKE "%heparin%"
    OR drug_name_generic LIKE "%heparin%"
    OR drug_name_poe LIKE "%heparin%"
ORDER BY ndc
```

Harmonizing data with SQLite.   We can see there are 11 entries of interest, many with the same name but all with different NDCs. Remember that NDCs are very granular and change with different types of packaging, vendors, size/volume, etc. Example 4-4 shows a listing of the NDC and drug name, making it easier for us to decide which values we want to embed in our next query.

Example 4-4. Distinct entries for heparin (results)

```
+-------------+--------------------------------------+
| ndc         | drug                                 |
+-------------+--------------------------------------+
| 63323026201 | Heparin                              |
| 00641040025 | Heparin                              |
| 17191003500 | Heparin CRRT                         |
| 17191003500 | Heparin Flush                        |
| 08290036005 | Heparin Flush (10 units/ml)          |
| 00409115170 | Heparin Flush (10 units/ml)          |
| 64253033335 | Heparin Flush (100 units/ml)         |
| 63323026201 | Heparin Flush (5000 Units/mL)        |
| 00641040025 | Heparin Flush CRRT (5000 Units/mL)   |
| 63323026201 | Heparin Flush CRRT (5000 Units/mL)   |
| 64253033335 | Heparin Flush CVL  (100 units/ml)    |
| 64253033335 | Heparin Flush Hickman (100 units/ml) |
| 64253033335 | Heparin Flush PICC (100 units/ml)    |
| 00409115170 | Heparin Lock Flush                   |
| 00338055002 | Heparin Sodium                       |
| 00074779362 | Heparin Sodium                       |
| 00264958720 | Heparin Sodium                       |
| 00409779362 | Heparin Sodium                       |
| 63323054207 | Heparin Sodium                       |
+-------------+--------------------------------------+
```

Based on these results, we decide we want to keep seven of the entries:

```
    63323026201
    00641040025
    00338055002
```

```
00074779362
00264958720
00409779362
63323054207
```

So, as we see in Example 4-5, we now update our query to only pull prescriptions containing these NDC codes instead of doing a string-based search.

Example 4-5. Prescriptions by NDC

```
SELECT ndc, drug FROM `PRESCRIPTIONS` WHERE ndc in (
  "63323026201",
  "00641040025",
  "00338055002",
  "00074779362",
  "00264958720",
  "00409779362",
  "63323054207"
)
```

We can now use this query within nested SELECT statements or in JOIN statements to analyze patients, admissions, or other items of interest that focus solely on heparin prescriptions that were not simply flushes. As you can see, we would need to carry this list throughout our code and different queries. What if we made a mistake and need to add or remove another NDC from this list? It would become quite problematic to manage and maintain, particularly if we end up sharing this code with other data scientists.

In the next section, we will walk through the same example but using a graph-based approach instead. This will highlight how we can use the database itself to mitigate the need to copy and paste a list of NDC codes across a bunch of different analyses/projects.

Property graph with Neo4j

Using graphs to harmonize data is where the magic and fun happens! One of the key benefits of a graph database is the ability to connect/join individual data points. For our particular use case, we will define a new concept, representing medications that contain heparin but that are used to treat conditions (thus excluding flushes). Once we have created this concept, we can use it in future queries. This is something that we can't easily do in a relational database—create nodes that we will connect to the actual prescription data within the MIMIC dataset.

One thing to note is that if we were to do this at scale (creating hundreds or thousands of these new concepts), we would want to add some properties to the new nodes so that we can track and manage them. For example, we might include a description of the concept and why we created it, a date/timestamp of when it was created and last modified, and tags or other metadata to help organize the concepts. Otherwise, you might end up with a pile of concepts with no way to manage and maintain them.

Unfortunately, Neo4j doesn't neatly embed into our Python code like SQLite did. So, the first thing we need to do is create a Docker instance of our database. We can use the same command to start a Docker container as we used in Example 3-9, or we can just reuse the same container.

Importing data into Neo4j.   To load the data into Neo4j, we need to follow pretty much the same process as with SQLite. Example 4-6 should look quite familiar since it's nearly identical to what we did before except we are now switching from the sqlite3 Python module to Neointerface (*https://oreil.ly/2vEn2*). It is a wrapper of the Neo4j Python library and also provides functionality around pandas dataframes.

Example 4-6. Importing MIMIC-III into Neo4j

```
import os
import pandas as pd
import numpy as np
import neointerface

mimic_path = "mimic-iii-clinical-database-demo-1.4"
# In case we are using ~ for path
mimic_path = os.path.expanduser(mimic_path)

db = neointerface.NeoInterface(
    host="bolt://localhost",
    credentials=("neo4j", "test"),
    apoc=True
)

csv_files = [f for f in os.listdir(mimic_path) if f.endswith(".csv")]

# Sort to make it easier to debug since tables are in predictable order
csv_files.sort()

print(f"Found {len(csv_files)} files, expected 26")

for f in csv_files:
    path = os.path.join(mimic_path, f)
    table_name = f.split(".")[0]
    print(f"Importing: {path} into table: {table_name}")
    data = pd.read_csv(path, dtype=str)
    data = data.replace({np.nan: None})

    # This is the only line different compared to SQLite
    db.load_df(data, table_name)
```

Optimizing Imports

For the MIMIC-III demo data, the code in Example 4-6 works well enough and takes only a minute or two to load the data. If you are attempting to load the entire MIMIC-III dataset, you will want to follow an approach similar to what we used for loading the UMLS in Chapter 3 since the previous code will take quite a long time.

Now that we have the base concepts loaded, we will want to connect all of the nodes per the MIMIC-III schema. While there are certainly opportunities to optimize the overall data model, we will stick to replicating the existing structure we find within the MIMIC schema to keep things consistent and simple. In Example 4-7, I've created a single dictionary that contains the relationships we will be creating. I've trimmed it for the book, but the complete version is available in the associated repo.

Example 4-7. MIMIC-III relationships in Neo4j

```
relationships = {
    ('PATIENTS', 'subject_id'): [
        ('has_admission', 'ADMISSIONS'),
        ('has_callout', 'CALLOUT'),
        ('has_chartevent', 'CHARTEVENTS'),
        ('has_cptevent', 'CPTEVENTS'),
        ('has_datetimeevent', 'DATETIMEEVENTS'),
        ('has_diagnoses_icd', 'DIAGNOSES_ICD'),
        ('has_drgcode', 'DRGCODES'),
        ('has_icustay', 'ICUSTAYS'),
        ('has_inputevents_cv', 'INPUTEVENTS_CV'),
        ('has_inputevents_mv', 'INPUTEVENTS_MV'),
        ('has_labevent', 'LABEVENTS'),
        ('has_microbiologyevent', 'MICROBIOLOGYEVENTS'),
        #('has_noteevent','NOTEEVENTS'),
        ('has_outputevent', 'OUTPUTEVENTS'),
        ('has_prescription', 'PRESCRIPTIONS'),
        ('has_procedureevents_mv', 'PROCEDUREEVENTS_MV'),
        ('has_procedures_icd', 'PROCEDURES_ICD'),
        ('has_service', 'SERVICES'),
        ('has_transfer', 'TRANSFERS')
    ],
    ...
    ('MICROBIOLOGYEVENTS', 'spec_itemid'): [
        ('specimen_item', 'D_ITEMS', 'itemid')
    ],
    ('MICROBIOLOGYEVENTS', 'org_itemid'): [
        ('organism_item', 'D_ITEMS', 'itemid')
    ],
    ('MICROBIOLOGYEVENTS', 'ab_itemid'): [
        ('antibody_item', 'D_ITEMS', 'itemid')
    ],
```

```
    ('OUTPUTEVENTS', 'itemid'): [
        ('item', 'D_ITEMS')
    ],
    ('PROCEDUREEVENTS_MV', 'itemid'): [
        ('item', 'D_ITEMS')
    ]
}
```

For this, I set up the dictionary such that the keys are a tuple consisting of the source node label as well as the attribute within the source node: (SOURCE_NODE_LABEL, ATTR). The values are a list of all the relationships from the source node as tuples consisting of the relationship and the target node label: (RELATIONSHIP, TARGET_NODE_LABEL). It is assumed that the name of the attribute to be matched in the target node is the same as the source node. As you can see with the microbiology events, there is a third item in the relationship tuple. In this situation, the third item is the attribute/property name within the target node.

So, the very first relationship we will be creating is

```
(PATIENTS)-[has_admission]->(ADMISSIONS)
```

and "joined" by the subject_id property.

Similarly, for the microbiology events, we have the relationship

```
(MICROBIOLOGYEVENT)-[specimen_item]->(D_ITEMS)
```

and "joined" by spec_itemid in MICROBIOLOGYEVENT and itemid in D_ITEMS.

To execute this and actually create the relationships, I have created a simple function that constructs and executes the query against the database as shown in Example 4-8.

Example 4-8. Function for creating Neo4j relationships

```
def merge_relationship(source, sattr, rel, target, tattr):
    print(f"Creating: ({source}:{sattr})-[{rel}]->({target}:{tattr})")

    query = f"""
    CALL apoc.periodic.iterate(
        "MATCH (s:{source}), (t:{target})
        WHERE s.{sattr} = t.{tattr}
        RETURN s, t",
        "MERGE (s)-[r:{rel}]->(t)
        RETURN s,r,t",
        {{batchSize:1000, parallel: true}}
    )
    """

    print(query)

    result = db.query(query)
```

As you can see, I am using one of the APOC functions `apoc.periodic.iterate`, which requires that we break up the query into two parts—the query and the action. We also specify the batch size to avoid building up one massive transaction. We will end up creating several million edges/relationships and trying to do that in a single transaction can be problematic. Lastly, we also ask Neo4j to parallelize the operation using a Java `ThreadPoolExecutor`.

Now that we have our data loaded into Neo4j, let's start querying it.

Querying data in Neo4j. So, back to our heparin example—we can query for all prescriptions that contain "heparin" (case-insensitive), and then we can immediately connect that to individual patients, as shown in Example 4-9.

Example 4-9. Cypher queries for Heparin

```
MATCH (p:PRESCRIPTIONS)
WHERE toLower(p.drug) CONTAINS "heparin"
    OR toLower(p.drug_name_generic) CONTAINS "heparin"
    OR toLower(p.drug_name_poe) CONTAINS "heparin"
RETURN DISTINCT p.drug

MATCH (pt:PATIENTS)-[r:has_prescription]->(p:PRESCRIPTIONS)
WHERE toLower(p.drug) CONTAINS "heparin"
    OR toLower(p.drug_name_generic) CONTAINS "heparin"
    OR toLower(p.drug_name_poe) CONTAINS "heparin"
RETURN DISTINCT pt
```

The Cypher queries look very similar to their SQL counterparts, though that isn't surprising given the depth and complexity of the queries. Next, we will take the queries one step further, focusing on those NDCs that we are actually interested in.

Harmonizing data with Neo4j. Now, let's look at how we handle this situation where we want to filter the prescriptions to ignore heparin flushes. We follow the same process as in the previous section. However, we will add the additional step of capturing this within the database itself, as shown in Example 4-10.

Example 4-10. Creating a new heparin concept

```
CREATE (parent:Drug:Knowledge {
    date_created: "2022-01-01",
    drug: "Heparin (non-flush)",
    description: "MIMIC-III, Heparin, excluding flushes"
    purl: "http://some-ontology.org/12345"
}) WITH parent

MATCH (p:PRESCRIPTIONS)
WHERE p.ndc IN [
```

```
   "63323026201",
   "00641040025",
   "00338055002",
   "00074779362",
   "00264958720",
   "00409779362",
   "63323054207"
]
```

```
MERGE (p)-[r:for_drug {derived: true}]->(parent)
RETURN DISTINCT parent,p
```

There are essentially three parts to this query:

1. Create the new concept to which we will link prescriptions.

2. Match the prescriptions of interest.

3. Link the matched prescriptions to the new heparin concept.

While this is the simplest and most straightforward way to link the new concept for "Heparin (non-flush)" to the prescriptions, the downside is that we don't have intermediate concepts for each of the seven individual NDCs. However, this is a theoretical downside; that is, academically, we may want to track concepts for each NDC, but the reality is that we may never use that information or knowledge. This is an example of the sort of decision we need to make when working with graphs—do we want to track things we may not ever use? Generally, the answer is *no*, but it's not always obvious to us what we might need in the future. On the other hand, how much should we invest in a future that may not exist?

Another point of note is the use of the `purl` property. PURL is a *persistent uniform resource locator* and is a way to uniquely identify resources accessible via the web. Many use PURLs simply as a way to create unique identifiers. However, the intent is that the PURL is a valid URL that leverages HTTP response codes to communicate to consumers the type and status of a particular resource.[7] The Open Biological and Biomedical Ontology (OBO) Foundry (*https://oreil.ly/WZWvx*) is another example of how PURLs are used for identifiers. Here, we are using it simply to create an identifier for the purpose of the example. The hostname used is not real, and the PURL will not actually resolve to anything.

So, given this new concept, how can we query our database for all patients on heparin, excluding flushes? We can basically follow our nodes and relationships using Cypher as we see in Example 4-11.

---

7 The DOI System uses PURLs (*https://oreil.ly/NlTgI*) and they provide a short discussion regarding how they use PURLs.

Example 4-11. All patients connected to heparin concept (Neo4j)

```
MATCH (pt:PATIENTS)-[rx:has_prescription]->(p:PRESCRIPTIONS)-[:for_drug]->
    (d:Drug {purl: "http://some-ontology.org/12345"})
RETURN pt
```

As you can see, our query is quite simple and intuitive. Depending on our internal governance process, we can add as many properties as we need to the new concepts we create as well as the relationships linking them. This will allow us to filter and follow only those nodes and relationships pertinent to our given question. For example, I included a `date_created` property that captures when the relationship was actually created in the database. This would allow us to track how the relationship might change over time (if we create a new relationship each time) but use the latest one only when performing queries such as the previous one.

Given this ability to connect patients to prescriptions, and prescriptions to our new drug concept, you might be wondering why we don't have other drug concepts. If we look at the `PRESCRIPTIONS` table within the demo database, we would actually see that there are 2,489 unique entries if we consider only the columns with drug information (excluding the prescription dates and links back to patients, admissions, or ICU stays).

We would want to introduce a new type of node to capture just the drug details and move the start and end date, admission, and ICU stay details to the `has_prescription` relationship. If we continue remodeling the data, we may also want to connect any given prescription to a hospital admission or ICU stay. This is where the property graph approach begins to show its limitations. If we model a prescription as a relationship, there would be no direct way to link this relationship to a hospital admission node. Given the details of the MIMIC data, we could work around this by storing the hospital admission ID (`hadm_id`) in both the admission node as well as the prescription relationship and make sure that our Cypher query filters on both. In Example 4-12, we would be querying all prescriptions connected to emergency department admissions for patient with `subject_id` 12345.

Example 4-12. Connecting an admission to a prescription relationship

```
MATCH (pt:Patients {subject_id: 12345})-[:has_admission]->
    (a:ADMISSIONS {admission_type: "EMERGENCY"}),
    (pt2:PATIENTS)-[rx:has_prescription]->(d:Drug)
WHERE a.hadm_id = rx.hadm_id
RETURN pt, rx, d
```

While this certainly makes the queries easier as compared to SQL, the trade-off is that you now need to manage the knowledge stored within the database and make sure that your queries are using the right concepts. What if you someone changes the underlying mappings that we created in the previous section? How would this affect your query? How would you even know that such changes had been made so that you could retest your queries to make sure they still made sense? This highlights that while this approach is "clean" in a semantic sense, it does highlight some of the key challenges around knowledge management, regardless of your chosen technological solution.

In the next section, we will walk through the heparin example again with TypeDB. In addition to the hypergraph aspects, we will also look at the use of an inferencing or reasoning engine. This adds another element to how we can maintain data harmonization mappings through the use of rules.

Hypergraph with TypeDB

We continue with TypeDB but will also look at a feature specific to TypeDB—their built-in reasoning engine, which allows us to manage our data harmonization mappings with two different approaches:

1. Similar to property graphs and RDF triple stores, we can create new relationships that connect the various heparin concepts together, embedding this knowledge directly in the graph.
2. We take advantage of the reasoning engine and create rules that handle the mappings, loading and unloading the rules based on our query needs.

There is no clear "best approach" between our two options, and the choice will largely depend on the details of the specific use case. For example, if your mappings are unlikely to change often and will be frequently queried, it is probably best to just write them directly into the database and manage them as you would other ETL jobs for modifying the contents of the database.

On the other hand, if your mappings are likely to change frequently, constantly updating your database will be challenging to manage and can increase the probability of inconsistent knowledge. These types of "bugs" can be difficult to track down because they are difficult to reproduce. In this situation, you could create the mappings as rules, managing them as you would any other code. Once loaded into the database, your queries would benefit from the most up-to-date mappings.

Before we get into the nuts and bolts of working with the data, we need to create and load the TypeDB schema, just as we did in Chapter 3 when working with the UMLS. Example 4-13 shows the schema for `Patient`, which corresponds to the `PATIENTS` table definition within MIMIC-III.

Example 4-13. TypeDB Schema for Patients

```
define

  patient sub entity,
      plays prescription:patient,

      owns row_id,
      owns subject_id,

      owns gender,
      owns dob,
      owns dod,
      owns dod_hosp,
      owns dod_ssn,
      owns expire_flag;

  row_id sub attribute,
      value long;
  subject_id sub attribute,
      value long;
  gender sub attribute,
      value string;
  dob sub attribute,
      value string;
  dod sub attribute,
      value string;
  dod_hosp sub attribute,
      value string;
  dod_ssn sub attribute,
      value string;
  expire_flag sub attribute,
      value long;
```

We have defined each column of the PATIENTS table as an *attribute* within TypeDB along with an associated data type. I have made everything a string to keep the code and parsing simple though I kept the various _id fields as long data types. You can also see that the patient entity corresponds to the PATIENTS table and links each of the columns via the owns keyword. While this may be a different syntax compared to other database definition languages, it is conceptually equivalent. The one key difference is the plays prescription:patient line, which highlights the fact that a patient "plays" the role of a patient within the *prescription* relation.[8] Example 4-14 shows another snippet of the schema definition specific to how we will be modeling prescriptions and drug instances.

---

8 Please see the TypeDB documentation (*https://oreil.ly/nF5Kr*) for additional information on entities, attributes, roles, and relations.

Example 4-14. TypeDB schema for prescriptions

```
prescription sub relation,
    relates patient,
    relates prescribed_drug,

    owns startdate,
    owns enddate;

druginstance sub entity,
    plays prescription:prescribed_drug,

    owns startdate,
    owns enddate,
    owns drug_type,
    owns drug,
    owns drug_name_poe,
    owns drug_name_generic,
    owns formulary_drug_cd,
    owns gsn,
    owns ndc,
    owns prod_strength,
    owns dose_val_rx,
    owns dose_unit_rx,
    owns form_val_disp,
    owns form_unit_disp,
    owns route;
```

I've split the original definition of the PRESCRIPTIONS table into an entity and a relation. The druginstance entity captures all of the drug information (e.g., name, dose, route, etc.), while the prescription relation captures the details of the prescription itself. Within the relation, we define two *roles*: *patient* and *prescribed_drug*. Roles allow TypeDB to capture and model an additional layer of context—the role that an entity plays within a particular relation.

Import data into TypeDB.   As I'm sure you are used to by now, we need to make sure our Docker container is running. You can use the same configuration as shown in Example 3-14 from the previous chapter.

The overall skeleton of our code remains the same as with the previous examples for SQLite and Neo4j. This is pretty straightforward though TypeDB does require the explicit use of transactions to manage our interactions. Before we start importing the actual data, we need to first load our TypeDB schema as we saw in Example 3-16.

Now that our database is primed and loaded, we will need to iterate through each of the CSV files and load them into TypeDB as we have done previously. Unfortunately, there is not yet a library that provides convenient loading of dataframes into TypeDB. Additionally, we need to do some processing of the data first so that we can extract unique drug instances that we can then connect using prescription relations.

Example 4-15 contains our top-level code that iterates through the CSV files and loads them.

Example 4-15. Loading the MIMIC-III data into TypeDB

```
csv_files = [f for f in os.listdir(mimic_path) if f.endswith(".csv")]
csv_files.sort()

print(f"Found {len(csv_files)} files, expected 26")

db = "test2"

with TypeDB.core_client("localhost:1729") as client:
    if client.databases().contains(db):
        client.databases().get(db).delete()

    client.databases().create(db)

with TypeDB.core_client("localhost:1729") as client:
    with client.session(db, SessionType.SCHEMA) as session:
        with session.transaction(TransactionType.WRITE) as tx:
            with open("../data/mimic-schema.tql") as f:
                q = f.read()
                tx.query().define(q)
                tx.commit()

with TypeDB.core_client("localhost:1729") as client:
    with client.session(db, SessionType.DATA) as session:
        for f in csv_files:
            path = os.path.join(mimic_path, f)
            table_name = f.split(".")[0]
            print(f"Importing: {path} into table: {table_name}")
            data = pd.read_csv(path, dtype=str)
            data = data.replace({np.nan: None})

            queries = processors[table_name](data)

            with session.transaction(TransactionType.WRITE) as tx:
                for q in queries:
                    tx.query().insert(q)
                tx.commit()
```

We have wrapped most of the import in transactions and other TypeDB-specific code compared to our previous examples. The other notable differences compared to Example 3-17 are the lack of batching and the use of more generic "processors." Each of our processor functions takes a dataframe as input and returns a list of query strings to be executed against the database. For straightforward tables such as PATIENTS, the processor function does a straight conversion. For prescriptions, we do

---

a bit more processing, as we can see in Example 4-16. I have left out the definitions of the template functions from the example since you saw some in Example 3-18.

Example 4-16. Patient processor function

```
def process_patients(df):
    queries = [patient_template(x).strip()
                    for x in data.itertuples()]
    return queries

def process_prescriptions(df):
    queries = []

    # Extract unique drug instances
    drugs = df[[x[0] for x in drug_fields]].drop_duplicates()

    queries.extend([druginstance_template(x).strip()
                        for x in drugs.itertuples()])

    queries.extend([prescription_template(x).strip()
                        for x in df.itertuples()])

    return queries

processors = {
    "PATIENTS": process_patients,
    ...
    "PRESCRIPTIONS": process_prescriptions
}
```

However, since we are separating our prescriptions into a druginstance entity and a prescription relation, we will need to do a bit more processing. First, we need to extract only those columns needed for a druginstance, and then we need to construct two sets of queries—one to insert druginstances and another to insert the prescription relations. Example 4-17 highlights the processor function as well as the associate template functions that generate the query strings.

Example 4-17. Prescription processor function

```
drug_fields = [
        ("drug_type", str),
        ("drug", str),
        ("drug_name_poe", str),
        ("drug_name_generic", str),
        ("formulary_drug_cd", str),
        ("gsn", str),
        ("ndc", str),
        ("prod_strength", str),
        ("dose_val_rx", str),
```

```
        ("dose_unit_rx", str),
        ("form_val_disp", str),
        ("form_unit_disp", str),
        ("route", str)
    ]

def druginstance_template(p):
    return f"""
    insert $p isa druginstance,
        {", ".join(filter(None, [has_clause(p, f) for f in drug_fields]))}
        ;
    """

def prescription_template(p):
    return f"""
    match
        $pt isa patient, has subject_id {getattr(p, 'subject_id')};
        $drug isa druginstance,
        {", ".join(filter(None, [has_clause(p, f) for f in drug_fields]))};
    insert $prescription (patient: $pt, prescribed_drug: $drug) isa prescription,
        has row_id {getattr(p, 'row_id')},
        has startdate "{getattr(p, 'startdate')}",
        has enddate "{getattr(p, 'enddate')}";
    """

def process_prescriptions(df):
    queries = []

    # Extract unique drug instances
    drugs = df[[x[0] for x in drug_fields]].drop_duplicates()

    queries.extend([druginstance_template(x).strip()
                    for x in drugs.itertuples()])

    queries.extend([prescription_template(x).strip()
                    for x in df.itertuples()])

    return queries
```

The most important difference is the match/insert query in `prescription_tem`
`plate()`. Since relations assume that the associated entities are already loaded in the
graph, we start with a `match` clause to find the patient and drug that form the prescription. Given the MIMIC-III data, we are matching the patient by `subject_id` and
the drug by all the drug fields and then creating the relation in which the start and
end dates of the prescription are captured.

Now that we have our data loaded into TypeDB, let's run some of our standard
queries.

Querying data in TypeDB. First, we want to see which drugs contain heparin using basic string matching. Note that, unlike previous examples, we are querying for our newly created drug instances and not prescriptions as we did for SQLite and Neo4j. Then, all we would need to do is add an additional clause to match prescription relations if we wanted to return all prescriptions related to our drugs containing the string "heparin". Both of these queries are shown in Example 4-18.

Example 4-18. TypeQL queries for heparin

```
# Query just the drug instances
match
    $drug isa druginstance;
    {$drug has drug contains "heparin";}
      or {$drug has drug_name_generic contains "heparin";}
      or {$drug has drug_name_poe contains "heparin";};
get $rx;

# Add clause for prescriptions
match
    $drug isa druginstance;
    {$drug has drug contains "heparin";}
      or {$drug has drug_name_generic contains "heparin";}
      or {$drug has drug_name_poe contains "heparin";};

    $rx (prescribed_drug: $drug) isa prescription;
get $rx;
```

Now, let's move on to how we might harmonize our drug instances with our heparin concept.

Harmonizing data in TypeDB. Now that we have our data loaded into TypeDB, the next step in our heparin example is to create a new drug concept for the subset of heparin in which we are interested. There are two approaches we can take when harmonizing the data. The first (Example 4-19) follows the same pattern as we used with property graphs—to just directly update the database.

Example 4-19. Example TypeDB rule

```
match
    $d isa druginstance, has ndc "63323026201";
    $c isa concept, has purl "http://some-ontology.org/12345";
insert
    (parent: $c, child: $d) isa hierarchy;
```

The second approach we will take involves creating rules. As you can see in the following query, it looks similar to the TypeQL query for inserting directly into the database. When using rules, the TypeDB reasoning engine dynamically "adds" new data to the database upon rule execution without actually persisting anything. This allows queries to interact with the data as if the data was in the database, essentially providing a mechanism that inserts data, runs the query, and then removes the data.

Example 4-20 shows a single rule that matches a particular `druginstance` (indexed by NDC) to our "Heparin (non-flush)" concept. Rules can infer relations and attributes but not new entities, so we would have previously inserted this concept into the database. Once the rule is triggered, the graph is effectively the same as if we had inserted the new relation as the previous example.

Example 4-20. Example TypeDB rule

```
define

rule heparin-non-flush-subset-ndc-63323026201:
when {
    $d isa druginstance, has ndc "63323026201";
    $c isa concept, has purl "http://some-ontology.org/12345";
} then {
    (parent: $c, child: $d) isa hierarchy;
};
```

This rule matches all drugs that have the specified NDC code and the concept to which we want to link them and creates a hierarchal relation. As you can see, we are specifying only a single NDC. We would need to create a separate rule for each NDC we want to match because TypeDB rule conditions are conjunctive. Disjunctive conditions can simply be created as separate rules.

OR Versus AND Conditions

TypeDB condition clauses (the "when" section) are conjunctive—they are combined using "AND" so all conditions must be met for the rule to trigger. If you need to specify disjunctive conditions (using "OR"), you would need to create separate rules for each condition.

So, to create the seven rules we need for the different NDC, we can either manually create the rules as we did earlier or can write a little block of code to generate the rules for us, loading them the same way we loaded schemas. We use the same template approach as before so our code is pretty straightforward as we see in Example 4-21.

Example 4-21. Autogenerate TypeDB rules

```
def heparin_ndc_rule_template(ndc):
    return f"""
```

```
define

    rule heparin-non-flush-subset-ndc-{ndc}:
    when {{
        $d isa druginstance, has ndc "{ndc}";
        $c isa concept, has purl "http://some-ontology.org/12345";
    }} then {{
        (parent: $c, child: $d) isa hierarchy;
    }};
    """

ndcs = [
    "63323026201",
    "00641040025",
    "00338055002",
    "00074779362",
    "00264958720",
    "00409779362",
    "63323054207"
]

with TypeDB.core_client("localhost:1729") as client:
    with client.session(db, SessionType.SCHEMA) as session:
        with session.transaction(TransactionType.WRITE) as tx:
            for rule in [heparin_ndc_rule_template(ndc) for ndc in ndcs]:
                tx.query().define(rule)
            tx.commit()
```

Now that we have loaded our rules to connect particular drugs to our new heparin concept, let's query our database. As we see in Example 4-22, the syntax is a bit more complicated than what we say with Cypher (in Example 4-11), but the conceptual approach is the same.

Example 4-22. All patients connected to heparin (TypeDB)

```
match
    # Find all drug instances linked to http://some-ontology.org/12345
    $p isa concept, has purl "http://some-ontology.org/12345";
    $c isa druginstance;
    (parent: $p, child: $c) isa hierarchy;

    # Find all prescriptions related to those drugs
    (prescribed_drug: $c, patient: $pt) isa prescription;
get $pt;
```

The first block of the `match` statement finds our new heparin concept (using the PURL), finds all connected drug instances, and then finds all of the prescriptions connected to those drug instances. As you can see, we achieve the same functionality as we did with property graphs. However, the link between our new heparin concept and existing drug instances is inferred by the reasoning engine and not persisted within the database. So, our database contains the facts as taken from the electronic health record, but our use-case specific grouping of the drugs is inferred in real time.

The main benefit to such an approach is that we don't clutter our database with mappings that are specific to a subset of use cases. We can load and unload rules as our needs change and limit the database to storing our facts. Of course, while this may sound appealing, we still need to balance this against our business case and whether this technical solution is actually fitting our needs. TypeDB has become quite performant (compared to earlier versions when they were Grakn), but making inferences in real time may become a bottleneck. Ultimately, whether you load knowledge as rules in the reasoner or directly in the graph would largely depend on how often you plan on using the inference, how likely it might change, and how performant the particular rule(s) are.

As we saw with each previous solution, the medication normalization problem can be solved with any database. The choice of which approach largely depends on other requirements, many of which may be difficult to determine when a projects starts. It is easy to over-engineer a solution especially if we are trying to account for poorly defined requirements. So, it is important that we spend the time up front to really understand the context in which we are building our solution.

For example, are we working with data from a disease area that is being updated frequently? In other words, is our understanding of the underlying science changing on the order of months or years? Aside from the disease itself, we also need to look at the associated clinical practice. We may understand the underlying pathophysiology of the disease process, but clinical management may be highly complex or nuanced.

Generally speaking, anything that increases the frequency or complexity of the mapping process will increase the chance that we will need to remap the data at some point. We then need to weigh this against how long it would take for us to remap the data and then apply those mappings to the underlying data. This is a great example of the intersection of data and engineering.

We need to balance working with the data (creating and maintaining the mappings) with engineering and operational considerations (applying the mappings to the data). It may be that the rule-based approach discussed earlier is the best approach from a data perspective. However, what if it makes our query so slow that it is unusable? We may need to persist these mappings simply to make queries usable, thus forcing us to find ways to better manage the migrations of the mappings.

So, this concludes our whirlwind tour through our heparin example in the context of different types of databases. As we discussed briefly in Chapter 2, RDF triple stores are a form of graph database based on semantic web standards. We did not go into specific implementation details of RDF triple stores and SPARQL because the modeling approach would be conceptually the same as with property graphs and hypergraphs. However, unlike property graph databases, RDF triple stores treat everything as a triple of subject-predicate-object. As a result, they can appear a bit more complex. Please visit the GitLab repo for specific implementation examples.

Similar pros and cons exist with RDF graphs as with property graphs. However, given that RDF triple stores follow an established standard, this approach can make it easier for us to share our knowledge with other systems. For example, instead of creating triples capturing the relationship between our new concept and the data directly as represented by MIMIC, we could use standardized PURLs for the medication concepts. We could then send these triples to others for inclusion in their systems.

In the next section, we quickly discuss how we could connect the previous approaches with terminologies such as the UMLS or specific sources such as SNOMED CT.

Connecting to the UMLS

As you saw in the previous set of examples, we were able to connect the data from an electronic health record to structured concepts. Though our example, focused on a new concept that we created and assigned our own definition and semantics, this could easily be a concept within the UMLS or other terminology/ontology.

In the SQL example, if we don't already have structured codes or concepts, we generally add this as a new column. Data scientists typically handle this within their code (e.g., R or Python) after they've exported the data from the database. An alternative would be to update the database schema and persist the structured concepts as a new column in the database or via more complex join tables (as we see with OMOP and the integration of the Athena vocabularies).

However, when working with graphs, you saw how quickly we could create a new connection between the data point and a structured concept that we created. If we have terminologies loaded into the same graph as our data, we can perform the same linkage with existing concepts from the terminology. When working with UMLS, we could look up concepts by CUI instead of a PURL. If we are integrating with the NCBO BioPortal, we could use the BioPortal PURL. Even if we are linking directly with a single terminology, we would simply use the source's unique identifier (e.g., RXCUI, LOINC code, SNOMED CT identifier).

To make it a bit more concrete, we can combine our example in this chapter with the heparin example from Chapter 3 where we found the concepts corresponding to the heparin pharmacologic substance. We also identified the therapeutic or preventative procedure that was "heparin therapy." With the MIMIC data, instead of creating a new heparin concept and linking the drugs, we could also just link the patient or admission directly to the "heparin therapy" concept. Not only would this cleanly link us to the UMLS, it may be more semantically correct. After all, it's not the drug itself that is therapeutic or not; it's the idea that it was used as a therapeutic to treat the patient.

After quite a bit of a technical deep dive, let's take a step back and, in the next section, discuss some of the difficulties and challenges we have when normalizing structured medical data.

Difficulties Normalizing Structured Medical Data

The medication normalization scenario discussed in this chapter is a relatively simple situation. There are certainly some complexities and potential ambiguity in mapping something like heparin, but medications are generally objective data. Things become much more challenging when working with data that may be subjective or where there is no clear consensus.

For example, as we discussed earlier in this chapter, cancer staging is a complex topic. In addition to different approaches to staging (group versus TNM), there are also the AJCC staging guidelines that are routinely updated. Though the guidelines were originally created for human consumption (i.e., for oncologists to read, understand, and apply in their practice), they are also evolving to reflect the shift to a data and computationally-centric future.

So, how does this affect us from a data harmonization perspective? When we work with oncology data that has staging guidelines, we need to identify which edition/version was used and whether we will need to account for differences between the versions. In other words, a cancer staged using one version of the AJCC guidelines might actually result in a different stage using a later version of the guideline. So, if we are combining datasets or analyzing patients across many years (during which time there was an update to the guidelines), we need to be careful about how the data were coded. Of course, there are too many examples to list, but similar nuances exist across all medical specialties, so it is critical that we engage appropriate domain experts to help us identify such pitfalls.

Conclusion

In this chapter, we dove into working with electronic health record data, using the MIMIC dataset to illustrate many of the challenges. We also looked at Synthea, a synthetic data generator. The MIMIC dataset is a real dataset and thus preferable in many ways over synthetic data. However, it focuses on intensive care data so is not reflective of the majority of data you are likely to encounter when working with EHR data. Synthea provides more generic data though they are synthetically generated. With Synthea, we can also get data in different formats, allowing us to test data transformation pipelines.

The most obvious trade-off between the two is that we can use the MIMIC data to both develop data pipelines as well as generate actual insights—as long as our use case aligns with intensive care data from an academic medical center. On the other hand, the Synthea data allows us to create and test data pipelines but can't be used for any actual analysis.

The MIMIC data also reflects true data quality issues that creep into EHR data because they were collected during actual patient care. Though the Synthea data generates pseudorandom data, the algorithms to generate the data are those that were engineered into the underlying software. So, while Synthea data can approximate many of the real-world data issues we see, it may still have many gaps.

Within the context of EHR data, we looked at some of the methods for storing and querying the data in the context of a medication harmonization example. This allowed us to compare and contrast SQL- and graph-based approaches for representing patient-level data, and Table 4-2 highlights the pros and cons to each type of database.

Table 4-2. Pros and cons of each type of database

Database	Pros	Cons
PostgreSQL (SQL)	• Integrates with existing analytics and business intelligence tools. • SQL is ubiquitous and accessible to both business and technical users. • Performance and scalability are well understood.	• Strict schema can make it difficult to update the data/information model. • Aligning the data model to account for different business needs can be intractable. • Querying graph-like data can result in very cumbersome and hard-to-read SQL queries.
Neo4j/ArangoDB (property graph)	• Naturally aligned with the use of terminologies and ontologies. • Schema can be updated as understanding of the data changes. • Graph algorithms can unlock hidden insights based on connections between the data and associated terminologies.	• NoSQL approaches can lead to poorly managed schemas and create fragile systems. • Performance characteristics are highly dependent on the structure of the data (e.g., supernode problem).[a]
GraphDB (RDF triple store)	• Use of semantic web standards makes the knowledge more portable (across organizations as well as databases). • RDF graphs are inherently self-describing, enabling tooling around the management of the graph itself. • Established ecosystem of tools and libraries for interacting with RDF graphs.	• Very steep learning curve and the perception that it is suitable only for academic use. • Can result in an overly complex solution with a high-maintenance stack. • Performance can become a problem.

Database	Pros	Cons
TypeDB (strongly typed hypergraph)	• More expressive graph schema with strong typing allows for richer modeling of RWD. • Integrated reasoning engine makes it easy to query and interact with transient/inferred relationships and nodes.	• Very new technology with limited ecosystem of tools and support. • Integrations with analytics and business intelligence tools require additional software development.

[a] ArangoDB: Do Graph Databases Scale? Yes! No! Let's See! (*https://oreil.ly/afRWa*)

By now, you should have a foundational understanding of the many issues that arise when working with real-world data. There is no way to capture all of the many nuances and challenges that you might encounter, but I chose the medication harmonization challenge since it is representative of many common issues.

In the next chapter, we continue our deep dive into RWD but we shift gears a bit and look at claims data that are generated as part of the reimbursement process. You may think that claims data are specific to the United States given our heavy focus on private insurers. However, even those countries with single payer or nationalized health systems still generate claims data—essentially, the government becomes the sole insurance company.

## CHAPTER 5

Deep Dive: Claims Data

In the previous chapter, we looked at clinical data from electronic health records. EHR data are often the most highly sought data given the depth and richness from the perspective of care delivery. However, many analyses require a combination of both the clinical data as well as associated financial data. Although it may feel immoral or unethical to discuss financial considerations in the context of patient care, the reality is that the cost of care is an important input to all levels of decision-making in the healthcare industry.

For example, say a new drug was just approved with an effectiveness that is 3% better —83% of patients show improvement on the drug versus 80% on the current drug. This is great news until we realize that the new drug is not only more expensive but also more invasive—it is 5x the cost and requires an IV infusion versus being a simple shot. While the clinical decision to choose the drug with the simpler delivery mechanism may be simple, the cost decision is not. Is the additional efficacy or effectiveness worth the 5x increase in cost? What about 10x? At what point does the relatively small increase in performance no longer justify the increase in cost or complexity?

Efficacy and Effectiveness

The *efficacy* of a drug (or vaccine) is its performance in a highly controlled environment (e.g., a clinical trial), usually to remove or mitigate confounding factors.

Effectiveness, on the other hand, is the performance in the real world, under normal conditions.

To start tackling some of these questions, we need to integrate claims and other financial data alongside the clinical data. Although there is a common misperception that claims are an artifact of the U.S. healthcare system, they are commonly found in nationalized or single-payer healthcare systems as well. At their core, claims are an accounting mechanism for the cost of care. While the U.S. healthcare system is much more complex given the number of payers and providers, all healthcare systems need a way to track healthcare spending.

In this chapter, we will review a publicly accessible dataset that will give us a taste of working with claims data. The dataset is synthetic and, while modeled after real data, is not suitable for any actual conclusions. However, it would be possible to get access to the real underlying dataset should you want to replicate your analysis on real data.

Publicly Accessible Data—SynPUF

Like much of healthcare, getting access to publicly accessible data is quite the challenge. Claims and financial data are very difficult since there are at least a couple factors at play—they contain identifying information such that the data would need to be de-identified or anonymized, and there is little incentive to share financial data. Given the delicate negotiations among hospitals, physician groups, and insurance companies, there is actually a disincentive to sharing claims data.

That said, if you end up working in the healthcare industry, there is a good chance that you will work on a project that involves something akin to claims data. It may be that you are working at an integrated health system (e.g., Kaiser Permanente) where there is a single overarching organization over both the provider and the payer. In this case, the organization as a whole is focused on delivering the best care possible in a way that is financially sustainable.

One accessible claims dataset is released from the Centers for Medicare and Medicaid Services (also known as CMS). Known as the *Data Entrepreneurs' Synthetic Public Use Files* (*https://oreil.ly/cdUVn*), or simply *SynPUF* for short, the dataset contains synthetically generated data based on real CMS claims data. As a result, the dataset is a great way to start working with claims data without needing to make the up-front investment of licensing actual claims data from CMS. The trade-off is that the results of any analyses performed in SynPUF data are generally meaningless.

The SynPUF data are based on actual claims from 2008–2010. The most obvious limitation is that, while based on real claims, the data is synthetically generated. The algorithms used to generate the synthetic data may be able to capture simple characteristics of the data (e.g., matching mean/variance of a single variable), but it is unlikely to capture higher-order interactions between variables.

However, even if you opt to license the nonsynthetic data from CMS, keep in mind that CMS covers a specific demographic of people in the United States. For those beneficiaries "under 65," the average age is in the early 50s for each state. For those "over 65," the average age is in the 70s. This is not surprising given the focus of CMS as a payer.

This highlights one of the inherent biases in any healthcare dataset—demographics can have a huge impact on any analysis that we do. One of the most commonly cited biases is geographic location, with many headlines offering some version of "your ZIP code matters more than your genetic code."[1] So, when considering different healthcare datasets, it is important to consider the patient demographic that is captured within the dataset. For example, in the San Francisco Bay Area, companies often look to the University of California, San Francisco (UCSF), and Stanford for access to both data and domain experts. As two of the top medical centers in the world, they are an obvious choice for potential collaborations. However, it is important to ask whether the patients captured within these hospital systems are reflective of the patient populations of interest. Are the people who live or work in the San Francisco Bay Area and carry private insurance representative of undocumented migrant workers in the California Central Valley? Would a model trained on one group of patients be applicable to the other group? These are important questions to ask though not always easy to answer.

Detailed Documentation on SynPUF

For detailed documentation regarding the SynPUF data, please check the user manual (*https://oreil.ly/LQxZx*).

So now that we have some understanding of claims data and know about a publicly accessible claims dataset, let's switch gears a little bit and focus on data models. If you have worked with data architects in the past, you will see some similarities in our overall discussion. However, in most projects, the data architects are helping with the modeling itself and defining the data model (and sometimes vocabularies). When working with RWD, we often don't have a choice—the data is given to us in whatever model the data provider is using. In this next section, we'll discuss data modeling a bit and then look at how we can use OMOP to integrate EHR and claims data.

Data Models

As with EHR data, there are many data models being used throughout the healthcare industry. In most cases, they are proprietary models developed for internal use within various systems such as electronic health records or revenue cycle management systems. Additionally, companies focused on interoperability or data aggregation are also flirting with their own data models. For example, Redox is an electronic health record integration company that seeks to work with companies looking to integrate

---

1 Jamie Ducharme and Elijah Wolfson, "Your ZIP Code Might Determine How Long You Live—and the Difference Could Be Decades" (*https://time.com/5608268/zip-code-health*), Time, June 17, 2019.

with various EHRs such as Epic and Cerner. They have created their own JSON-based data model (*https://oreil.ly/BtpW2*) including some support for claims (*https://oreil.ly/rYrBj*). On the other hand, many companies (e.g., IQVIA and Optum) are starting to offer their data in proprietary, native formats in addition to OMOP.

Choosing a Data Model

While data and information models are a necessary part of any data and analysis project, I have seen way too much focus on choosing the "right" or "best" data model too early on in the project lifecycle. For example, I often get asked something along the lines of "We are starting this new project where we're working with a local hospital to extract data for analysis. Should we use a common data model? What do you think about OMOP?" My initial response is usually a series of questions: What exactly are you trying to do? What types of data are you extracting? What scientific questions are you asking of the data?

This highlights the dependency between the data model and what we, as data scientists and engineers, are trying to do with the data. For example, the OMOP data model is gaining popularity and traction (as evidenced by vendors such as IQVIA and Optum making their data available in OMOP) and may be a great fit. However, it is designed around longitudinal analysis of observational data. This means that it takes a patient-centric approach so that we can query a single patient's progression over time. The tables in OMOP are structured to capture events and episodes throughout a patient's journey through the healthcare system. As a result, it may be unnecessarily complicated for analyses that are looking only at cohorts of patients at a single instance in time.

There are many angles to consider when choosing a data model (in no particular order):

- What data model is currently being used by the source data? Can we just continue to use this model?
- What data model is currently being used by our data scientists or analytics tools and models?
- What types of analytics are we planning over the next 6, 12, 24, etc., months?
- If we are going to develop an ML model, what model would work best when we push the model to production?
- How often do we anticipate processing new data?
- Do we have an external terminology management solution?
- Where do we have the most informatics expertise and resourcing? Closer to model development, or closer to production deployment?

Academically, you may be tempted to find the "best" data model that can be extended indefinitely to support any number of potential use cases. However, experience shows that this usually results in an excessively complicated solution that becomes a "one size fits none" solution.

Pragmatically, it becomes a delicate balance between getting the most benefit and keeping things relatively simple and easy. For example, say we are trying to develop a clinical decision support tool that will help decide whether a patient is at risk of sepsis and therefore should be admitted to the hospital and transferred to the ICU. In one scenario, we may be working with a very diverse group of hospitals, each with varying degrees of IT and informatics capabilities. However, they all are using electronic health records that support FHIR. We may choose to design our architecture around this since it would drastically simplify the process of pushing our model to production in an MLops sense. Of course, this means we may incur higher up-front costs to harmonize the data that we have acquired from Optum, UCSF, and Stanford to train and develop our model.

On the other hand, imagine a scenario where we are working with the same academic medical centers on a similar sepsis prediction algorithm. However, these medical centers all have robust IT and informatics capabilities and prefer to handle the integration and deployment of machine learning models themselves. In this case, we know that IQVIA, UCSF, and Stanford all have existing efforts to standardize data into OMOP. It then makes the most sense to leverage this existing effort and build our ML models based on the OMOP data model. Then, it would be up to each of UCSF and Stanford to integrate this model into production.

While oversimplified, the previous examples highlight the thought process behind choosing one data model over another based on operational considerations. Of course, there may also be reasons to choose one over the other based on the capabilities of the data model. For example, the FHIR model is built around the notion of using an external terminology management system. Concepts and the terminology sources to which they belong are directly supported within the standard. OMOP, however, uses its own vocabulary management system, and connecting with an external terminology server is nontrivial and requires additional engineering with both data architecture and data engineering.

So, we know that choosing a data model can be an involved decision that balances multiple facets ranging from the scientific question, use of external terminologies, or even operational considerations. In this next section, we will discuss the combination of claims and EHR data to see if we can extract any additional insights that we would not be able to when looking at either dataset independently.

Combining Claims and EHR Data

Whether we are trying to combine different datasets into a single analyses or we are simply trying to run the same analysis on different datasets, many of the topics that we will cover are applicable. There are specific considerations when combining and then analyzing multiple different datasets, particularly from the perspective of clinical validity of the analysis. For example, taking CMS claims data (which generally skews toward an older population of patients) along with the Federal Adverse Events Reporting System (FAERS) may conflate age groups of patients, possibly masking confounders. Consequently, we must bring in the appropriate clinical domain experts to help think through these potential pitfalls.

First, let's look at how this might work with OMOP.

Using OMOP

Referring to OMOP as just a data model does it a disservice—the OMOP community, documentation, and management of the Athena Vocabulary Service are all components that make OMOP successful as a data model. There are established best practices that can guide us when transforming data from an existing data model into OMOP. This helps ensure some consistency as we query data across datasets and organizations. So, when choosing a data model, it may be worthwhile to consider the community support and documentation as important nonfunctional requirements.

In this section, we work through some of the considerations when transforming both the MIMIC and SynPUF data to OMOP. That said, we will be relying on existing projects from the open source community to do the heavy lifting for us. This will allow us to discuss the complexities without spending the time developing all of the ETL code from scratch!

Generally, there are two big buckets of work that we need to take care of. One, we need to map the structured concepts that appear in the source data to concepts within Athena (as we'll discuss in the next section). Two, we need to map the tables and columns of the source schema to tables and columns within OMOP. The process of mapping data to OMOP is nontrivial and is a topic of ongoing discussion within the OMOP community. Some are more clinically focused (e.g., how we map adverse events into OMOP), while others are more technically focused (e.g., how do we structure the overall ETL process).[2]

---

2 Dave.Barman, "Lessons learned and advice needed for ETL (of Medicaid data (or other) data)" (*https://oreil.ly/QceMG*), OHDSI Forums.

Integrating vocabularies using Athena.   As we discussed in Chapter 3, vocabularies are a powerful aspect of working with healthcare data. We have developed quite a robust set of standardized concepts capturing many elements of healthcare data. There are many different ways to manage these concepts, and OMOP provides a mechanism for querying them directly using SQL, referred to as Athena (*https://athena.ohdsi.org*).

Athena is essentially a series of tables that allows us to store and map concepts from UMLS and various source terminologies so that we can reference them from other OMOP tables. So, the main goal here is to make sure we choose the best concept possible. In some cases, this is fairly straightforward—for example, diagnoses in the MIMIC tables are already stored as ICD-9 codes, so it is simply a matter of doing a lookup in Athena.

However, even when dealing with structured codes, there may still be some challenges. To continue the example from the previous chapter, we need to look up and map NDC codes for the medications. The challenge is that NDC codes are reusable. Once deactivated, the code can be reused for a new product. So, the NDC codes used in the MIMIC dataset (which has patients from 2001 to 2012) may have been reused since then. On the other hand, one of the quirks of OMOP is that the Athena vocabulary service is not versioned. That is, Athena is routinely updated, and there is no native support for capturing which version of the vocabularies you are using. So, if we start a new project today using the MIMIC data, we will be attempting to link MIMIC's NDC codes from 2001 to 2012 with Athena's NDC codes from 2021.

One way to address the previous issue with NDC codes is what we typically need to do for many semistructured fields—some form of text processing. In some cases, we need a full-blown natural language processing (NLP) solution. However, when dealing with relational databases, we can often take shortcuts since we have somewhat static context—we know that the column contains only drug names, so we do not need all of the complexity that comes with NLP. That said, similar to the discussion we had in the previous chapter about heparin, we still need to make sure that we have the appropriate domain experts (e.g., a pharmacist) to help curate the process to ensure that we are matching the concepts correctly. To help with this process, the OMOP ecosystem provides a tool, Usagi (*https://oreil.ly/a9kgQ*). that helps us map codes.

Another common challenge is the need to match concepts that are pre-coordinated in one data model and post-coordinated in another. For example, OMOP supports only fully pre-coordinated terms. On the other hand, most RWD sources capture post-coordinated data.

Pre-coordination Versus Post-coordination

As a reminder, pre-coordinated terms/concepts are when a single term/concept captures all aspects of the underlying concept. One simple example of pre-coordination is "fracture of the left ulna" where we have a single term capturing this concept; there would then be another term that captures "fracture of the right ulna." On the other hand, if we were using post-coordination, we would have one term for each of the concepts "left" (versus "right"), "fracture" (versus "sprain" or other injury), and "ulna" (versus "radius" or other bone).

In the MIMIC dataset, we might have an ICD-9 code that provides a coarse definition of the patient's diagnosis, and then we look into the chart or note events tables to find more granular details. Then, we need to identify the single concept that best represents the level of detail that we want to capture. The challenge here is that creating all possible combinations of terms so that we can use pre-coordination creates an unwieldy number of combinations (and some may not even make any clinical sense). This is another example of some of the complexities we face with RWD, and the answer is not always evident.[3] One solution is to simply capture each facet of the overarching concept as a different row in the respective table (e.g., CONDITION_OCCUR RENCE for diagnoses or OBSERVATION for other observations), linked to the same visit, date/time, etc. However, this will push the complexity of recombining all of these concepts to your query. What if the patient has multiple overlapping conditions that require post-coordination? How will we capture this in the database and then correctly recombine them in the future?

Mapping tables and columns. The need to map tables and columns is not a new problem nor is it specific to healthcare data. This process sits at the heart of ETL (and, increasingly, ELT) pipelines, so we won't spend too much time reviewing this. However, within the OMOP ecosystem (*https://oreil.ly/fgU59*), there are a couple tools that we can use to help us with the process:

White Rabbit
> White Rabbit (*https://oreil.ly/Sigj6*) is a tool to scan source databases and produces a report of the tables, columns, and values that appear in the source database.[4]

---

3 Borim_Ryu, "Post-coordinated SNOMED CT concept expression?" (*https://oreil.ly/y3NN7*) OHDSI Forums.

4 Book of OHDSI, White Rabbit (*https://oreil.ly/BphzF*).

Rabbit in a Hat

Rabbit in a Hat (*https://oreil.ly/2o0pm*) is a tool that takes the output of a White Rabbit scan and provides a graphical user interface for creating the mapping specification document.[5]

While many fields may be straightforward to map to their OMOP counterparts, most mappings will require some degree of complexity. For example, in OMOP, there is a `CONDITION_OCCURRENCE` table that "contains records of Events of a Person suggesting the presence of a disease or medical condition stated as a diagnosis, a sign, or a symptom, which is either observed by a Provider or reported by the patient."[6] Because this table contains any condition that a patient may have, irrespective of any particular visit or encounter with the healthcare system, each row contains its own start/stop dates.

However, if we are mapping the MIMIC data, we will need to pull data from multiple tables. Specifically, we need to look in the `DIAGNOSES_ICD` table to capture the ICD-9 code and then follow the primary/foreign key relationship (`hadm_id`) to the associated hospital admission in the `ADMISSIONS` table. Within the `ADMISSIONS` table, we actually have a few dates to choose from (though the most obvious ones are the hospital admit and discharge times), but we could also choose the emergency department (ED) registration time instead of the hospital admission time. So, which timestamp do we use? In most cases, it probably wouldn't matter since these timestamps are usually a few hours off, at most. But, take row 12283 in the `ADMISSIONS` table from the MIMIC data. The patient has a hospital admission time of "2132-12-05 02:46:00" and an ED registration time of "2132-12-04 20:11:00". If we map just the date component, choosing one or the other could result in what appears to be a difference of one day.

The difference of one day could have significant impact depending on the size of the patient cohort being analyzed. Imagine the situation today where county Departments of Public Health and the CDC are trying to determine the duration of symptoms and length of time that a person might be infectious with COVID. We are seeing the guidance change on the order of days. Per the CDC, people are infectious one to two days prior to onset of symptoms and two to three days after. Being a single day off in the data could skew results 30%! This isn't to say that we always need to track the granularity of timestamps to hours and minutes (since this might be overkill in most situations), but it does mean we need to be aware of each decision we make and how it may impact the interpretation of the data, particularly when our own understanding is rapidly changing (as it is with COVID).

---

5 Book of OHDSI, Rabbit in a Hat (*https://oreil.ly/RTk47*).

6 OMOP CONDITION_OCCURRENCE table, v5.4 (*https://oreil.ly/YwVAf*).

Even after we choose which date to use, we run into another even deeper challenge. From the perspective of the MIMIC data, we see that a patient has a particular ICD-9 diagnosis code and look to map this to the CONDITION_OCCURRENCE OMOP table. However, there is a fundamental mismatch in the underlying *semantics* of the MIMIC data model and the OMOP data model. The dates associated with an ICD-9 code in MIMIC capture only the official diagnoses that are attached to a patient for the purpose and duration of the hospital admission. In other words, when we look at the MIMIC data, all we know is that a patient was diagnosed with a particular ICD-9 code as part of a particular hospital admission, and we know the dates associated with the hospital admission. On the other hand, within the OMOP data model, the dates for each row in the condition occurrences represents when the patient was diagnosed with a particular condition and when that condition resolved.

So, what if a patient was previously diagnosed 10 years ago with diabetes and we don't have any record of this patient in the MIMIC data until their admission last week? If we look only at their MIMIC data, we may falsely conclude that their condition started last week. Similarly, given that the MIMIC data is an inpatient dataset, it is hard to tell if patient's particular condition resolved or if the patient was simply discharged and still lives with the condition.

This highlights that while we think it is fairly straightforward to join the ADMISSIONS and DIAGNOSES_ICD MIMIC tables to populate the CONDITION_OCCURRENCE OMOP table, the results can be quite problematic when it comes to accurately capturing the intended meaning of the data, what we often refer to as *semantics*.

The OMOP data model was created to facilitate and enable observational research across multiple different organizations and datasets, and it supports both EHR/clinical and claims data. In the next section, we see how this could work if we used graphs instead of OMOP and SQL.

Using graphs

There is often a misconception that graphs will magically align the data, harmonize the semantics, and be a silver bullet. As with anything else, they are a tool that can help us address and mitigate many of the challenges. Take the previous example about which date to choose and whether we should map the admission and discharge timestamps to the OMOP condition occurrence table. In reality, we can likely make this assumption for some diagnoses but not others. For example, if a patient is coded as a diabetic (ICD-9 250.x), there is a good chance that they were diabetic prior to admission and remain diabetic even after discharge. However, for a patient coded as having been septic, this may have started prior to admission (but not by very many days) and was most likely resolved by discharge.

What this highlights is that we often need to make mapping decisions based on the specific details of a particular row or patient. When working with relational data models such as MIMIC and OMOP, data mapping and transformation rules typically require that the data get mapped at a structural level. If we choose to use the admission timestamp as the start of a condition, this rule gets applied to all data that we are ETL'ing. It is difficult to do this on a case-by-case basis using native SQL tools. So, we either need to change the schema or need to do the mapping using an external process (e.g., Python or Java).

The reality is that transforming data between healthcare data models is an iterative process that requires a blend of technical competencies as well as subject-matter and domain expertise. Typically, we iterate through the following steps:

1. Explore the source data.
2. Map the data to the target schema.
3. Compare analyses of the source and target data (this can be as simple or as complex as you need but typically involves basic epidemiological or biostatistical analyses).
4. Determine which data have been mismapped and the potential underlying reasons.
5. Repeat step 2 onwards.

One fundamental assumption that I make is that this process is inevitable—there will always be a need to map and then remap the data. Given this, approaches such as graph databases and knowledge graphs could help shorten the iteration cycle or even decrease the number of cycles needed. In many project that I have been involved in, this mapping process has easily taken more than six months. As a result, we often slowed the process down even more so that we could "get it right the first time." The challenge is that it is basically impossible to theorize and then implement the perfect solution. So, all we did was make the process even slower!

If we assume (and embrace!) the iterative nature, then our goal shifts—instead of trying to develop a foolproof mapping approach for any particular combination of source and target data models, we focus on mapping the data as quickly as possible, identifying what is working and not working and remapping the data as needed. This is where I see tremendous potential for graph databases as well as other technologies such as Apache Spark (*https://oreil.ly/DXqFh*), Apache Beam (*https://oreil.ly/AvcHH*), and similar.

We have looked at both OMOP and graphs as potential options for combining clinical and claims data. In the next section, we dive into a case study where we combine clinical and claims data and, more specifically, diagnoses and medication data. Please keep in mind that this is a representative example using publicly available datasets with a particular focus on the data wrangling. We will be ignoring whether the data are actually compatible in a clinical sense.

Case Study: Combining Diagnoses and Medications

Let's go back to our two datasets—we have patient-level clinical data in the MIMIC-III dataset, and we have patient-level clinical *and* claims data in the Synthea dataset. There is a common desire to bring different datasets together and "combine" them so that we have a larger dataset (and theoretically more *power*[7] given that any dataset is essentially a sample of the underlying population).

Given our two datasets, would it be possible to ask questions such as *which medications are commonly prescribed to patients with XYZ diagnoses?* Naturally, it is tempting to consider just merging as many datasets as we can find. However, if we look at the high-level differences between MIMIC and Synthea, we see that the MIMIC is biased toward inpatient (more specifically, intensive care) data, whereas the Synthea dataset focuses on outpatient/ambulatory settings. So, would looking at an ambulatory patient dataset help if we're studying heparin (as we discussed in the previous chapter)? Answering such questions truly requires subject-matter and domain experts. While some nuances can be clarified by any experienced clinician (e.g., regardless of their medical specialty or specific type of medical license), other nuances may be specific to a particular institution or region.

Our understanding of biology, physiology, pathophysiology, and the practice of medicine is constantly evolving. This means how we interpret data is also constantly in flux. One technique for cleaning or processing data today may be inapplicable or even incorrect a year from now. Additionally, there is also a natural delay in the dissemination of information throughout the medical community. Academic medical centers often incorporate changes earlier in the process given that their physicians are also researchers. Community hospitals, on the other hand, may lag behind their academic counterparts. No amount of technology will be able to eliminate these challenges. However, we can use technology to help us mitigate them.

We have a bit of an understanding of OMOP as a data model, and we've spent a bit of time with graphs relative to the UMLS as well as EHR data. Let's look at both OMOP and graphs as potential solution options in the next section.

---

7 Retrospective Power Analysis (*https://oreil.ly/HWoJl*).

OMOP Versus Graphs

As we discussed earlier, we can combine different datasets by transforming them into the OMOP common data model (CDM). We simply need to agree on which version of the OMOP CDM to use and follow the guidelines provided by the OMOP community. That said, if you spend any time on the OHDSI OMOP forums,[8] you will see many threads of situations where the answer may not be immediately obvious until there is some discussion,[9] sometimes without a broadly accepted convention.[10]

For those situations where the solution isn't immediately obvious, we fall back to an iterative approach. With graph databases, we can often apply multiple different mappings within the same instance, making it easier to compare/contrast the different mappings. All we would need to do is add a property to nodes/vertices and relationships/edges that identifies particular mapping attempts (e.g., a timestamp or unique mapping identifier). In a relational database, this approach to coexisting different mapping attempts is much more challenging. Of course, this type of an approach can incur significant performance penalties. There are also many tools out there (both those specific to OMOP as well as generic business intelligence/visualization tools) that seamlessly integrate with SQL-based systems. These would need to be reimplemented for each type of graph database out there. Remember, there is no silver bullet!

If you have a good and clear understanding of your source data model and how it maps to OMOP (e.g., Optum when they map their own datasets to OMOP), sticking to the standard approach is your best bet. There are tons of resources from training to tools/libraries to support from a well-established community. In this situation, there are few benefits to using graphs despite the additional costs.

However, if you're still in the exploratory phase of a particular dataset and you're still experimenting with how best to map the data, then graphs present an interesting opportunity. The iterative process discussed earlier becomes easier to manage since you can track all of them in the same database. Validating one mapping approach over another could be as simple as updating the unique mapping identifier when querying the data.

---

8 OHDSI Forum (*https://forums.ohdsi.org*).

9 Diego_Bosca_Thomas, "Allergy to Drugs, What Happens with Drugs with More than One Active Ingredient?" (*https://oreil.ly/HWoJl*) OHDSI Forums.

10 Christian_Reich, "Procedure_occurence Table—Examples of Procedure Codes That Can Last Multiple Days" (*https://oreil.ly/8r67w*), OHDSI Forums.

What's the Best Approach?

When discussing the best machine learning or statistical model, a quotation from George EP Box is often cited: "All models are wrong, but some are useful."

Though we're discussing data models and not statistical models, the same notion applies. Every data model will have its trade-offs and force us into a certain set of assumptions. No data model will accurately capture all of the context and nuance underlying the data. However, for any particular use case, some data models will be more useful than others.

So, it's important to maintain a pragmatic approach and not fall into the trap that there is a single, perfect data model.

We could endlessly debate and experiment on the best ways to use OMOP and relational databases, or graph databases, but this frames the problem in a purely technical sense. Now, we take a step back and look at some of the considerations independent of the specific technology solution. Once we have a better understanding of the considerations from the perspective of the data, we can then identify the most technically appropriate solutions.

Considerations When Combining Different Sources of Healthcare Data

As we just discussed in the previous section, there are many things to consider even at the database level. Some of these considerations are clinically oriented, while others are more technological. In this section, we will dive a bit deeper into a couple key areas that I have frequently encountered over the years, starting first with the distinction between structural and semantic harmonization.

Structural versus semantic harmonization

Figure 5-1 shows the relationships of three levels of harmonization. This model is adapted from the HIMSS levels of interoperability (*https://oreil.ly/leoOt*). As we discussed earlier in this book, there is a lot of overlap in how we think about interoperability (typically framed in the context of the transactional exchange of [healthcare] data) and harmonization (typically framed in the context of bringing different [healthcare] datasets together).

The *foundational* level usually refers to the basic technical foundation necessary to achieve harmonization, such as databases and networking. For example, as we attempt to merge data from two different clinics, we could use a cloud provider such as Amazon S3 or Google Cloud Storage. Solutions to foundational issues are an IT function and not usually something we need to worry about as data and analytics engineers.

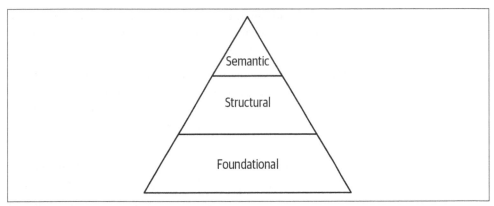

Figure 5-1. The pyramid of interoperability

The next level is *structural* harmonization. This is where we typically see discussions around data models, the challenge of unstructured data, and how we deal with all of the scanned documents in healthcare. For example, we may digitize all of the patient charts in a clinic and upload them to a cloud provider. Now, how do we actually combine a pile of PDF documents with structured data we extracted from an electronic health record?

Structural harmonization highlights one of the first pitfalls we typically see when technologists first get their hands on RWD. Choosing a data model (e.g., OMOP) addresses the structural harmonization challenge. If we choose to use the OMOP data model, we have defined specific data fields and clarified the syntax and format of data. This gets us closer to our goal of harmonizing two datasets, but we're not quite there yet! Structural harmonization is necessary but insufficient. Take our example earlier in this chapter about using the hospital versus emergency department admission time as the proxy for the onset of a condition—we know that the field is a date-time field, and we know that it should capture the date and time a particular condition started. However, we still need to reconcile which source field we should use. This requires that we understand the underlying meaning and context of the source data (i.e., what's the difference between a hospital admission timestamp versus an emergency department admission timestamp?) and of the target data model (i.e., what does OMOP intend to capture as part of the condition start time?).

This takes us to the top of this pyramid, *semantic* harmonization. The ultimate goal is to be able to send and receive healthcare data in such a way that the full context and meaning of the data are preserved. Our previous example about the start of a condition versus the hospital or emergency department admission time really highlights this issue. The semantics of the OMOP CDM condition start time clearly defines the intended meaning of that column. However, the source data that we have access to has captured data that has a similar meaning. Therein lies the key challenge—the meaning of a data element or data field in one model is often similar, though not identical, to the data element of another model. So, when attempting to combine these two models, we need to make decisions on how to interpret the meaning of the source data and how to transform it to meet the meaning of the target data model.

How we interpret the source and target data models, and the decisions we make regarding how best to transform the data, is entirely dependent on the surrounding context—what is the scientific question being asked of the data, how/why were the data collected in the first place, how accurate do we need to be, among other questions.

Let's go back to the MIMIC data but consider another aspect of it—the "ordering" of diagnosis codes. If you examine the schema for the DIAGNOSES_ICD table, you will notice a column SEQ_NUM. This column stores an integer value that is intended to order or rank the diagnosis codes attached to a particular hospital admission. Specifically, the MIMIC-III documentation states: "Priority of the code. Sequence 1 is the primary code." The primary diagnosis code is typically the reason or the cause for the encounter. In other words, why did the patient visit the clinic or hospital? However, if we start to dig into what this value really means, we start to encounter some ambiguities.[11] While the SEQ_NUM column certainly conveys some sort of ordering, there is a question of whether it truly captures relevancy or priority accurately. It is also unclear what the relatively weight is as the SEQ_NUM increases—how much *more* relevant is a value of 1 versus 2 versus 3?

As data scientists and engineers, we often want a clear answer so that we can reliably transform and interpret the data. However, the reality of medical diagnoses is much more nuanced. For example, when I was working on an ambulance as part of the 911 system, I came across quite a few car crashes where the driver was injured and needed to be rushed to a trauma center. Say we have a patient who suffered a head injury as a result of the crash and is taken to the nearest trauma center. During the trauma assessment, the trauma team also discovers that the patient is in hypoglycemic shock, a condition where the patient's blood sugar level reaches critically low levels. Many of the signs and symptoms of hypoglycemic shock overlap with the signs and symptoms of head trauma.

Given the obvious signs of head trauma, we may conclude that the "primary" reason for the patient's visit to the trauma center is the head injury, thus assigning a SEQ_NUM value of 1 to the corresponding ICD-9 code, and a value of 2 to the ICD-9 code for hypoglycemia. In reality, we may consider both of these to be significant aspects of the patient's clinical profile since each will be the reason for many of the tests and procedures ordered as a part of the patient's hospital admission. It would be inaccurate to assume that the primary diagnosis code is the main reason for the battery of

---

11 MIMIC Code Repository, "Sequence in diagnoses_icd table" (*https://oreil.ly/xbv2B*).

tests and procedures. Also, even if the patient had not crashed their car, they may still have been admitted to the hospital for their severe hypoglycemic event. On the other hand, what if the car crash patient had a severe head injury but it was noted that the patient also had high blood pressure? In this situation, hypertension would be coded with a SEQ_NUM of 2, but it is much less significant to this patient's admission when compared to the previous patient.

If we are pulling this data into our own system for analyses, we then need to ask ourselves if we want to maintain some sort of ordering of the diagnosis codes or if we want to "flatten" them and treat them all as equal. If we can't trust the ordering or if there is inconsistent weighting of different values, we may need to treat all of the diagnoses as a "bag of diagnoses." On the other hand, if our analysis is trying to study the length of stay as a function of the patient's admission diagnosis, we may opt to keep the first item knowing that it is the most relevant (even if we don't know how much more relevant than the next code) and treat the remaining items as a "bag of diagnoses."

This level of harmonization falls under *semantic* harmonization and is extremely difficult. There is rarely a single "right" answer, so we need processes and tools/technologies to help mitigate this issue. When I approach a new dataset, I make the assumption that we will need to transform/map the data multiple times. This is why I immediately look to technologies that help speed up the iterative process.

I have also seen people quickly jump onto the "yes, we need semantic harmonization" wagon and immediately look to integrating terminologies and crosswalks/mappings, as I'll share in the next section.

Using coding systems and crosswalks

Another common issue that arises when mapping datasets that contain coded data (e.g., ICD-9/10 codes, CPT codes, etc.) is the overconfidence in using crosswalks. Crosswalks are basically a list of codes from a source coding system with corresponding values to a target coding system. For example, as the United States made the transition from ICD-9 to ICD-10 codes for billing, there were a number of crosswalks released by both commercial and noncommercial organizations. One example was the General Equivalence Mappings (GEMS) provided by CMS (*https://oreil.ly/ TpBeT*).

During the ICD-9 to ICD-10 transition, I encountered a few chief medical information officers who were very quick to say something along the lines of "We are using the GEMS mappings so we should be good to go." As the transition began, there were numerous academic papers as well as white papers that highlighted the challenge.[12,13] There are many more examples than captured in the footnotes, but the general synopsis, as written by Jones and Nachimson in their white paper *Use Caution When Entering the Crosswalk: A Warning About Relying on GEMs as Your ICD-10 Solution*, is simple: "In fact, the very description of GEMs as 'crosswalks' is seriously flawed, as they contain numerous shortcomings and deficiencies as a coding translation method, and were not designed for this purpose at all."

Like our discussion about semantic harmonization, crosswalks are typically created using a specific set of data for a specific purpose. Whether that crosswalk applies to your unique problem is the first question to answer. If your problem is largely aligned with the methodology used to create the crosswalk, then it might work well for your purpose. In most cases, however, it will be a starting point (at best) or downright misleading. This applies to all crosswalks you may encounter whether they are from academic institutions, government agencies, or commercial entities. Like everything else, it is critical to understand the requirements of your specific project and align them with the methodology and data used to generate the crosswalks. It is also important to test and validate the application of crosswalks to your data. An example of such an exercise is available in the paper *Standardizing Clinical Diagnoses: Evaluating Alternate Terminology Selection*, from Burrows et al. (*https://oreil.ly/Ivcjy*), where they compare mappings using several different approaches. This helps you understand both the crosswalk itself as well as how it affects your data.

Conclusion

To recap, combining or merging different datasets is becoming increasingly popular. Whether we are combining EHR and claims data, or multiple different EHR sources, or even incorporating patient-generated and patient-provided information, we generally encounter the same challenges. These challenges largely parallel those encountered when dealing with interoperability for transactional systems. However, when dealing with real-world data that have already been collected, we are at the mercy of the existing systems. Often, our jobs as data engineers and data scientists involve reverse engineering the clinical workflows, business processes, and source systems.

---

12 *The Complexity and Challenges of the ICD-9-CM to ICD-10-CM Transition in Emergency Departments* (*https://oreil.ly/qj3dO*) is a paper that provides an example of how crosswalks and mappings impact a specific service line of a hospital, in this case, the Emergency Department.

13 *Conducting Retrospective Ontological Clinical Trials in ICD-9-CM in the Age of ICD-10-CM* (*https://oreil.ly/2LpkQ*) highlights the impact for clinical trials in contrast to the previous paper about clinical care and reimbursement.

As we work to determine how best to process, clean, and curate the data, one frequent task is to pull the data into a CDM. The use of CDMs could improve efficiency of data scientists, ensure reproducibility of analyses, and simplify the data stack and toolchain. However, we must not fall into the trap of thinking that there is a single "best" data model to use. Choosing a data model will often depend on what type of data we are working with (e.g., claims versus EHR), what clinical specialty (e.g., oncology versus primary care clinics), what scientific questions we are trying to ask, or who our collaborators are and what data model they are already using.

The use of graphs and graph databases is not intended to be a cure-all or a silver bullet for these challenges. They are simply another tool for us to keep in our toolbox, to be used when helpful. That said, my hypothesis is that the combination of graph databases with other technologies (e.g., Spark) can help us be more efficient during the iterative process of transforming and mapping RWD. In essence, we can shift the ETL problem to be ELT where the L loads data into a graph database for subsequent transformation.

Aside from the technological considerations, we also need to think about the implications of merging two different datasets together to effectively create a larger dataset. This is an area that requires a very intentional and rigorous approach for mapping the data and then verifying the final dataset. Given the range of how and why data are collected, it is often not possible to combine or merge datasets from a semantic perspective. Sure, we can map columns to one another or transform strings into integers or dates (i.e., we can structurally harmonize the data), but we need to be careful that we have not combined data elements with inherently different meanings, especially if they are similar to someone without clinical expertise.

No amount of graph databases or data processing pipelines will address this issue. Simply put, we need domain experts with the necessary knowledge whether it's biology, (patho)physiology, or medicine. However, technology can help us iterate quickly, especially when even our domain knowledge is rapidly changing.

In this chapter, we dove into working with claims data and some of the challenges when looking to combine datasets. OHDSI MOP was introduced as one potential data model and approach for linking EHR and claims data. In addition to the data model itself, the OHDSI community also provides tools such as White Rabbit and Rabbit in a Hat to help with the data mapping process as we harmonize data from multiple different sources into an OMOP instance. While OMOP is typically thought of as a data model, it also closely integrates a set of terminologies, Athena. One of the core tenets of Athena is that all concepts are pre-coordinated, so we spent a little time comparing the pros and cons of pre-coordination and post-coordination when working with terminologies and controlled vocabularies.

You should have a deeper appreciation for the challenges and solutions for combining different datasets, particularly if they are from entirely different sources. In the next chapter, we will continue our journey and begin to link some of these concepts, and particularly the graph-based approach to harmonizing data, with analytics (from stats to machine learning/deep learning).

## CHAPTER 6

Machine Learning and Analytics

Up until now, we have spent quite a bit of time focused on how to think about healthcare real-world data, and how we can start engineering it. Of course, we are engineering these data so that we can analyze them and extract insights! When most of us (myself included) started working with data, we probably wanted to dive straight into machine learning and build predictive models. Then, we found ourselves constantly manipulating data, transforming it from one dataframe to another. Nearly every library out there doing something with data expects the input to be in the form of a dataframe, a tabular structure that fits well with data from CSV files and relational databases, but less so with data from document or graph databases.

So, we have spent all this time looking at the complexities of RWD and talked about how graphs would be great. How do we connect this to all of these analytics tools that want things in neat little tables? Or, are there alternative approaches?

In this chapter, we start to discuss how we can connect RWD (especially if in a graph) to analytics, and machine learning in particular. We start with a simple approach to extract a subset of the graph (also known as a *subgraph*) into a table/dataframe. Following that, we look at the machine learning pipeline overall and how graphs fit into the process of exploratory data analysis and feature engineering (including feature stores). Finally, we finish with integrating the graph data directly with deep learning through the use of graph embeddings. Given the focus of this book, we will not be diving deeply into the machine learning or deep learning itself so we will not be tuning models or discussing how to set up or design the network.

So, let's start with a high-level discussion of machine learning.

A Primer on Machine Learning

Before we dive into the nitty-gritty details of prepping data for analytics, let's start with a brief discussion about machine learning, deep learning, and feature engineering. This might be review for those with experience in the area, but my goal is to establish a baseline vocabulary and understanding to help provide context for the remainder of the chapter.

Let's start with a review of *feature engineering* and how this is changing in light of deep learning techniques. This is especially interesting if we consider that, in many ways, the process of feature engineering is the incorporation of domain knowledge and context. Of course, some feature engineering is highly abstract, unlocking higher-order interactions between variables, but that will always be the case.

What Is Feature Engineering?

I like the general idea that feature engineering is the process of transforming data and then selecting the most relevant data when performing some sort of analysis, typically machine learning. This process is becoming increasingly subsumed by deep learning techniques where much of the feature engineering is occurring within the neural network itself. Even so, there is still an explicit need for feature engineering and, more importantly, to ensure that the processing and transforms during model development and validation are carried through to the use of the model in production.

While feature engineering is typically discussed as a part of developing models, I have seen too many projects fail as models are brought to production (or at least as this process is attempted). As a medical informaticist/informatician by training, I very often look at the end-to-end big picture—from how the data is collected through to how a model is going to be integrated into the clinical workflow.

Clinical workflow integration is quite a complex topic and involves more than just user experience (UX) design regarding where the buttons go or the order of the screens. As data and informatics professionals, we need to make sure that models we develop can actually guide clinical practice. For example, we may develop a model that uses the latest and greatest deep learning algorithms that is 98% accurate in predicting three-day mortality (i.e., predicting that the patient will die within the next three days). However, unless we can give the clinical team some idea of why the patient might die or what to do, this information is generally useless. The features are the first place we go to get these insights. If we can highlight that the most important features are related to particular organ function, we have narrowed the search space that the clinical needs to operate within. So, the feature engineering stage is of particular importance when working with healthcare RWD.

Aside from clinical implications, the feature engineering process is a critical component of the MLops philosophy and is captured as part of the *feature store* (as shown in

---

Figure 6-1). A feature store is a service that allows data engineers and data scientists to create, register, store, find, and integrate features from the model development process all the way to model deployment. If properly developed and maintained, a feature store addresses the technical challenges of managing the feature engineering process. We would have a process for ensuring that the transformations we apply during model development are carried all the way through and applied when calling `predict()` or the equivalent function.

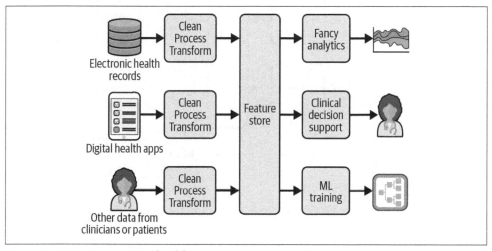

Figure 6-1. Feature store in healthcare

However, in healthcare applications, it's often not possible for us to deploy the feature store approach highlighted in Figure 6-1. This approach assumes that all data is processed and stored in the feature store, regardless of whether these data are used for model training or for prediction. This assumption facilitates the MLops approach and assumes a closed world where all access to and control of data is unified.

As discussed earlier, what we need is a way to ensure that any data processing or transformation is applied at the "point of prediction" using the exact same algorithms and parameters. This might be as simple arithmetic (e.g., subtracting admission and discharge times to extract length of stay) or quantitative normalization (e.g., standard scaling or min-max normalization) or as more complex, domain-specific processing (e.g., extracting cancer line of therapies).

Figure 6-2 shows a similar diagram that highlights this requirement in the context of a clinical decision support tool that makes patient-level predictions. The diagram is quite similar to Figure 6-1, but notice the dotted lines at the bottom, highlighting that we can follow the typical MLops approach using a feature store for aggregate analytics and for developing and validating machine learning models. However, when presented with a single patient's data for the purpose of making an actual prediction (in production), we need to make sure that the same clean/process/transform steps are applied, as highlighted by the dotted lines. This is where the typical feature store approach doesn't apply as cleanly.

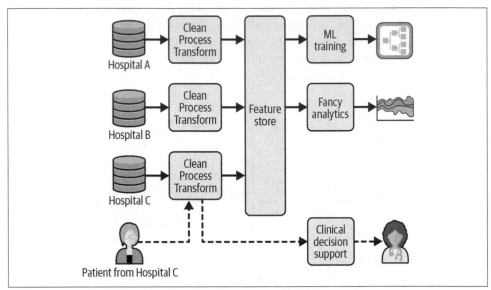

Figure 6-2. Feature store in healthcare for clinical decision support

There are different ways to try to address this problem ranging from tools such as Dataiku or dbt to Keboola or Kylo. More often than not, I've seen data teams create their own in-house solutions based on the combination of pipeline tools along with data cataloging and lineage tools.

The conversation around feature engineering is starting to shift given the focus on deep learning where much of the feature engineering is being handled by the algorithms themselves. Let's take a quick look at how graphs and deep learning are coming together in healthcare before getting back to the technical aspects of machine learning pipelines.

Graph-Based Deep Learning

As I mentioned earlier, when we start getting into deep learning, the feature engineering process gets a little blurry. The type of deep learning network (e.g., recurrent versus convolutional), the number of layers, and how we ultimately connect them will all have an impact on what we would traditionally refer to as feature engineering. In essence, the choices we make in setting up the neural network are part of the feature engineering process. This also includes incorporation of approaches such as multitask learning.

Similar to the use of ontologies and knowledge graphs within the context of NLP, we have a similar opportunity when looking at how to integrate graphs with deep learning in general. Graphs and graph embeddings can be used to encode the underlying knowledge itself (e.g., encoding the UMLS) or to encode patient-level data that is linked to existing knowledge graphs or ontologies. The latter idea is particularly interesting since clinicians often refer to the signs and symptoms a patient reports as a *constellation*, suggesting that even what we observe of a patient is itself a network or graph of data. A paper from UCSF by Nelson et al. (*https://oreil.ly/KubSW*) explores this idea by linking patient data with a knowledge graph that incorporates both clinical as well as biological knowledge.

This is still very much an active (and increasingly popular) area of research. Figure 6-3 shows a histogram from a very crude search of "graph embedding" within PubMed. This is a rough proxy for academic interest in using the embedding-based approach for integrating graphs that has become so popular with NLP. We can see a dramatic increase over the past three years; the number of papers in the first two months of 2022 alone nearly match all of the papers published in 2017.

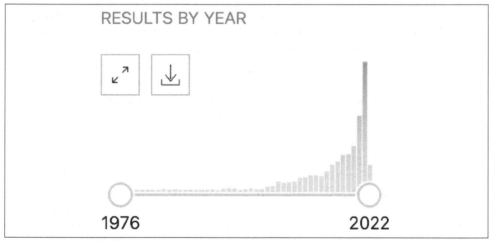

Figure 6-3. "Graph embedding" on PubMed

As you can see, there is growing interest and a lot of potential for graphs and deep learning in healthcare. We will go into a bit of detail later this chapter, but let's get back to our machine learning pipelines and how we can integrate graphs into the current dataframe/table-centric workflows.

Extracting Data as a Table

As data scientists, you are well accustomed to working with and analyzing tabular data. You probably started with Excel and kept making your sheets more and more complex until you needed something more powerful. Or, you went straight into using R or Python/numpy/pandas in which case dataframes are now intuitive.

If your data is already in a relational database of some sort, then there's not much to do explicitly except query and extract your data. At the heart of nearly every query when working with OMOP is the nested SELECT statement and JOIN. Given how OMOP stores and manages the vocabulary tables, you will often need to use nested queries in order to extract relevant concepts; then you will need to join the concepts with other tables of interest whether they are drugs, observations, demographics, etc.

In this next section, we'll discuss some trade-offs between handling complex SQL queries directly in SQL versus doing it in your programming environment (e.g., R or Python). If you are not familiar with more advanced SQL features such as nested sub-queries,[1] case statements,[2] or joins,[3] I've included a few footnotes with links to The Data School, though there are a plethora of resources ranging from blogs to videos to MOOCs.

To SQL or Not to SQL

As data scientists, you probably push most of the work directly into the SQL query itself. After all, you need to extract a very specific subset of data to answer a very specific question. Why extract data from your database (incurring query, network traffic, and memory costs) that you don't need? However, as data engineers, you are probably supporting multiple data scientists, projects, or use cases. You notice that in most projects, the queries are extremely similar, so you then ask yourself if there's a better way to structure everything to make the code more reusable across projects.

One option would be to have simpler queries to the database and then perform the joins and other manipulations directly in R, Python, or any other programming language of choice. The downside to this approach is that you might be extracting significantly more data than you ultimately need, putting unnecessary load on your database and network. However, this would allow you to better manage the complexity as a software library. It would also abstract the processing such that you could potentially manage it without being dependent on the specific source database.

For higher-level transformations (e.g., harmonizing ICD-10 codes as discussed in Chapter 3) that are at the semantic level, maintaining them outside of the database makes them portable, reusable, and independent of any particular data model. For example, you might be looking at seasonal trends—assuming that the dates in your dataset are accurate, the cutoffs between seasons are nonspecific to the data source, so embedding this in the SQL query itself would be overly restrictive. Similarly, if you are working with oncology data and trying to overlay treatment regimens based on

---

1 The Data School, "How SQL Subqueries Work" (*https://oreil.ly/gqBPd*).

2 The Data School, "How CASE WHEN Works" (*https://oreil.ly/VfziX*).

3 The Data School, "SQL Join Types Explained Visually" (*https://oreil.ly/prKpH*).

medication prescriptions, you could manage and maintain this separately since it's based on third-party treatment guidelines from organizations such as the American Society of Clinical Oncology (ASCO) or the National Comprehensive Cancer Network (NCCN). If you embed this directly in the SQL query and later determine that the hospital deviated from the guidelines, you would need to fix your query and rerun it against the database.

Like many things when it comes to software and IT, it is important to remain pragmatic and always balance how often you might need to change/update the query, how often the data may change, and how likely the query or data may be reused. Most importantly, you need to consider the performance implications of embedding your logic directly in the query versus handling it later in the pipeline. For example, maybe we are trying to encode an external treatment guideline and we know it will be reused across the organization. As a result, we decide to do this in Python as a separate library that can be imported by others in the future. However, if the process ends up being so slow that it takes hours to process a dataset versus a few minutes as part of a SQL query, you must consider the needs of the project and use case overall.

This is a key area where our needs as data engineers intersect very technical considerations by our infrastructure team. The speed of our database systems and network, availability of read replicas, cache, or parallelization are all factors we need to consider as engineers. Sometimes, the theoretically "correct" solution is simply too slow or onerous to maintain.

One such situation that is becoming an increasing area of focus is integrating with terminology systems as we'll discuss in this next section.

Terminology systems

As we discussed in Chapter 3, terminologies and controlled vocabularies are a core part of most healthcare RWD. If you have data in a relational database yet you need to integrate these data with some sort of terminology service, things get a bit more complicated. Most terminology services are accessible via a REST API, but this immediately pushes much of the data harmonization code away from the query and into your code (e.g., R or Python) as highlighted in Figure 6-4. The dotted arrows represent each step of your data pipeline and will most likely involve sending a dataframe from one step to the next.

The use of terminology services to perform lookups and mappings between different coding systems is one area where we need to work across both engineering teams as well as data science teams. Regardless of the specific terminology service you are using, you will most likely be accessing it via a REST API. If you are processing a dataset with millions of rows of data to look up in the terminology service, you will find that the data processing will take a very long time. Though generally outside of the scope of this book, you will need to work with your engineering team to add caches such as Memcached or Redis. In addition to caching, you may also consider parallelization of the data processing, using frameworks such as Apache Spark or Apache Beam.

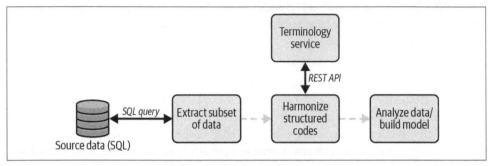

Figure 6-4. SQL queries with an external terminology service

One alternative to this would be to extract the subset of terms/concepts of interest, capturing any relationships of interest (e.g., synonyms, broader/narrower concepts, etc.). A challenge you will encounter is the need to create some sort of intermediary data model to represent the concepts and their relationships. Example 6-1 shows one very simple example created as an illustration.

Example 6-1. Sample JSON representation of semantic concepts

```
{
  "C0011849": {
    "preferredName": "Diabetes Mellitus",
    "cui": "C0011849",
    "icd10": "E14",
    "synonyms": ["DM"],
    "relationships": {
      "narrower": ["C0011860"]
    }
  },

  "C0011860": {
    "preferredName": "Non-Insulin Dependent Diabetes Mellitus",
    "cui": "C0011860",
    "icd10": "E11",
    "synonyms": ["NIDDM"],
    "relationships": {
      "broader": ["C0011849"]
    }
  }
}
```

As you can see in this contrived example, there are two concepts, one that is broader than the other—"diabetes mellitus" being the broader concept that encompasses "non-insulin dependent diabetes mellitus." Ultimately, how you design or architect the data model depends on how you plan on incorporating the semantic concepts into your pipeline.

If your data consists of a column of ICD-10 codes that you would like to replace with UMLS CUIs, the format shown previously would be quite inefficient since the ICD codes that you would need to look up are buried in the depths of the JSON objects. On the other hand, if you have a column of CUIs and would like to replace them with the associated ICD-10 code, the previous structure could easily work.

Yet another alternative would be to integrate vocabularies alongside your data, integrating the terminologies directly into the SQL database. This would simplify the data pipeline since you could combine everything into the SQL query itself. Of course, the trade-off is that your SQL queries would be much more complex overall. This is the approach that the OHDSI community uses for OMOP and is the topic of our next section.

Querying OMOP Data

Given the number of options for integrating terminologies, the OMOP community has decided to completely integrate them directly into the database. This allows the same SQL queries to be used across any instance of OMOP, allowing clinical researchers to share their queries in federated data sharing/research networks (but not in the "federated learning" sense).

Book of OHDSI

The Book of OHDSI (*https://oreil.ly/QzRkA*) is a great resource and should always be considered the most up-to-date resource on working with OMOP. As with any software library, OMOP is constantly being refined and updated, so it's always best to go straight to the source.

If you are querying data in OMOP and dealing with structured concepts that are linked to controlled vocabularies, you will need to get intimately familiar with the vocabulary tables. This is one of the major reasons many OMOP SQL queries are nested.

In Example 6-2, from the OHDSI community repository (*https://oreil.ly/7IqoT*), we are trying to count the number of patients who have had an "exposure" to a certain set of drugs. "Exposure" is used since it encompasses everything from medication administration (presumably by a caregiver) to something the patients take over the counter.

Example 6-2. OMOP query example

```
SELECT concept.concept_name, drug_concept_id, count(person_id)
AS num_persons
FROM drug_exposure
JOIN concept
  ON drug_concept_id = concept.concept_id
WHERE lower(domain_id)='drug'
  AND vocabulary_id='RxNorm'
  AND standard_concept='S'
  AND drug_concept_id IN (40165254, 40165258)
GROUP BY concept.concept_name, drug_concept_id;
```

As you can see, the query is joining the drug_exposure and concept tables, searching for those concepts that are part of RxNorm (a terminology of drugs/medications) and match a specific set (those with a concept_id of 40165254 or 40165258). In this example, we are looking for two specific concepts, represented by their concept_id, that correspond to Crestor (rosuvastatin), a "statin" that is used to treat high cholesterol. If you search Athena for the keyword "crestor," limiting results to valid and standard drug concepts within RxNorm, you will see that there are still 11 concepts (*https://oreil.ly/IZfYC*) that could potentially be used (assuming we ignore the specific dose). If our dataset is tracking drugs by National Drug Code (NDC), we can see that there are 143 matching concepts (*https://oreil.ly/XHqVd*).

Our options are to expand the query to include all 143 NDC concepts, or we can use a nested SQL query to map the nonstandard NDC codes to standard RxNorm codes. Before we work on nested queries, let's look at how we can query all NDC codes related to the two RxNorm concepts of interest, as shown in Example 6-3.

Example 6-3. Mapping RxNorm and NDC codes

```
SELECT concept_id_2 AS standard_concept_id
FROM concept_relationship
INNER JOIN concept source_concept
  ON concept_id = concept_id_1
WHERE concept_id IN (40165254, 40165258)
  AND vocabulary_id = 'RxNorm'
  AND relationship_id = 'Maps to';
```

This query will return all concepts that are mapped to Crestor 20mg and 40mg. With this query, we can use nested SQL queries (*https://oreil.ly/fx6Ro*) (as shown in Example 6-4) without needing to copy out every single concept_id manually. This cleans up our code, reduces the likelihood of an error/bug, and makes our query less fragile.

Example 6-4. Nested SQL query for vocabularies

```
SELECT concept.concept_name, drug_concept_id, count(person_id)
AS num_persons
FROM drug_exposure
JOIN concept
  ON drug_concept_id = concept.concept_id
WHERE lower(domain_id)='drug'
  AND vocabulary_id='RxNorm'
  AND standard_concept='S'
  AND drug_concept_id IN (
    SELECT concept_id_2 AS standard_concept_id
    FROM concept_relationship
    INNER JOIN concept source_concept
      ON concept_id = concept_id_1
    WHERE concept_id IN (40165254, 40165258)
      AND vocabulary_id = 'RxNorm'
      AND relationship_id = 'Maps to';
  )
GROUP BY concept.concept_name, drug_concept_id;
```

The astute reader will notice that the previous query may not do exactly what we intended. While we want to count all patients who are on either Crestor 20mg or 40mg, the previous query will actually group patients by each NDC code that is connected to the two RxNorm codes that we provided. At this point, cleaning up this query further is a standard SQL exercise, but you can see how the OMOP community has combined both the patient-level data with terminologies and controlled vocabularies. This makes it easy to integrate the system with any number of existing tools and platforms that are built on top of SQL.

From Graphs to Dataframes

In the previous section, we spent a bit of time looking at how to extract data from SQL databases, particularly in the context of working with controlled vocabularies or terminologies. Given that relational databases store data in tables, SQL queries naturally return data in a tabular structure.

In this section, we will look at extracting data from graphs into dataframes. Conceptually, converting a graph to a table is nontrivial given the inherently different ways of storing and representing the data. However, we are not trying to broadly represent the graph itself in a tabular format. Instead, we are trying to extract a subset of the data from a very specific perspective. For example, say we have a fully connected graph of patients, their medications, all of the standardized representations of medications in RxNorm and NDC, their diagnoses, and ICD-10 codes. We would not want to extract all of this into a single dataframe (or even a handful of dataframes). To do so, we would basically need to re-create a data model similar to OMOP—one that has tables for the healthcare data and for the vocabularies—and to join the two.

Neo4j

When working with Neo4j, we can control exactly what is returned in the RETURN statement. Typically, we return the nodes and edges themselves, as shown in Example 6-5, using the same model that we introduced in Chapter 2.

Example 6-5. Cypher: returning nodes and edges

```
MATCH (p:Patient)-[o:has_order_for]->
      (m:Medication {Medication_name: "Acetaminophen (Tylenol)"})
RETURN p
```

If we tried to turn this into a table, we would need to add additional code to "unpack" the properties of the node p and edge o into columns. However, we can unpack them directly as part of the Cypher query, as highlighted in Example 6-6. To highlight working with properties of edges, say that the edge/relationship connecting our patients and medications also contains the property date_prescribed.

Example 6-6. Cypher: returning properties

```
MATCH (p:Patient)-[o:has_order_for]->
      (m:Medication {Medication_name: "Acetaminophen (Tylenol)"})
RETURN p.Patient_ID, p.DOB, o.date_prescribed, m.Medication_name
```

As you can see, we will get a list of four columns—patient ID, patient date of birth, date of the prescription, and name of the medication. If you use a driver such as py2neo and execute the previous query, you can feed the return value directly into pandas to create a dataframe, as shown in Example 6-7.

Example 6-7. py2neo: Cypher to dataframe

```
from py2neo import Graph
import pandas as pd

# Setup a session for interacting with the database
session = Graph("bolt://somehost:7687", ...)
query = '''
MATCH (p:Patient)-[o:has_order_for]->
      (m:Medication {Medication_name: "Acetaminophen (Tylenol)"})
RETURN p.Patient_ID, p.DOB, o.date_prescribed, m.Medication_name
'''
# Execute the query against Neo4j
result = session.run(query).data()

# Create dataframe based on `result`
df = pd.DataFrame(result)
```

As you can see in these examples, it is more of a programming and software engineering exercise than anything to get the results of the queries into a dataframe. Between Python iterators and dictionaries, this is often handled by the database drivers themselves. As the popularity of pandas dataframes continues to grow, I suspect we will see more and more libraries for easily converting data to/from dataframes.

Aside from the engineering aspects of getting data into dataframes, the previous examples also highlight that the conceptual approach for querying graphs is no different than the examples we discussed in Chapters 3 and 4. Once we understand the structure of the graph and the queries, we simply turn these results into a dataframe.

So, if it's a matter of querying the graphs and turning them into dataframes, why even bother? After all, we could just use a relational database in the first place and our data would already come out as tables. The next section begins to answer this question.

Why Add the Complexity of Graphs?

So, we've spent a bit of time looking at how we can extract data from a graph into a table. You might be wondering—why bother with all this back and forth if we are going to ultimately convert everything back to tables? The main benefit is that we can take advantage of the graph databases to capture and represent data in a way that is more natural while preserving as much of the context and meaning of the data as possible. Figure 6-5 highlights our two options with the hypothesis that the traditional, nongraph approach (a) is inherently more resource intensive and complex than the graph approach (b).

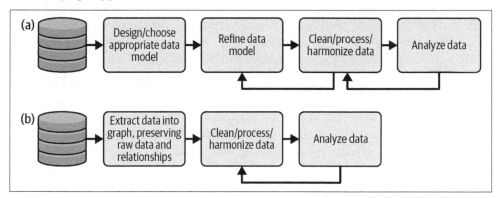

Figure 6-5. Nongraph (a) versus graph (b)

Currently, we conflate the processes of structuring, cleaning, normalizing, and harmonizing the data. While all of these steps will be necessary in nearly every project and are always dependent on both the source data as well as the downstream analysis, decoupling them and injecting the use of graphs early on in the process could simplify the overall process of prepping the data for analysis. Each step becomes much easier to manage, and the complexity of the overall system is reduced.

This last point is particularly interesting and something that seems to be underappreciated in data science. From a software engineer's perspective, trying to write a monolithic codebase is a recipe for disaster. For example, imagine a web application that incorporates a machine learning model, user interface, and network communication with the server—the user interface would interact with the network code, which sends data to the ML model for prediction, and results are sent back to the user.

If this entire app was written as a single, continuous process, it would be extremely complex and brittle and require significant rework every time something changed. If we needed to change some of the features for the ML model, we would need to update the network code as well. However, software engineers will quickly tell you that standard practice is to separate each of these components/modules, decoupling them as much as possible so that changes to one minimize impact to the others. If engineered correctly, a change to the ML model might require a new field to be added to the UI, but the network code would be unaffected.

We should think about our data pipelines the same way. I see many projects where the data teams treat it as one monolithic problem where we try to harmonize our data, design (or choose) our data model, and clean the data, all in one go. Instead, let's split this up into distinct phases. This is where we start to encounter challenges in more traditional approaches. While designing or choosing our data model in a SQL system, we need to make many up-front decisions such as how we treat null values, how to link data together, what can/should be linked, etc. The very features that make SQL databases excellent choices for reliably capturing structured data for transactional use cases make them brittle platforms for analytics use cases where there are many ways to interpret, process, normalize, and harmonize the data.

The integration of graphs allows us to standardize certain parts of our data pipeline, while allowing us to defer other parts to as close to the analytics as possible. For example, instead of worrying about the nuances and details of our data model early on (especially if we're still working through exactly how to interpret the data), we capture the data in a graph where we can easily link a particular data point to multiple different coding systems or semantic concepts. Then, as we clarify our use case and better understand how to interpret our data, we perform some graph traversals and extract the data into tables that align with our existing tools.

Now that we have a better understanding of why we might incorporate graphs into an otherwise table-centric workflow, we will walk through some examples on how graphs can help us with machine learning, especially during feature engineering.

Machine Learning and Feature Engineering with Graphs

While the main focus of this section is how we can incorporate graphs into machine learning and feature engineering, the same ideas apply when manipulating data for other analyses (e.g., survival curves, mixed effect models, etc.). Feature engineering is often generally defined as some combination of transforming or processing and then filtering or choosing what to include in machine learning. However, these are also the same things we need to do when performing any analysis.

Transforming or processing the data is not usually defined and can really include almost anything. Data scientists often think of things like quantitative normalization (e.g., standardizing the data to zero mean and unit standard deviation or normalizing data to be in a certain interval such as [0,1]) or even more sophisticated techniques such as principal components analysis (though, sometimes this may be considered a part of "filtering" the data). However, as we have seen throughout this book, when working with healthcare RWD we need to add another level of transformations, factoring in the semantics (the context and meaning) of the data.

So, when we decide to combine a bunch of NDC codes into a single RxNorm code, this is feature engineering at some level. Sometimes, this decision is made by the data scientist as part of their analysis and very specific to the use case. Sometimes, this decision is simply a function of knowing a hospital's internal processes or something about the source data.

Within our discussion in this section, I will be very specific and break down the process even further with the following specific definitions:

Cleaning
> Cleaning is the process of ensuring that the data meets basic syntactic and structural requirements before we can proceed with more complex transformations. Examples of specific tasks include fixing data types (e.g., number versus string), ensuring that strings are compliant with a regular expression (e.g., dates or ICD codes), or changing the case of a string (e.g., "male" to "MALE"). Simply put, this is where we clean up the data at a syntactic level so that future steps are more likely to succeed and not result in errors. Cleaning is the least dependent on specific use cases and is mostly dependent on the data source given. Those transformations that are dependent on the specific analytic algorithm or the context and meaning of the data are handled as part of harmonization.

Harmonization
> Harmonization encompasses the bulk of the topics we have discussed throughout this book and often includes processing the data at a semantic level. This includes (but is not limited to) converting codes from one code system to another, merging or combining different datasets, limiting quantitative data to physiological limits, or matching drug names to RxNorm concepts. During this phase, we

rarely remove a column but instead add additional columns. For example, say we have a column of drug names or NDC codes and want to convert the NDC codes to RxNorm concepts; we would simply add a new column that contains the mapped RxNorm codes. Unless you have limitations in memory or it's simply too slow, this is a recommended practice because it reduces the loss of information. As we perform our analytics, we have access to both the mapped data as well as the pre-mapped data.

Feature Engineering

Feature engineering is the processing of data given the specific nuances of an analytic algorithm, and the ranking and filtering of variables/data elements. In one example, when dealing with algorithms that rely on "distance" calculations between data, we often see scaling of numeric ranges so that one variable does not have more influence than another (e.g., min-max scaling). Another example may be the application of principal components analysis as we attempt to reduce the dimensionality of a dataset while minimizing the loss of information. This may also be where we ignore a particular variable or data element because we know it is simply unrelated such as ignoring the patient's blood pressure readings when comparing chemotherapy regimens. Another common example is the use of one-hot encoding when working with categorical data. The list continues endlessly, but the key point here is that we are processing the data in the context of a very specific use case and often given the mathematical or biostatistical requirements of a particular analysis technique.

We just spent all this time breaking down cleaning, harmonization, and feature engineering to highlight that graphs are particularly useful for harmonization (generally requiring "cleaned" data) and not for feature engineering. However, most data pipelines that I have seen bundle all of these steps together, as shown in Figure 6-6. After some initial exploratory data analysis (EDA), we iterate the process of cleaning/harmonizing/feature engineering and analyzing the data until we achieve the desired output/insight.

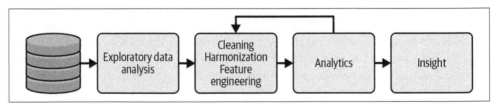

Figure 6-6. Basic data pipeline

The challenge with this approach is that we end up repeating this process over and over for every single project or use case (Figure 6-7). This is extremely inefficient since data scientists, epidemiologists, and biostatisticians end up repeating much of their work. Imagine if you had three main data sources used by your data team with ten data scientists. A change to the format of one of the columns would need to be addressed by each data scientist despite that they would all be making essentially the same change to their code.

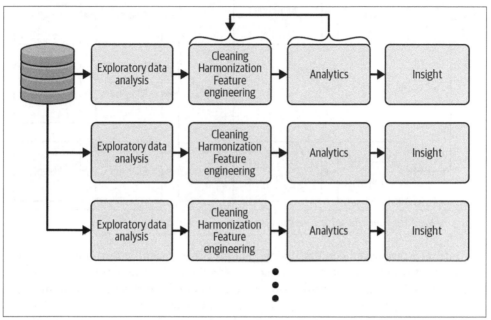

Figure 6-7. Basic data pipeline, repeated

You may be thinking—what about feature stores? This is a relatively new idea that is gaining popularity because it provides a framework to better manage the data engineering process. Some of the details of feature stores are specific to machine learning pipelines such as ensuring that any data processing applied to training data is applied to new data for prediction. Figure 6-8 shows a simplified representation of how our data pipeline evolved to include feature stores. We see that there is a feedback loop between the analytics phase and the data processing phase, as we saw in our basic pipeline. In the middle of the diagram, you may also notice that (if we're lucky), we have additional use cases that can reuse the features in our feature store. While this is certainly a step up from our basic data pipeline, there is still some duplicate/redundant work as we process our data.

Even for use cases involving descriptive statistics or biostatistics, the idea of a feature store is still applicable even though we do not need to worry about machine-learning-specific ideas such as training data or making predictions. The ideas of lineage, reusability, reproducibility, and governance are still applicable and useful.

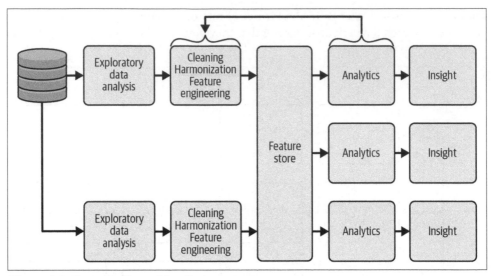

Figure 6-8. Data pipeline with a feature store

Up until now, we have been discussing data pipelines, machine learning, and feature stores, all of which have plenty of nongraph solutions. Despite improving the overall data pipeline by adding a feature store, we are still bundling cleaning, harmonization, and feature engineering into a single pipeline. This is often the fastest and easiest solution from the perspective of a data scientist—you would get access to a particular dataset, perform EDA, and then starting processing the data for your use case. As we discussed earlier, there are a number of drawbacks to this approach, particularly as the data science team grows.

Software engineers often say that if something is repeated over and over, it should be abstracted and maintained as a library. The same is true in this case, and we can start to do this by adding another layer to our pipeline. Figure 6-9 incorporates a knowledge graph at the beginning, after cleaning and harmonization.

Knowledge graphs are gaining traction, but there is not a single, rigorous definition of what exactly comprises a knowledge graph. In this context, I am defining a knowledge graph as the combination of patient-level data along with standardized concepts from terminologies and ontologies. By adding this additional step in our data pipeline, we have now created a process where data cleaning and harmonization are handled once per data source. Data scientists work with the data downstream of the knowledge graph, following the same workflow they would normally use otherwise.

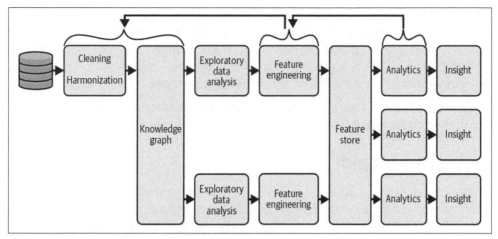

Figure 6-9. Data pipeline with a knowledge graph

You are probably wondering how this knowledge graph can be created once and used for any number of use cases. This is a great question, and there is no intention to do this once and for all. One thing we have not discussed are the feedback arrows at the top of these figures. They represent the process where data scientists develop a deeper understanding of the data in the context of a specific use case and improve how they process the data. During the analytics phase, you might realize that you want to clean, harmonize, or engineer features differently. When we incorporate knowledge graphs, we have two opportunities for feedback—we may choose to engineer features differently, or we realize that there is something more fundamental and we need to update our knowledge graph.

This particular approach makes some basic assumptions:

1. Patient-level data (e.g., diagnoses, medications, etc.) is stored alongside concepts from terminologies/ontologies in the same graph.

2. Nodes/relationships (vertices/edges) are tagged with metadata that provides additional context about the underlying data as well as the analytics use case. Examples include:

   a. Original/raw data versus derived nodes or relationships.

   b. For derived data, some link back to the underlying code or process (e.g., git commit hash, date/timestamp, or clinical guideline).

3. The knowledge graph is a supergraph from which subgraphs are extracted for specific use cases.

Now, you have a sense of why graphs can be a valuable part of your data science workflow and pipeline, even if your analytical stack is centered around dataframes and a tabular representation of your data. While it might be hard to justify this approach for very small teams working with fairly homogenous data, we see more value as the size of the team or number of use cases increases.

In the next section, we look at ways to analyze the graph structure directly, many of which are based on deep learning.

Graph Embeddings

If you are trying to analyze your data using descriptive statistics/biostat, extracting your data into tables generally makes the most sense. You can take advantage of existing tools and libraries without needing to reinvent that wheel. Depending on how you are storing your graph, you might be able to embed the computation directly as part of the query, including the use of stored procedures or other custom ways of embedding logic into the query.

However, as we move into advanced analytics and machine learning use cases, an increasingly popular approach involves the use of embeddings. Embeddings have become quite popular in fields such as natural language processing (NLP) and have been shown to be powerful and much more cost effective when working with large datasets. They allow data scientists to leverage the implicit information/knowledge contained within datasets without needing to manually annotate all of data.

If you have looked at NLP or embeddings at all, you have probably seen the classic example looking at the words *king*, *queen*, *man*, and *woman*. While this captures the underlying conceptual aspect of embeddings and vector math, it does oversimplify the challenge. As with anything else in data science, such examples require a lot of tuning. However, they do offer us another tool for our toolbox, one that we will take and adapt to graphs.

Similar to word embeddings, graph embeddings create a vector representation of the structure of graphs, allowing us to use these vectors in machine learning approaches such as neural networks. In essence, they allow us to translate the spatial structure of graphs into a vector of numeric values that can be fed into any number of algorithms. In this section, we walk through several example applications of graph embeddings, starting with node2vec.

node2vec

While some of the later examples are specific to biomedical applications, *node2vec* is a generic approach to creating embeddings of graph data. At the core, node2vec leverages the approach used by *word2vec* to create embeddings. If you are not familiar with the details of how word2vec works, it is a popular topic, and there are numerous blog posts and videos that provide detailed walk-throughs. In essence, a neural network is trained to predict the next word in a sequence of words. However, we don't actually use the predictive model—what we really want are the weights of the hidden layer. These weights constitute the vector representation of a word.

For graph embeddings, Grover and Leskovec[4] devised an approach that applies a random walk to nodes in a graph, generating a sequence of nodes. The key element of their approach is to randomly walk a graph to generate a series of sequences. These sequences of nodes are analogous to a sequence of tokens and fed into the same approach as used for word embeddings. In other words, we can think of text as a sequence of nodes where each node is a token in a sentence or phrase; so, the approach to generate word embeddings can be adapted to an arbitrary graph given that we can reduce the graph into a set of sequences of nodes.

There are two key things you need to know to understand node2vec—the first, as we discussed earlier, is to understand word2vec; the second is to understand the application of a random walk to a graph in order to generate the sequences of nodes. At its simplest, a random walk starts at a particular node and randomly chooses which edge to follow next, traversing the graph and creating a sequence of nodes visited. node2vec builds upon the random walk, biasing the traversal given two parameters, p and q. These two parameters allow us to influence the walk as follows:

- p—the "return" parameter, which influences the likelihood that we will return to our previously visited node
- q—the "in-out" parameter, which influences the likelihood of following an edge that either keeps us in the neighborhood or moves us out farther away from our current node

In both cases, we are actually using the inverse of p and q. A high value of p means we are less likely to revisit nodes, and a low value of p means we are likely to backtrack, keeping us more local. On the other hand, a high value of q means we are more likely to focus *in*ward (staying close), and a low value of q means we are more likely to focus *out*ward (exploring the network further away).[5]

When dealing with node2vec, you will see two ideas that come up when discussing the in-out parameter: *homophily* and *structural equivalence*. Homophily is a type of similarity that indicates if nodes generally belong to the same community. If you look at a graph spatially and group nodes together based on their location, you are most

---

4 Aditya Grover and Jure Leskovec, "node2vec: Scalable Feature Learning for Networks" (*https://arxiv.org/abs/1607.00653*), in *Proceedings of the 22nd ACM SIGKDD International Conference on Knowledge Discovery and Data Mining*, July 3, 2016, Cornell University arXiv.

5 MemGraph provides a great explanation (*https://oreil.ly/ynsdk*) of p and q.

likely using homophily. In terms of q, you can probably guess that homophily is a function of high q values, biasing the traversal to stay close to a particular starting node.

On the other hand, if we lower q, encouraging the traversal to explore farther nodes, we will see similarity around *structural equivalence*. This indicates nodes that play a similar role in the graph given the connections to surrounding nodes.

So, let's think about homophily and structural equivalence in the context of patient data. Let's say we are loading a patient dataset consisting of three types of nodes—patients, diagnoses, and medications. We would expect that homophily would return clusters of nodes, most likely corresponding to a patient-centric view of the data. In other words, the most similar nodes will likely be those associated with a particular patient. On the other hand, if we look at structural equivalence, we may expect to see diagnoses and medications each grouped together.

As we saw with NLP, this is an active area of research and innovation—node2vec is not the only way to create embeddings from graph data.[6,7,8] However, given its relatively simple approach, it is a great starting point.

In the next section, we will quickly discuss embeddings of clinical concepts since they are such an important part of working with RWD. However, it is important to note that some embeddings are created using nongraph approaches, such as using text representations and co-occurrence versus their actual graph structure.

cui2vec

Since we discussed UMLS and CUIs a bit in Chapter 3, we will start with *cui2vec* (*https://arxiv.org/abs/1804.01486*), an approach that generates embeddings of concepts. When working with the UMLS and considering embeddings, our first thought might be to load the UMLS into a graph and then generate graph embeddings. The downside to this approach is that the embeddings would only contain representations of knowledge that the field has previously incorporated into the UMLS. In other words, if there is a yet unknown relationship between a medication and a diagnosis, this would not be captured in the UMLS or any other ontology or knowledge base.

---

6 Haochen Chen et al., "HARP: Hierarchical Representation Learning for Networks" (*https://arxiv.org/abs/1706.07845*), Cornell University arXiv, November 16, 2017.

7 Bryan Perrozi et al., "DeepWalk: Online Learning of Social Representations" (*https://arxiv.org/abs/1403.6652*), Cornell University arXiv, June 27, 2014.

8 Jian Tang et al., "LINE: Large-Scale Information Network Embedding" (*https://arxiv.org/abs/1503.03578*), Cornell University arXiv, March 12, 2015.

Off-Label Use and Adverse Events

Previously unknown interactions between multiple medications or between medications and diagnoses are of particular interest in healthcare. Providers want to make sure that they aren't ordering treatments that, when administered at the same time, cause adverse events in patients due to unknown interactions between the treatments.

Similarly, we are also interested in discovering new diagnoses for which an existing drug on the market might have therapeutic benefit though is not marketed as such. This is called *off-label* use and allows providers and patients to treat conditions with existing drugs that may have well-established safety profiles in both clinical trials and real-world use.

The *cui2vec* approach leverages the structured concepts within the UMLS but also incorporates the use of RWD to generate the embeddings. It looks for co-occurrence of pairs of CUIs but uses slightly different algorithms depending on the data source, as we'll discuss next. For all types of data, the data is first preprocessed such that the concepts are converted to CUIs:

Journal articles
Pairs are CUIs are identified (after preprocessing the text) and counted as a co-occurrence if they are identified within a 10-word window.

Claims data
Given the patient-centric nature of claims data, co-occurrences are counted as the number of patients for which two CUIs appear within a 30-day window.

Clinical notes
The specific approach for clinical notes is slightly more complex given the differences with clinical NLP.[9] The general idea is that co-occurrences are counted per 30-day window (which might be multiple times per single patient).

This approach allows embeddings to be generated based on data from multiple different contexts. Each provides a different perspective on co-occurrences whether it's from research papers, what is billed/reimbursed, or how clinicians communicate about their patients.

While there is a certain intuition to training any sort of model on several different types of RWD, it that you first test the model and its output relative to your use case. We want to include as much data as possible, but we also run the risk of creating a

---

9 Youngduck Choi et al., "Learning Low-Dimensional Representations of Medical Concepts" (*https://oreil.ly/0nm9E*), *Proceedings—AMIA Joint Summits on Translational Science* (2016): 41–50.

schizophrenic model that is trying to learn several different (yet conflicting) things at the same time. So, while it is enticing to build an all-encompassing embedding model that factors in multiple different types of data, it is always important to test your approach against the specific nuances of your use case.

Like many forms of analytics, cui2vec focuses on analyzing data with little consideration for temporal relations between the data. Temporal windows are used to determine the co-occurences, but the embeddings themselves don't actually account for changes in the clinical record. Next, we'll look at med2vec, which attempts to build embeddings that retain temporal context.

med2vec

Similar to cui2vec, med2vec (*https://arxiv.org/abs/1602.05568*) also attempts to incorporate RWD. However, instead of bringing together multiple different types of RWD, med2vec focuses on EHR data, specifically on the temporal aspects of a longitudinal patient record. Simply put, med2vec assumes that a particular visit or encounter is a point in time and can be used to predict what has happened in the past or what will happen in the future. This allows the generation of embeddings that potentially capture the temporal relationships between concepts, instead of just treating a single patient as a "bag" of concepts.

In addition to tracking temporal differences from one visit to the next, med2vec also tracks co-occurrences of concepts within a single visit. As a result, med2vec provides a visit-centric context for clinical concepts. We often think of patients at a single point in time, but many patients have multiple interactions with the healthcare system, often around a set of conditions that get better or worse over time. By taking a visit-centric approach, med2vec embeddings begin to surface these clinical changes. If we take a purely patient-centric approach, we naturally commingle elements of a patient's history from 50 years ago with their current status. Again, it is important to consider the implications of these nuances on our use cases.

These approaches have relied primarily on co-occurrences, so let's look at one that leverages the graph nature of ontologies, particularly SNOMED CT.

snomed2vec

We have looked at a few embeddings that incorporated RWD and not just encoded knowledge. In this section, we'll revisit the SNOMED ontology. As we discussed in Chapter 3, SNOMED is a comprehensive source of concepts and relationships between them across biomedicine. These concepts range from basic science to clinical practice across multiple body systems and disease areas. Although approaches that integrate RWD are great at capturing previously unknown context and relationships between concepts, they also forget all of the knowledge that we have gained over the years. Though a bit of a hyperbole, I used to tell new students that if they looked only at the data without any understanding of context, the models they trained would conclude that people should never go to hospitals since there is a high mortality among those who are admitted. In other words, it is important to still use our knowledge of biomedicine and the delivery of healthcare to guide our interpretation of any data. One source of such knowledge is SNOMED (which we discussed a bit in Chapter 3).

The snomed2vec (*https://arxiv.org/abs/1907.08650*) project compared several different embedding approaches as applied to SNOMED CT concepts. They introduced two other embedding techniques, metapath2vec (*https://oreil.ly/u7CA7*) and Poincaré embeddings (*https://arxiv.org/abs/1705.08039*). Though we won't go into the implementation details of these, they offer alternatives to node2vec, and the snomed2vec paper does a good job of comparing them with respect to SNOMED.

At a high level, metapath2vec targets graphs that have a much higher level of heterogeneity in the nodes themselves or how they are connected. Take, for example, our earlier discussions of patients versus visits. Approaches like node2vec may conflate the two since they would have similar connections to diagnoses or medications. In other words, to the embedding algorithm, there may not be much difference between patients and visits. However, approaches such as metapath2vec focus on preserving both the structure and the semantics that we find in heterogeneous graphs (though the authors refer to them as *networks*).

This is particularly helpful given the size and scope of the SNOMED graph. It captures many different levels of hierarchy along with a multitude of concept types with varying degrees of semantic differences. For example, the active ingredient of a drug and a specific formulation of the drug have much more similar semantic meaning than a drug and an anatomical body part.

They also discuss the use of Poincaré embeddings, which provide yet another alternative to generating embeddings of graph data. In this case, the embeddings are focused on both hierarchy and similarity. Though we do have some understanding of hierarchical structures within biomedicine and have captured many explicitly within SNOMED, we also know that there are potential latent hierarchies as well—that is, hierarchies that are implicit within the data.

Of course, this technique can also be applied directly to electronic health records or other real-world data sources, as we saw with cui2vec and med2vec.[10]

Now that we have reviewed the specifics of a few embeddings, let's take a step back and look at embeddings overall.

---

10 Quihao Lu et al., "Learning Electronic Health Records through Hyperbolic Embedding of Medical Ontologies" (*https://oreil.ly/K1D12*), BCB '19: Proceedings of the 10th ACM International Conference on Bioinformatics, Computational Biology and Health Informatics, September 2019, pp. 338–46.

Some Final Thoughts About Embeddings

As you can see, there is tremendous potential in working with healthcare RWD using graphs and without needing to pull that data back into tabular structures. Though embeddings are only one set of examples on how to work with graph data directly, they are certainly an exciting area given the pathway from graphs to embeddings to deep learning. The use of embeddings (and innovation on how to generate embeddings) catalyzed a new era of NLP that leveraged deep learning to better understand (and now generate) free text. Personally, I am quite excited and see tremendous and similar potential with graphs and graph embeddings. Data generated during the treatment of patients is naturally a graph, and I am looking forward to the innovation that lies ahead with both how to generate better embeddings at scale, as well as leveraging the embeddings to solve many of our complex problems in healthcare.

However, as exciting as it is, there are some key things we need to consider when working with graphs and graph embeddings. These are not necessarily specific to graphs (we see them in other applications as well, such as NLP), but I wanted to make sure to call them out in the context of graphs.

First, if you start searching for graph embeddings, you will quickly find pretrained models to generate embeddings such as the Medical Concept Embeddings for SNOMED CT (Jan 2019 version) (*https://oreil.ly/Ym64n*). The first question you need to ask is what source data were used to train the model. In this case, we see that SNOMED CT was used. If we would like to use these embeddings within our project, we need to make sure that the version of SNOMED they used and the version of SNOMED in our project are compatible. SNOMED is released periodically, and concepts are constantly being added, removed, and amended, so we just need to make sure we understand the impact given any mismatches.

However, if we look at embeddings trained on RWD, it is important that we understand the source data and how it might compare to our data. For example, the cui2vec project uses claims data to help train the underlying model. What if the claims data were provided by the United States Center for Medicare and Medicaid Services (CMS)? Given the focus of CMS, it would be heavily biased toward an older population. Embeddings generated from such data could create many challenges if we were to use the embeddings to conduct analyses of data from a general hospital population, ranging from neonates to geriatrics.

Second, you now have an additional model and pipeline to manage and maintain, thus increasing the overall complexity of your project. Let's say you are trying to create a model for the early detection of sepsis (as we briefly discuss in Chapter 6) and decide that you will incorporate embeddings. You now need to create your own embedding model or use pretrained embeddings. You also need to tune your actual deep learning model that takes the vectors generated by the embeddings as inputs (in addition to any other data). Consequently, you have two levels of models to tune, optimize, and validate. As with any data analytics use case, keep the models and your overall approach as simple as possible despite the temptation to use the latest and greatest techniques! You should increase the complexity of your approach if and only if simpler methods fail to work.

Third, as you navigate the many different methods for creating embeddings or considering pretrained embeddings, you will see many comparisons to benchmarks. These serve as good tools for comparison of the different options at a very coarse level. You also need to consider how well your particular use case aligns with a particular benchmark. Not only do you want to consider your source data versus the data used in the benchmark, you also want to look at the specific question you're asking and the corresponding learning tasks as they compare to the benchmark.

Lastly, as with any machine or deep learning project, it is absolutely critical that you consider how overfit your models have become—defined here as overly specific to a particular dataset and not generalizable to others. As we just discussed with pre-trained embeddings and benchmarks, there is a chance that the model used to generate embeddings has been overfit and not generalizable to other data. For example, say you are using a pre-trained embedding model that was "trained on diagnoses, medications, and lab values" and are applying that to a use case based on similar data. Additionally, the data used to train the embeddings was focused on differentiating between specific formulations of medications. On the other hand, your use case involves predicting adverse events in patients, and you are interested only in the active ingredient of a medication, not how it was formulated. I consider this one of many examples of an overfit embedding model since it has been trained on a specific perspective of medication data and is no longer generalizable to your use case.

This is a very active area of work, so I hope this has given you a foundational introduction of one of the more exciting areas of graph-based analytics when working with RWD. In the next section, we will adapt some of these concepts in the context of federated learning. We will also spend a little time discussing the implications of graphs and federated learning, even outside of embeddings.

Making the Case for Graph-Based Analysis

Ideally, this very quick tour of extracting data from graphs and also analyzing graphs directly has inspired you to experiment more with graphs and healthcare RWD. Many of our analytics tools and techniques today assume tabular data, so if we are to use graph techniques to help with data harmonization, we need to extract this data into a format with which our current tools can integrate.

Given the complexity of healthcare RWD and the close integration of coding systems, terminologies, and ontologies, graphs can be a powerful tool for data and analytics engineering. We can use graphs and graph databases to harmonize different datasets or to create reusable data pipelines. As a result (and even despite the additional complexity), graphs should remain a tool in your toolbox even if your entire analytics stack today requires tabular data. There is always a chicken-and-egg problem with new technologies such as graph databases. People are hesitant to adopt new technologies such as databases until there are tools to consume the data.

We started this chapter looking at how to integrate graphs into our current tools (one way to break the chicken-and-egg cycle!) and then continued with an exploration of graph embeddings. I have little doubt that graphs-based analytics is the future when it comes to leveraging healthcare RWD at scale. Even though many often look to embeddings and deep learning in the context of predictive models, there are many opportunities to leverage embeddings in other ways.

We are already seeing additional work in areas such as using transformers with graphs (e.g., Graph-BERT (*https://arxiv.org/abs/2001.05140*)).

We will see quite a bit of innovation as people learn how to incorporate graphs as part of the data harmonization process and as we tackle other problems in healthcare such as patient matching, cohort definition, and generally helping ensure that the right patients get the right therapies and interventions at the right time.

In the next chapter, we will explore other trends in healthcare such as federated learning and NLP where we will revisit some aspects of graphs.

Conclusion

This chapter was a bit different than the others given its focus more on the data science and deep learning rather than how to harmonize or wrangle data. However, it was an opportunity for us to see how graphs can be used as part of the data wrangling regardless of what type of analytics we will use.

If we do need to extract the data back out into tables or a dataframe, it is primarily a coding/software engineering exercise. The key is that we can use the graphs to manipulate and process the data using graph traversals. This allows us to take advantage of the fundamentally different way of representing and querying the data and then converting the results back to a graph.

While this is great to bridge the gap between the "old" ways of working (dataframes) and the "new" ways (graphs), we spent a bit of time looking at how we can start to work with the data directly in graph form. This allows us to take advantage of the richness of the graph-based representation, including the ability to maintain better context of the data.

Lastly, not only can we work with data directly as graphs, but new approaches to capturing embeddings from graphs could allow us to generate embeddings that are much more meaningful overall. These embeddings can combine what we know about patients with knowledge gained from journal articles to generate a vector representation whose features capture much more context than we would otherwise have.

Deep learning is just one of many exciting topics on the horizon for us, whether we are looking at real-world data overall or at graphs in particular. In the next chapter, we look at some emerging trends in healthcare analytics such as federated learning.

## CHAPTER 7

Trends in Healthcare Analytics

While data engineering is a critical component in how we leverage real-world data, it is not the most glamorous of topics. Of course, all of this cleaning and processing of the data is a means to an end. Whether we are on the IT side, the data side, or even the business/clinical side, the end goal is to derive insights of the data that will improve decision making.

For business use cases, this may be to support more efficient care, improve cost savings, or even increase revenue (which is still important, even for nonprofit institutions). For clinical use cases, this may be to enable earlier and more accurate diagnoses of diseases, connecting care teams to the right information about the patient at the right time or determining the appropriate staffing levels based on patient acuity. This last point is particularly interesting since it represents a subset of use cases where there is both a clinical and business benefit.

On one end of the spectrum, data analysts rely on business intelligence tools such as Tableau or Cognos. On the other hand, data scientists rely on NLP and machine learning (including deep learning) to build predictive models. While we often break "data science" or "analytics" tasks into simple buckets like "business intelligence" and "machine learning," the reality is that these lines are becoming increasingly blurred as we integrate data deeper into both our clinical and business workflows.

In this chapter, we will discuss some general trends and advances in analytics as well as a few specific examples from the literature. We will start with a discussion of federated learning and federated analytics. This is an exciting area in data science as we all look for solutions that allow us to leverage the ever-increasing amounts of data while balancing privacy and security concerns.

The Old and New of Federation

The term *federated* has been used in healthcare, especially among researchers, for quite a while. The idea was that researchers could process their data into a common data model with common terminologies (OMOP being a prime example) and then share their SQL queries so that the same query was run at each site participating in the research network. The results could then be aggregated manually, thus increasing the statistical power of research studies. This approach allows researchers to collaborate across institutions without needing to deal with de-identification or anonymization, which are quite time and resource intensive.

Today, however, the idea of federating data access has taken on an entirely different meaning. For most, the first thoughts that come to mind are federated (machine) learning, federated average/stochastic gradient descent, differential privacy, and privacy-preserving analytics. In all cases, the assumption is that the federation of the analysis or machine learning is automated, handled entirely by software libraries.

So, as you interact with other data scientists and researchers, it would be a good idea to quickly align on definitions, especially if you are working with informatics and clinical researchers.

So, in the next section, we will dive into the current definitions of federated learning/analytics, particularly in the context of healthcare RWD.

Federated Learning and Federated Analytics

Our first stop is one of the hottest trends that we are seeing across many industries, not just healthcare. You may have heard the term *federated learning* in contexts such as Google's comic (*https://oreil.ly/ANaVP*). Such examples of federated learning combined with edge computing have enabled a level of data "sharing" that was unthinkable even a few years before. For example, consider all of the many keyboards in use on smartphones today. Companies ranging from Google to Apple to Samsung are trying to improve the predictive capabilities of their keyboards. However, to train such models, they would need access to everything you type on your phone. This would be a huge privacy nightmare given that we all use our phone to access banking services, healthcare records, and even details of our daily lives via our calendars and email.

In healthcare, we aren't (yet!) talking about tapping into every patient's individual phone. Initiatives are currently focused on federating across institutions or organizations. Over the next couple sections, we will look at how federated learning works and how some are differentiating between federating machine learning (e.g., training models on data across multiple organizations) and federated analytics (e.g., descriptive statistics, biostatistics). Then, we'll look at the intersection of federated approaches, data harmonization, and graphs. So, let's jump into how federated learning works.

How Does Federated Learning Work?

So, how are companies able to learn from our data while mitigating privacy concerns? Federated learning is the answer, but what is it exactly?

To many, federated learning is not a new idea—it is simply a natural extension of moving computation closer to the data. We have seen this trend of "bring the compute to the data" for a while, such as we did with the excitement around Hadoop. In the context of machine learning, bringing the compute closer to the data means training machine learning models on the data while leaving it in place. In the example of smartphone keyboards, this means training a keyboard's predictive model without needing to send all of the text someone types to a company's servers.

There are plenty of companies that leave the data in place and move the computation to the data. This ranges from map-reduce algorithms to distributed SQL queries. If these technologies have been around, then why the fuss over federated learning? Simply put, training a single machine learning model on distributed data sources is nontrivial.

Let us go back to the smartphone keyboard example and say we are training a neural network to predict the next word as we are typing. It is pretty trivial to call a `train()` function on the local data on each phone and call it a day. But, we would have a different model for every installed version of our keyboard. While this would certainly produce a model for each user that will predict text, we are missing out on the opportunity to train a model that is fed data from *all* of our users.

This is where things start to get complicated. If we are training a neural network, we need a way to view and update weights for every training instance.[1] However, if these instances are spread out all over every installed version of our keyboard, this process has become a bit more difficult. For each user of our keyboard, we need to download the weights (trained from other keyboards) onto a user's phone, update the weights based on that particular user's data, and then send the weights back to a central coordinating server.

For those who are really paying attention, you might be wondering, "Isn't this very similar to the transfer learning problem?" That is certainly one way that we can go

---

[1] For additional details regarding neural networks and the details of training, please see *https://oreil.ly/icRrC* and *https://oreil.ly/IoQYB*.

about the problem. We take a trained model, download it to a particular phone, update that model, and then send it back to a central server. From there, it can be sent to the next phone for training, etc. We would be following a similar process to transfer learning though we aren't necessarily adapting the model to a related or similar domain. While there are other approaches for federating the machine learning process, they are all quite sensitive to how well the data has been normalized/harmonized from one dataset to the next.

Throughout this chapter, I'll generally use *federated learning* as the primary example. However, there is a whole segment of *federated analytics*, focusing on those analytics that do not require training some sort of machine learning model. Though federated analytics isn't as clearly defined since it is basically anything that is *not* machine learning, we sometimes see the phrase *privacy-preserving analytics* or *differential privacy* used also. In this chapter, I am defining *federated learning* as the need to federate the training of a machine learning model, while *federated analytics* is any type of analytics (including things like visualization) that *does not* involve training a model. While the specific implementation details and underlying mathematics are different between federated analytics and federated learning, the biggest pitfalls when applying either of these to RWD are the same.

We now have a little bit of understanding about the difference between federated learning and federated analytics. We also see that it has the potential for mitigating privacy concerns, but the section goes into a little detail about why we would want to use federated analytics/learning.

Why Federated Analytics/Learning?

There is a certain allure to this notion that we can leverage data for statistics, analytics, or machine learning in a way that completely mitigates privacy risks and concerns. Of course, nothing is that easy and clearcut, but federated approaches do provide some potential benefits.

Imagine you're at a large pharma company and you are working on an evidence generation project—that is, you're trying to analyze RWD to help generate evidence that supports the use of one of your drugs for a particular subset of a disease. Your drug is approved by the FDA (meaning it meets minimum safety and efficacy requirements), but it is not yet considered the standard of care. So, your goal is to generate evidence "proving" that your new drug should be the first choice. In Chapter 4, we discussed *efficacy* versus *effectiveness*—here, we are trying to use RWD to quantify the effectiveness and make the scientific claim that our drug is better than the existing standard of care.

While you might be able to use some of the datasets that your company has already licensed, you and your team decide that you need to access external datasets at local health systems. Your internal dataset simply doesn't have enough patients for your study design.

Now, imagine the conversation that your partnership team might have with local medical centers: "We would like to copy all of your patients' data into our data and analytics platform so that we can run evidence generation studies. We will need you to de-identify all of it for us because we only want de-identified/anonymized data."

What the CIO and CMIO are thinking: "They want us to give them a copy of all of our patient data *and* they want us to be responsible for ensuring that all of the data has been de-identified/anonymized? This means it's our fault if any PHI/PII gets leaked."

PHI and PII

You may see the terms PHI and PII used somewhat interchangeably. PHI refers to *protected health information* and is a set of fields that may identify a patient (e.g., appointment dates/times or physician name). PHI is defined by statute as part of HIPAA.

PII refers to *personal identifying information* and is much more broadly applied across all industries, not just healthcare. As a result, things like your physician's name are not considered your PHI (but may be considered your physician's PII). PII is typically governed by consumer protection or general data laws (e.g., GDPR).

I have been part of many such conversations, and those who hold the data are often risk averse and quite fearful when it comes to making their data available. It also doesn't help when a commercial company is doing the asking from a nonprofit or academic medical center.

On the other hand, imagine the following alternative proposal to a CIO or CMIO:

"We would like to train a predictive algorithm on your data that identifies patients who are likely to do well on our drug. But, don't worry! The data will never leave your systems, and you will always retain full control of your data. We will send the algorithms to your systems, and the only things that ever leave are aggregated statistics or model weights! You can even control what data our algorithms are able to see in the first place."

The appeal of federated analytics and federated learning is that those who are responsible for patient data never need to relinquish control. It's also great from the perspective of data scientists and organizations that want access to the data. As consumers, we don't need to worry about being responsible yet we can still get all of the benefits of the data. From most angles, it is a true win-win situation where everyone gets what they want.

But if it is so great, why haven't we seen broader adoption across the healthcare industry? After all, it addresses one of the biggest hurdles commonly cited by all healthcare industry stakeholders—access to enough data. We definitely want more data, but the key isn't to just have more data; it's to have more *high-quality* data. This brings us back to the data harmonization theme that has followed us through the whole book.

The Data Harmonization Challenge in a Federated Context

If we go back to our initial example about federating the training of a keyboard's predictive algorithm, we can see that there really isn't a data harmonization problem. The creator of the keyboard controls how the data is collected on each phone. So, when they construct the federated learning system, every phone is guaranteed to provide data in the same format and structure, and the context and meaning of the data are uniform.

Real-world data is neither uniform nor consistent in its structure, meaning, or context. As we have discussed in previous chapters, there is a lot of nuance to how we interpret RWD and what we must do to clean and process it. Now, imagine if two different organizations need to make sure that their data is properly harmonized to one another, yet neither organization can see the other's data.

Imagine that the fictitious University Medical Center is setting up a federated learning network with Community Medical Center. Analytics engineers at both organizations decide they want to use the OMOP common data model along with the Athena vocabularies. Informatics and data teams at both organizations work furiously to transform their local data models to OMOP, do some quick internal data validation tests, and proudly announce to the other team that their data is ready for training a machine learning model.

The federated network is built using a popular federated learning framework (e.g., Substra, FATE, TensorFlow Federated, Nvidia, etc.), and the model training commences! However, you go to validate the resultant model and it does not perform very well. In your typical data science workflow, this isn't such a bad thing. We just go back, take a look at the data, and tweak our features or hyperparameters accordingly. But, given the federated setup, the data scientists at University Medical Center can see only their own data; they cannot see any of the data at Community Medical Center—and vice versa.

Here are a few potential scenarios that are affecting our model performance:

No "signal" within the data
> In other words, there is actually no pattern in the data, and no amount of feature engineering or tuning of hyperparameters would produce a good model. Any

model that would appear to perform well would just be an extremely overfitted model to the data.

Choosing the wrong model

There is a pattern to be found within the data, but you are using a model that simply isn't performing well. In the case of traditional machine learning, maybe you are using a support vector machine when a random forest might perform better. In the case of deep learning, perhaps you need a different topology.

More feature engineering needed

In this situation, there is a pattern to be found, but we haven't extracted the right features or we haven't normalized values adequately. For deep learning, this may be another instance where we have a particular topology that doesn't work for the data. The key is that there is a pattern: we just haven't been able to "unlock" it.

Mismatch in data transformations

Unlike the previously discussed issue, this is particular to those situations where we are combining multiple different datasets. The issue is that when we are combining datasets A and B, we transform each in a way that is mismatched with the other.

The second and third scenarios are true of any machine learning project and not something that we need to discuss here. However, when dealing with a federated learning project, we must ask ourselves how we can distinguish between the first and fourth scenarios. Why is this any different than with most machine learning projects? Namely, we cannot see data throughout the network other than our own. This makes it difficult for the data scientist to just sit down, look at the output of the model, and systematically analyze and work through the data.

As we will see in the following examples, the data harmonization problem isn't different when dealing with federated analytics or federated learning. It is simply made more difficult by the fact that data engineers and data scientists can see the data from their own institution but none of the others. They are essentially forced to conduct their analysis as they normally would but with one hand tied behind their back—with most of the data available to them only as aggregated statistics or other privacy-preserving methods.

Let's revisit our toy example from earlier with Academic Medical Center and Community Medical Center. As with many diseases, age is often a factor in determining risk factors and guiding treatment options. As one common technique to help preserve privacy of older populations, many organizations cut off the age of their older patients to a predetermined value. For example, anyone over the age of 85 has their age recorded as 85. So, anyone who is 85 and older appears as if they are just 85 years old. So, what would happen if Academic Medical Center used a cutoff of 85 years old and Community Medical Center used a cutoff of 90 years old? This may not affect diseases where the bulk of patients are younger. However, what if we are studying geriatric diseases where we think age is a significant factor, particularly around the 85–90 year old range? Our model will obviously not be able to capture anything meaningful given the mismatch in age.

Of course, this type of mismatch is relatively easy to identify. Even in a privacy-preserving framework, we might be able to trade histograms and other aggregate statistics of the data. A skilled data scientist would see the histograms across the institutions and begin to ask probing questions of the respective informatics teams.

However, what if the situation is a little more nuanced? Let's go back to the MIMIC-III dataset and the discussion we had in Chapter 4 about the "admission" date and time. Imagine if we are creating a machine learning model that uses length of stay as a predictor of 30-day readmission. At Community Medical Center, we map the date and time that a patient was first seen by any department within the hospital. This will likely be the emergency department admission time for most patients at this medical center. At Academic Medical Center, the decision is made to use the date/time that a patient is actually moved to a specific unit within the hospital outside of the ED. They made this decision because of the number of patients they admit to the hospital outside of the ED and because this makes their data cleaner. To make things even more complex, our data scientist developing the predictive model decides to use only the date portion, ignoring the time, when calculating the length of stay.

If the average length of stay across this dataset is 10 days, we are looking at a ~10% difference between length of stay between the two datasets. How would this impact the training and testing of the model? More critically, how does a data scientist even identify this particular mismatch? Unfortunately, this is one of those things that is quite obvious if we know to ask data teams from both medical centers. However, absent this discussion, we will most likely never know that this mismatch even exists.

Another example is a real scenario that I encountered while at a young startup that was focused on enterprise-scale management of data from electronic health records. We were discussing with the CMIO of a hospital system that was in the process of merging with another, and he brought up a very specific example involving *time under anesthesia*. They wanted to be able to run analytics on their surgical patients to optimize the use of their operating rooms. As a large hospital system, their operating rooms were a precious resource. If there were no operating rooms available when a trauma patient came in, essential, life-saving procedures could be delayed or would need to be performed in the suboptimal emergency department environment. On the other hand, if multiple operating rooms remained unused and unscheduled, that meant other patients were unnecessarily delaying elective surgery. Additional complexity creeps in when working with time under anesthesia because patients coming out of the ORs need to be managed in the post-anesthesia care unit (PACU). The hospital may be able to perfectly optimize the OR schedule, but this may overwhelm the PACU.

So, what was the challenge, and why are we discussing it in a book about data? After all, time under anesthesia seems like it would be pretty straightforward. You start the clock when the anesthesiologist puts the patient under and stop the clock once the patient wakes up and is no longer under anesthetics. However, when we dig into how the data was collected and the various influences from the clinical workflow, we start to see how this becomes a problem for us from the data end of things.

First, in one of the hospitals, their official "start time" was when an IV was started on the patient in pre-op. In the other hospital, the clock was started only after the patient went "wheels in" into the OR. Their reasoning was that the patient wasn't officially under anesthesia until they were put under by the anesthesiologist, which occurred within minutes of being wheeled into the OR.

Second, the first hospital (that started the clock when the IV was started) would track a patient as "under anesthesia" until they were discharged from the PACU. Their reasoning for both start and stop time was that once a patient was confirmed for surgery and being actively prepped for surgery, resources were now committed all the way until the patient was discharged from the PACU. This made total sense from the perspective of tracking these data to optimize the use of their operating rooms and, by extension, their PACU. For the second hospital, they started and stopped the clock when the patient was rolled into and out of the OR. They had originally started tracking this time because their main focus was tracking the availability of anesthesiologists. As a smaller hospital, their main concern had been the anesthesiologists themselves, not the OR or PACU.

So, from the data perspective, we were told that there was a field that had been calculated in the respective data warehouses that tracked "time under anesthesia." However, these two times could differ by up to hours between the two hospitals for some patients. Trying to develop a predictive algorithm to project estimated time under anesthesia based on a variety of inputs (e.g., diagnoses, medications, scheduled versus emergency procedure, etc.) would be extremely difficult if we were to train the same model on data from both hospitals, as we would be doing in a federated system.

As data scientists working for the larger hospital and trauma center, we may see that our model performs poorly and begin the process of investigating why. We may dive into our own hospital's dataset and see that the model performs pretty well. However, the moment we federate this query, the model performs poorly. But, because we are unable to see the specific data from the other hospital, we don't realize that our outcome variable is quite skewed between the two hospitals.

We discussed earlier the possibility of looking at histograms or other aggregate statistics to help clue us in to any potential data mismatches. However, we look at our trauma center's data and then we look at the aggregate data from the smaller community hospital. After discussing with colleagues, we conclude that the community hospital has a shorter time on average because their procedures are also generally less complex. Of course, the reliance on aggregate statistics masks the true underlying reason for the difference.

Time under anesthesia was seemingly quite simple yet turned out to be much more complex (even when trying to harmonize the data between only two hospitals). Other disease areas such as oncology or neurology are even more challenging. These diseases and their management (and the resulting data) are already highly nuanced. Additionally, our understanding of the diseases and treatments is constantly evolving. This makes the harmonization problem even more challenging.

In Chapter 6, we spent a bit of time looking at how we can use graphs when analyzing healthcare data to help harmonize the data as well as graph-specific analytics. Now, let's look at how some of these topics would look in the context of federated approaches.

Graphs and Federated Approaches

Given all of the excitement with federation, let's spend a little time looking at how graphs and federated approaches can come together. As we discussed earlier, the need for data harmonization is even greater in a federated context. Before we can analyze data across sites, we need to make sure that the data was harmonized at each site and consistently across the network. Graphs can certainly be useful here just as they are outside of the federated context.

However, in this section, we will discuss a few ways that we can incorporate graphs explicitly as part of federated analytics and federated learning. Just a point of note— much of what we will be discussing is an active area or research with many new ideas and approaches. Some of these may prove to be quite valuable, and some might be useful only in a small and specific set of use cases. But, as I mentioned in Chapter 6, I continue to be excited about graphs in general, so graphs with federated learning is a natural place to explore.

As we discussed in Chapter 6, we can directly analyze graph data through the use of embeddings (in addition to other methods such as graph traversals). An implicit assumption of techniques such as node2vec is that all of the data is available in a single place. This would be fine for embeddings based on ontologies or other encoded knowledge (e.g., SNOMED or UMLS) but will be challenging if we want to build embeddings based on real patient data (as we saw with cui2vec or med2vec).

The natural question then is how we would federate the training of models to generate embeddings, particularly given that there are some potentially huge benefits. While training an embedding model on our own data is a great starting point, we know that our data may be biased. For example, data on patients in the San Francisco Bay Area represents a very different demographic than patients in rural California. To train a model across all of these data, we have a couple choices. Either we can aggregate the data into a single location or we can use federated learning.

The former is the simplest and easiest from a technical perspective, but we would need to get the organizations aligned on the bureaucratic and legal aspects. Given the increasing scrutiny on security and privacy breaches, the leadership may still opt for a federated approach despite alignment otherwise—simply to mitigate risk overall.

The specific solution and approach would ultimately depend on the type of embedding you are trying to create. In the node2vec case, the first step would be to generate the random walks across the entire graph. The next step would be to train the model weights across the entire network of federated learning sites, using techniques such as *transfer learning* or federating the learning itself (e.g., using FedAvg (*https:// arxiv.org/abs/1602.05629*)).[2,3]

Instead of attempting to train an embedding model across the entire network, a simpler approach would be to use the same pre-trained models across the entire federated network as part of the feature engineering process. For example, we could distribute the same snomed2vec model to all sites in our federated network and then use that model to encode the data at each site (diagnosis codes, medication codes, etc.). Once the data has been encoded using the design, we execute the remainder of the machine learning/deep learning project as we would any other project.

This also highlights the potential to share embeddings of patient records across sites. Though we are still working through legal and ethical questions on how best to share patient data, particularly across national boundaries, sharing patient-level embeddings would be one way to mitigate privacy concerns. Of course, this assumes that we can execute and validate two key things:

- Harmonize the data *within* each site to common semantics across the entire network.

- Ensure that the embeddings have consistent semantics across the entire network.

---

2 Shalisha Witherspoon et al., "SEEC: Semantic Vector Federation across Edge Computing Environments" (*https://arxiv.org/abs/2008.13298*), Cornell University arXiv, August 30, 2020.

3 Daniel Garcia Bernal et al., "Federated Word2Vec: Leveraging Federated Learning to Encourage Collaborative Representation Learning" (*https://arxiv.org/abs/2105.00831*), Cornell University arXiv, April 19, 2021.

The first is something that we have discussed throughout this book at many different levels and applies just the same within the federated context. Though, as we discussed in the previous section, it is even more critical in the federated context. It is also more challenging given the general difficulty in identifying inconsistencies and particularly *why* there are inconsistencies. Because one site can see only their own data, the guidelines for semantic harmonization must be as clear as possible (similar to what the OHDSI community has done with OMOP mapping guidelines).

The second involves *semantics* but in a very different sense. Here, we are not talking about whether ICD-10 codes are consistent or that everyone is using SNOMED codes. Nor are we talking about whether a "medication order" means the same thing as a "medication prescription." Instead, we mean that as the embedding model is trained, the various weights that are learned are consistent across the network. This is an active area of research, and I have not yet seen consensus on best practices or "batteries-included," off-the-shelf libraries.[4]

Natural Language Processing

So, we have learned a bit about federated analytics and federated learning and seen how the data harmonization challenge is magnified in that context. We have also seen how graphs can be used to mitigate some of the challenges.

Another area of healthcare data analytics that often intersects many of the themes discussed in this book is natural language processing. Like most things in healthcare, the phrase "natural language processing" can mean many different things. I've seen projects range from indexing text using ElasticSearch, Solr, or Lucene, to full-blown transformer-based NLP to extract highly nuanced progression of disease from free text.

Two other areas of interest that have popped up over the past few years include *natural language understanding* (NLU) and *natural language generation* (NLG). Those who are deeply embedded in working with natural language often use these terms distinctively, but I often see them lumped together as simply natural language processing. While there is some work in healthcare around natural language generation, the majority of work mostly aligns with the idea of NLU.

---

4 Fengda Zhang et al., "Federated Unsupervised Representation Learning" (*https://arxiv.org/abs/2010.08982*), Cornell University arXiv, October 18, 2020.

This is an active area of both research and implementation across nearly every industry. After all, much of the data generated involves free text of some sort. From social media to IT ticket management to clinical notes, we end up with a lot of text that sits alongside the structured data. Sometimes, this text is overlapping, and sometimes it is complementary to the structured data (we'll look at the significance of this distinction in a bit). When it comes to healthcare NLP we break the data down into two categories—clinical text and nonclinical text. In this chapter, we focus primarily on clinical text. If working with nonclinical text, there are many resources out there across many industries.

Now that we have a basic introduction to NLP and NLU, let's focus on one specific task within NLP that is the most common task that I have seen across nearly every project that leverages clinical text.

Concept Extraction

More often than not, when I hear about an "NLP" project based on RWD, it is some form of *concept extraction*. Sometimes this is also referred to using the general NLP process of *named entity recognition*. In essence, the unstructured text is scanned, and terms/concepts are extracted that correspond to known terminologies/controlled vocabularies.

For example, autocoding during the medical billing process is one application of *concept extraction*. Hospitals and clinics often use an autocoding service that can match text detected in both structured and unstructured fields to identify the appropriate billing code (e.g., ICD-10, E/M, CPT, etc.) to be attached to a claim. Though autocoding is an automated process, a human is typically integrated into the workflow to validate the claim and fix an errors.

There are many degrees of sophistication when it comes to autocoding or, more generally, concept extraction. Some approaches may use simple keyword matching tools based on fuzzy string matching, as you might find in ElasticSearch (*https://oreil.ly/pPRv9*), Solr (*https://oreil.ly/ApEQr*), or Lucene (*https://oreil.ly/cLD1l*). Some of these tools do begin to use more sophisticated NLP techniques such as stemming or lemmatization (*https://oreil.ly/1DFuI*). Stemming and lemmatization involve breaking a word down into a more meaningful "root" rather than just blindly looking at something like the Levenshtein (*https://oreil.ly/NMdir*) or Damerau–Levenshtein (*https://oreil.ly/ZPPwc*) distance.

Distance Metrics

Levenshtein distance is a simple measure and quantification of the difference between two strings. It takes the form of a distance between strings by counting the number of single-character insertions, deletions, or substitutions. The Damerau-Levenshtein distance builds on this by also counting text transpositions, in addition to insertions, deletions, and substitutions.

These types of metrics do not require any understanding of the actual text yet can be effective in processing text with typos. As with other aspects of healthcare data, one thing to keep in mind when looking at text processing techniques is whether they are focused on the syntax or semantics of the text. Often, simpler syntactically focused solutions provide very good results.

Stemming is the process of breaking a token down to a word stem. This usually follows some basic rules of the English language to remove suffixes, such as the *s* from pluralized terms, the *ing* from gerunds, or the verb conjugations. For example, the words *humble*, *humbled*, and *humbles* could be reduced to the stem *humbl*. It is important to note that stems do not need to be valid words. By incorporating stemming, search and indexing engines would be able to match terms that may be separated by high Levenshtein distances yet are otherwise obviously related to a native English speaker.

Similarly, *lemmatization* also breaks a token or word down to increase the matching of very similar terms. However, it incorporates the context and meaning of the words. Similar to our discussion regarding interoperability and harmonization, stemming is syntactic while lemmatization is semantic. For example, the words *corpus* and *corpora* (terms we often use to describe sets of text on which we train NLP algorithms) would result in the stem *corp* while the resulting lemma is *corpus*. In another example, the words *bore*, *bearing*, *bears* would result in the lemma *bear* since they are conjugations of the verb *to bear*.

As you may have noticed, the last example involved words that could result in multiple lemmas. For example, *bore* could simply be the noun versus the past tense of *to bear*. Also, *bears* could simply be the plural of *bear*, the animal. These words all have multiple meanings depending on their context and part of speech. So, lemmatizing terms also incorporates part of speech. If you do not know the part of speech, then you may opt to return all possible lemmas.

So, back to this idea of *concept extraction*. Ideally, we would want to use some sort of lemmatizer vs. basic stemming given the complexity and nuance of healthcare terms. Of course, out-of-the-box models that were created based on text such as Wikipedia are not well-suited for clinical NLP. That said, the process of lemmatization itself is usually too broad and generic for most healthcare use cases involving RWD.

In the context of evidence generation, we often only need to extract a few types of concepts—diagnoses, medications, and lab/test values. These are all nouns, and all have a very specific context. However, identifying similar or synonymous terms requires more than just finding a common stem or the appropriate lemma. For example, "acetaminophen," "paracetamol," and "Tylenol" all mean the same thing in most contexts when trying to extract the medications that a patient may be taking. Identifying these overlaps in concepts requires much more knowledge than what we can train a lemmatizer to do using traditional NLP techniques alone. Things get even more complex when we look at something like DayQuil, which contains acetaminophen in addition to other medications. So, if we are trying to match all patients who are currently taking Tylenol, not only would we need to identify paracetamol and acetaminophen, we would also need to find DayQuil and other combination medications that contain it.

This is where the UMLS and the many terminologies and controlled vocabularies become extremely useful. As shown in Figure 7-1, one approach would be to use NLP-based tools and libraries (e.g., MetaMap, cTAKES, MedSpaCy) and then link the extracted concepts using additional context and knowledge.

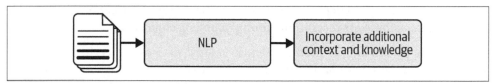

Figure 7-1. NLP followed by additional context

Currently, this is the most common approach. Tools such as MetaMap (*https:// oreil.ly/fHDdR*) will return *concept unique identifiers* that correspond to concepts contained within the UMLS (as we discussed in Chapter 3). Once we have the CUI of a concept, we can use the existing relationships within the UMLS to augment this concept with additional context and knowledge.

Let's take a look at a specific example involving a short piece of text and how we can extract concepts/CUIs.

Case study example: DayQuil

Let's say we have a block of text where someone has noted that "patient reports taking DayQuil PRN."

PRN

PRN is an abbreviation for "pro ne rata," a Latin phrase meaning "as the thing is needed." This is commonly used in clinical notes to signify that the medication (or other intervention) is used only as needed versus following a regular schedule (e.g., as we often see with antibiotics).

We run the MetaMap tool against this text, resulting in a list of one CUIs—*C0719665*. We then query our graph for *broader concepts*, which returns the following list of CUIs:

1. *C0000970* (acetaminophen)
2. *C1511537* (cough and cold preparations)
3. *C0350422* (dextromethorphan hydrobromide)
4. *C0304430* (pseudoephedrine hydrochloride)

Three of these CUIs correspond to the component medications: acetaminophen (pain and fever reliever), dextromethorphan (cough suppressant), and pseudoephedrine (decongestant). By querying the UMLS, we have incorporated additional knowledge to our system, knowledge that is quite common among clinicians.

This same approach can be used for semistructured data elements. In many of the commercial datasets that I have seen, there is often a column of diagnoses or of medications. While the terms may be consistent within the single dataset (e.g., there is only a single way "acetaminophen" appears in the column), the column still contains an uncontrolled set of terms. One of the first things we need to do is match these terms against a known terminology. In such situations, we can use this same approach even though it is not full-scale NLP.

As we saw with graphs (and many other areas of data science), the focus on deep learning extends to NLP as well. In the next section, we discuss how we can integrate several NLP tasks since we know one task can influence another.

Integrated approaches

Increasingly, we are seeing efforts to combine multiple tasks into a single algorithm. One obvious approach is multitask learning, the simultaneous training of different tasks at the same time. Figure 7-2 shows a high-level neural network that has several

---

shared layers followed by task-specific layers. The idea is that the layers of the various tasks can influence each other.

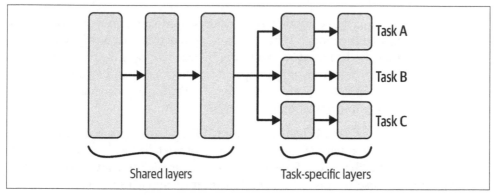

Figure 7-2. Layers of multitask learning

For example, let's go back to our discussion about stemming and lemmatization. We can train separate models for lemmatization and for part-of-speech detection. However, given that lemmatization benefits from knowing a word's part of speech, combining both of these tasks into a single neural network could improve overall performance.

Additional Resources on Multitask Learning

For some additional information on multitask learning, here are a few resources:

- An overview of multi-task learning (*https://oreil.ly/xxgX7*)
- Deciding Which Tasks Should Train Together in Multi-Task Neural Networks (*https://oreil.ly/IDS4D*)
- Natural Language Processing and Graph Representation Learning for Clinical Data (*https://oreil.ly/H6ONZ*)

One recent example of multitask learning in clinical NLP is the 2021 paper by Mulyar et al. titled *MT-clinical BERT: Scaling Clinical Information Extraction with Multitask Learning* (*https://oreil.ly/vmtPB*). They set up a model to perform tasks across several areas:

- Sentence pair similarity
- Sentence pair entailment
- Drug event and adverse drug event extraction
- PHI de-identification

- Problem, treatment, and test extraction
- UMLS semantic group identification

These tasks can all impact one another, so it makes sense to attempt to combine them into a single deep learning model. When attempting to detect various types of clinical concepts, increasing the likelihood that a term is a drug naturally decreases the likelihood that it's also a problem (a sign, symptom, or diagnosis), and vice versa. Similarly, knowing the semantic group (*https://oreil.ly/Fti2H*) of a string would help improve the detection and extraction of concepts.

When trying to address broad challenges with RWD that are nonspecific to any particular disease area, we often see approaches like those detailed earlier—extraction of problems, treatments, drugs, etc. Sometimes, we can narrow the search space a bit by focusing only on those treatments related to cancer or other disease area. However, from a data perspective, the techniques are still fairly generic.

However, we are seeing increasing focus on specific tasks that use multitask models that integrate NLP and knowledge (graphs). One example is a project by Alawad et al. titled *Integration of Domain Knowledge using Medical Knowledge Graph Deep Learning for Cancer Phenotyping* (*https://arxiv.org/abs/2101.01337*) that combines NLP with a knowledge graph based on UMLS to perform specific cancer phenotyping (site, subsite, laterality, behavior, histology, and grade) from pathology reports.

Up until now, our discussion around NLP has been largely focused on extracting structured concepts from text using a variety of different techniques and approaches. In the next section, we look at how we can build a model directly on the text without an explicit step to extract structured concepts.

Beyond Concept Extraction

In the previous section, we took a look at concept extraction and named entity recognition from a clinical perspective. I would say many of the use cases today focus on the extraction of pertinent clinical concepts, often as part of feature engineering with the intent that the clinical concepts can be compared alongside other structured data. There are also use cases that simply analyze the text directly, similar to sentiment analysis, without an explicit concept extraction phase.

Let's take a look at a use case around detecting sepsis by combining various clinical data and clinical text together to directly predict sepsis. Essentially, they are treating the text data as another stream of data. The embeddings approach (as we discussed in Chapter 6) implicitly captures some of the underlying semantics and context of the text. However, there's no set of concepts that can be inspected by the data scientist during feature engineering.

Sepsis prediction

Sepsis is a systemic dysfunction cof the body's organs that is triggered by an infection. Often, people refer to sepsis as a "blood infection" though sepsis is actually the body's response to the infection. Untreated, sepsis is most often fatal. The earlier the treatment, the better the chance of survival. As a result, there is increasing focus on sepsis early detection algorithms, some applied as soon as a patient meets the triage nurse in a hospital's emergency department.

There are many papers that apply various aspects of machine learning to sepsis detection, ranging from using vital signs to electrocardiogram monitors (EKG/ECG) to incorporating clinical text. One example is a project by Amrollahi et al. titled *Contextual Embeddings from Clinical Notes Improves Prediction of Sepsis* (*https://oreil.ly/eKF2F*). This is not the only example of such work, but it does highlight the alternative approach to incorporating clinical text without relying on explicit concept extraction or named entity recognition. The authors ultimately create a model that incorporates both structured data (e.g., vital signs) and embeddings from Clinical-BERT (*https://arxiv.org/abs/1904.03323*), without the need to first extract the concepts.

Additional Info on Sepsis, NLP, and ML

A recent systematic review of existing research was just published by Yan et al. in early 2022 (*https://oreil.ly/gwyeI*) and may be of interest if you would like to learn more about sepsis, NLP, and machine learning.

This example of using Clinical-BERT embeddings is only one of many ways to directly incorporate text data into deep learning and other advanced analytics approaches. Just as there is no single best practice when it comes to deep learning, such approaches for applying embeddings to text and combining multiple different vectors require experience and knowledge of NLP and deep learning in addition to clinical text and the clinical domain of interest.

Now that we have a bit of understanding of clinical NLP and some specific examples, let's look at some clinical NLP tools available to us. We will spend a bit of time with open source or publicly available tools. After, I'll list a few commercial tools that I've encountered over the years though we don't actually go into any detail about them.

Clinical NLP Tools

There are quite a few tools and products out there within the spectrum of "clinical NLP." As discussed earlier, some are much closer to search engines, while others are closer to natural language understanding solutions.

In this section, we will discuss a few solutions and some pros and cons. The solutions are discussed in no particular order.

NCBO BioPortal Annotator

The NCBO is the National Center for Biomedical Ontology (*https://oreil.ly/7Vfa8*), an NIH-funded initiative that is managed by Stanford University. NCBO is generally known for its main offering, the BioPortal (*https://oreil.ly/hRB3V*).

The BioPortal is a hosted platform that allows researchers to interact with terminologies, controlled vocabularies, and ontologies using a web interface and the REST API. In addition to hosting standard sources such as those in the UMLS, BioPortal also allows users to upload and share their own ontologies. What makes the BioPortal particularly powerful is the ability to link terms and concepts across ontologies. This allows anyone to create an ontology for their use case while also connecting this ontology to existing concepts such as those from ICD-10, SNOMED CT, LOINC, etc.

Within the BioPortal are two NLP tools, Annotator (*https://oreil.ly/e5ywJ*) and Annotator+ Beta (*https://oreil.ly/KxZGR*). These tools will take unstructured text as input and return a list of matching concepts across all "ontologies" within the BioPortal.

"Ontologies" Within the BioPortal

It is important to note that all uploaded sources within the BioPortal are referred to as *ontologies*. However, the formality of the ontologies varies depending on the background of the authors and intent/purpose of the ontology. Some are simply controlled vocabularies, while others are full-fledged ontologies that adhere to semantic web principles.

There is a web interface that allows you to test small amounts of text and refine your search parameters (e.g., specifying a subset of ontologies or semantic types). Let's go back to our case study involving DayQuil—"patient reports taking DayQuil PRN." If we enter this into the Annotator (Figure 7-3), we see that there are 150 results, as shown in Figure 7-4.

If you try this yourself in the Annotator, you will see many results that match the term *patient* across many different ontologies. For our particular use case, we probably don't care about most of these ontologies since they are specific to an unrelated use case (e.g., Malaria Ontology). The Annotator allows us to restrict to particular ontologies of interest as well as forcing certain restrictions such as "match longest only."

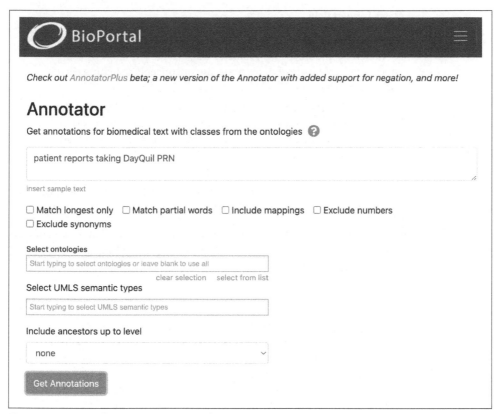

Figure 7-3. Sample input to BioPortal Annotator

Annotations

total results **150** (direct **150** / ancestor **0** / mapping **0**)

CLASS filter	ONTOLOGY filter	TYPE	CONTEXT	MATCHED CLASS	MATCHED ONTOLOGY filter
patient report	Ontology of Consumer Health Vocabulary	direct	**patient reports** taking DayQuil PRN	patient report	Ontology of Consumer Health Vocabulary
Patient	COVID-19OntologyInPatternMedicine	direct	**patient** reports taking DayQuil ...	Patient	COVID-19OntologyInPatternMedicine
patient	Viral Disease Ontology Trunk	direct	**patient** reports taking DayQuil ...	patient	Viral Disease Ontology Trunk
Patient	Cancer Research and Management ACGT Master Ontology	direct	**patient** reports taking DayQuil ...	Patient	Cancer Research and Management ACGT Master Ontology

Figure 7-4. BioPortal Annotator results

Match Longest Only

This is a feature within BioPortal but also most clinical NLP tools. By matching the longest possible string, we get the most specific concept possible instead of a smattering of concepts matching each part of the string.

For example, the string "prostate cancer" returns 189 results, matching prostate cancer itself in addition to concepts for prostate and cancer individually. If we check "Match longest only," there are only 46 results, each about prostate cancer.

By specifying additional search parameters, we are essentially integrating additional context into the process, improving the quality of the concepts that are extracted.

The BioPortal now has a new version of the Annotator in beta, referred to as Annotator+ (*https://oreil.ly/KxZGR*). It functions similarly to Annotator but adds additional functionality such as negation detection.

Negation Detection

Negation detection is the ability to detect "negative" statements in a clinical record. When we started our example, we were looking for patients who might be taking a drug that contains acetaminophen. However, if the clinical note says, "patient denies taking…" or "patient stopped taking…," we need to remove this entry from the results. Other examples include phrases such as "rule out," "no evidence," or "absent." When used alongside clinical concepts, we negate the presence of the concept as part of the patient's clinical record.

Negation detection is a challenging yet important aspect of clinical NLP and generally remains an open problem (*https://oreil.ly/aKBGN*). If we blindly perform concept extraction/NER tasks against a corpus of text, we will find all mentions of clinical concepts. This means that a search or filter for all patients who have recently taken acetaminophen would match our patient who "denies" taking it, resulting in many false positives.

Let's change our phrase to "patient denies taking dayquil," select negation detection, and limit the search to SNOMED CT and NCIT. In Figure 7-5, we can see that the concept for DayQuil is still detected but that it has been negated.

Annotations				total results *4* (direct *4* / ancestor *0* / mapping *0*)			
CLASS filter	ONTOLOGY filter	TYPE filter	CONTEXT	MATCHED CLASS	MATCHED ONTOLOGY	NEGATION
Veterinary Patient	National Cancer Institute Thesaurus	direct	**patient** denies taking dayquil	Veterinary Patient	National Cancer Institute Thesaurus	AFFIRMED
Patient	National Cancer Institute Thesaurus	direct	**patient** denies taking dayquil	Patient	National Cancer Institute Thesaurus	AFFIRMED
Patient	SNOMED CT	direct	**patient** denies taking dayquil	Patient	SNOMED CT	AFFIRMED
Dayquil	National Cancer Institute Thesaurus	direct	... denies taking **dayquil**	Dayquil	National Cancer Institute Thesaurus	NEGATED

Figure 7-5. Match longest only

While the web interface for the Annotator is a useful tool for a small amount of text or for determining the most appropriate parameters, there is also a REST API (*https://oreil.ly/Sss1v*) for automated interaction with BioPortal.

The Annotator API is a part of the broader BioPortal API, so it follows the same conventions as interacting with the BioPortal in general. This includes the use of API keys and support for both JSON (and JSON-LD) and XML.

cTAKES

Apache cTAKES is the *Clinical Text Analysis and Knowledge Extraction System* (*https://oreil.ly/BOXTf*) and is a project that began as an academic project at the Mayo Clinic. Since then, it has become an Apache top-level project and incorporates complex frameworks such as Apache UIMA (*https://uima.apache.org*).

For many years, cTAKES was a go-to framework for implementing complex clinical NLP pipelines. Given the use of UIMA, it was possible to integrate the cTAKES pipeline with other project-specific steps. UIMA also makes it possible to swap out steps of the cTAKES pipeline with custom processors. At its heart, cTAKES (and UIMA in general) allows us to create and manage *annotators* that integrate with the Common Analysis System (CAS), as shown in Figure 7-6.

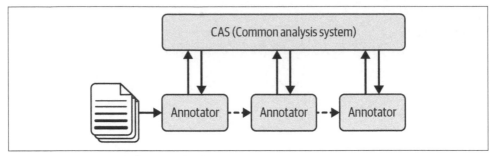

Figure 7-6. Overview of UIMA CAS

We can see that the input text is processed and loaded into the CAS. Then, it is processed and analyzed by each annotator (as highlighted by the dashed arrows). However, the annotators do not talk to each other directly; they interact with the CAS. Each annotator extracts the data/information that it needs from the CAS, processes and analyzes the text, and sends the results back to the CAS.

This allows annotators to be inserted/removed as needed by the project without being dependent on other annotators. For example, one annotator might be a sentence detection algorithm that splits the incoming text into a series of sentences. Another annotator could then take these sentences as input to perform part-of-speech detection. If the POS detector requires sentences and none are available, the overall *analysis engine* simply moves to the next step.

There are analysis engines provided for matching text against UMLS CUIs as well as other specific tasks (such as detection of smoking history). The main challenge with cTAKES is that it has a fairly steep learning curve and can be daunting to the new user. This complexity also means that there is a lot of overhead in setting up and integrating cTAKES into data science projects, particularly from non-JVM languages such as Python and R. Another challenge, as with any prebuilt model (and not specific to cTAKES), is that it may not meet expectations out of the box given the type of text that the models were originally trained on.

However, it does come with a visual debugger that allows us to peek into each step of the NLP process and can facilitate sophisticated tuning and optimization of NLP pipelines. Also, it comes with a standalone "processing engine" graphical user interface that allows the user to process a batch of documents or other text. One of the steps of the analysis engine pipeline could be to persist the output of the NLP to a database or other durable storage. Given that it is implemented in Java, one can set up an analysis engine to interface with pretty much any type of database, whether on-prem or cloud-based, assuming there is a supporting library available.

MedSpaCy

The last project that we will discuss is the MedSpaCy (*https://oreil.ly/QyOy3*) tool that is built on top of the SpaCy framework (*https://spacy.io*). One of the major reasons it is quickly gaining popularity is that it's written in Python and thus convenient to integrate into existing Python-based projects.

Similar to cTAKES, it is modular and takes an object-oriented approach as its underlying architecture (*https://arxiv.org/abs/2106.07799*). This allows data scientists to leverage functionality "out of the box" while also making it easy for data scientists to customize and augment pipelines as needed (which is pretty much always!). It also includes a module that will provide concept extraction/named entity recognition against the UMLS.

We've discussed a few FOSS (free, open source) clinical NLP projects. As with any FOSS approach, there may be a significant hidden cost, particularly if you are simply trying to solve a specific problem and don't want to be burdened with the nitty-gritty details of deploying an NLP pipeline. Next, we'll look at a few commercial clinical NLP solutions to round out our discussion.

Commercial Clinical NLP Solutions

There are a number of commercial offerings available providing some combination of on-prem and cloud-based solutions:

Amazon Comprehend Medical (https://oreil.ly/Pm0Z7)
> This is a web service provided by AWS that functions similarly to the BioPortal Annotator. It links against commonly used terminologies such as ICD-10 and SNOMED CT. They also provide some linkage with UMLS though identifying specific version information of source terminologies and UMLS releases is a bit buried in their documentation.

Google Healthcare Natural Language API (https://oreil.ly/xKzZ2)
> Similar to AWS, Google also provides an API for clinical concept extraction that is linked against the UMLS. Google also provides the ability to integrate your own custom models if the prebuilt ones do not fit your specific needs.

Melax Tech (https://www.melaxtech.com)
> Melax Tech is a startup that is commercializing the Clinical Language Annotation, Modeling, and Processing (CLAMP) (*https://clamp.uth.edu*) toolkit. CLAMP began as an academic project (from the School of Biomedical Informatics at the University of Texas Health Science Center) and is available for free for academic users working on individual research projects.

Spark NLP for Healthcare (https://oreil.ly/UzwOe)
This is a solution offered by John Snow Labs built on top of its Spark NLP solution. It has published comparisons of its solution against AWS, Google Cloud, and Azure for common NLP benchmarks (*https://oreil.ly/JsBky*) as well as for clinical entity extraction (*https://oreil.ly/lLs9c*) (though it calls it *clinical entity resolution*).

IQVIA NLP (https://oreil.ly/NSQTc)
IQVIA provides analytics and technology solutions, clinical research services, and data assets to the broader healthcare industry. As part of its solutions, it also provides an NLP platform.

Linguamatics (https://www.linguamatics.com)
As another healthcare-specific company, Linguamatics has provided NLP solutions for all levels of the industry, ranging from hospitals and health systems to pharma companies. They were recently acquired by IQVIA in 2019, so I would suspect that they are being integrated into the broader IQVIA set of solutions.

Wolters Kluwer Health Language Clinical NLP (https://oreil.ly/UBE1R)
Similar to IQVIA and Linguamatics, Wolters Kluwer provides an NLP solution as part of a broader suite of solutions for the healthcare industry.

Whether you are evaluating open source or commercial tools, it's important to consider which tools are built specifically around clinical text. There are some key differences between clinical NLP and "regular" NLP that we'll discuss next.

Key Differences Between Clinical NLP and Other Applications of NLP

As you can see, there are many options when tackling the clinical NLP problem. These options are all highly specific to dealing with clinical text, and we often hear that clinical NLP is different and more challenging than other use cases. How true is this? After all, the English language (or any language for that matter) is quite nuanced, and there is often room for multiple interpretations. After all, this is what allows us to enjoy poetry and literature!

Every data science project has nuances and specific considerations that are different than the next project. Even in industries such as finance, the needs of one organization differ from others; this trickles down to the data scientists who need to account for these nuances during the course of their analysis. So, what about clinical NLP makes it "more challenging"?

This question is a bit of a red herring, a misdirection that unnecessarily focuses us on the NLP aspects. In fact, the challenges we see with clinical NLP are the underlying challenges we see with all healthcare data. The application of free and unstructured text does make things a bit more challenging, but the text itself is not necessarily more difficult.

As we discussed in Chapters 1 and 2, healthcare data suffers from a huge "variety" problem. There are many different ways to say the same thing and many different ways to interpret what appears to be the same thing. In many ways, this heterogeneity is a symptom of the variations in how healthcare is practiced. The delivery of healthcare and practice of medicine are always playing catch-up to our understanding of human physiology and pathophysiology. Consequently, it's near impossible to ensure that healthcare is delivered uniformly in a way that follows "standards."

So, when tackling problems that require NLP, we need to always factor this into our thinking and problem solving. For example, the "bag of words" technique is often used as an initial, simple way to incorporate text data into an analysis. Similarly, term frequency-inverse document frequency (TF-IDF) (*https://oreil.ly/VuxYr*) is also often used. These approaches rely on differences between strings and are sometimes coupled with stemming or lemmatization. However, as we discussed earlier, stemming and lemmatization are not enough when dealing with clinical text. As a result, we need to factor this in. So, instead of a "bag of words" approach, we need to consider something akin to "bag of concepts." That is, instead of just looking at the text as a bucket of (minimally) processed strings, we need to instead process and analyze the data at the conceptual level.

You might be wondering—wouldn't we want to do this with any NLP approach? Generally, yes! However, we often don't need it in other use cases because we have such large amounts of text; terms with similar meaning often get automatically factored into the underlying model. Relatively speaking, the amount of clinical text available is minuscule compared to the amount of text we can access from the Wikipedia, Twitter, or other public corpora of text.

Obviously, of all the text that we can analyze, a very small percentage of it is clinical text. However, to make things more challenging, clinical text is not easily shared due to privacy concerns and the leakage of PHI/PII (see "PHI and PII" on page 177). Text is extremely difficult to de-identify/anonymize though this is also an active area of research and development. Given this challenge, organizations seldom make clinical text available to researchers and data scientists looking to improve their models. As a result, available NLP models are highly specific to the organizations at which they were trained.

This leads us to another key challenge when dealing with clinical NLP—dialects. Again, this challenge is magnified due to the lack of available data. So, when we have a project such as cTAKES that provides pretrained models based on text from a single institution (in this case, the Mayo Clinic), we end up with models that are trained to a single dialect only. Even within a single institution, we often see "subdialects" that differ from one service line to the next—how cardiologists capture their notes may be different from psychiatrists and emergency physicians.

So, the lack of data magnifies many of the challenges we already see with NLP and text analysis. To make things even worse, the expectations around model performance (typically measured by sensitivity and specificity) are much higher than in other industries. Take our recent experiences with COVID—say we were working on an algorithm to help improve our ability to detect patients with COVID very early on in the pandemic, when tests weren't yet widely available. The "cost" of a false positive means the patient would be prevented from going to work for two weeks; a false negative would be even worse with the same patient now infecting multiple other co-workers, friends/family, and others. Of course, we would want to increase sensitivity (i.e., decrease the number of false negatives) though doing so would result in increased false positives. So, to prevent the spread of COVID, we subject people to missing work and isolating from family and friends.

Now, let's compare this to Spotify, Netflix, or any other media streaming provider and their recommendation engines. You wouldn't know if there was a false negative since a song or movie simply wouldn't be recommended to you. On the other hand, a false positive could even be marketed as a feature! An "errant" recommendation could be sold as a way to broaden your horizons, introducing you to content that you would never have looked for on your own. Simply put, the stakes are higher, so the data science challenges are harder because of increased expectations (and rightfully so).

Conclusion

Each of the topics we covered in this section could be a book in and of itself. They are highly complex and nuanced, and they remain very active areas in both academia and industry, from digital health startups through big pharma.

However, the key theme is that how we harmonize the data is a very important aspect of data science, even if your focus is primarily on machine learning, deep learning, or even federated learning. In fact, the intense focus and excitement around federated analytics and federated learning highlights that effective data harmonization is more important than ever.

As such, graphs continue to play an important role in data harmonization. However, even aside from improving how we can map concepts between different coding systems or terminologies, graphs are getting integrated into the model development process more and more. Whether we are integrating them into NLP use cases or into decision support use cases, the information and knowledge captured in graphs is becoming a key feature of deep learning algorithms. The expansion of embeddings into the graph space unlocks many of the key learnings and techniques from the NLP world where word embeddings have become a key item in the data science toolbox.

## CHAPTER 8

Graphs, Harmonization, and Some Final Thoughts

We have spent the past several chapters diving deeply into various aspects of working with real-world healthcare data. We started with a pretty high-level view of healthcare data, starting with an overview of common sources of healthcare data. One of the most challenging aspects of working with RWD is that the number and types of data sources is virtually unbounded. As clinicians, researchers, entrepreneurs, and tech companies continue to innovate, we will continue to see an increase in the different types of RWD available.

When we use the phrase *real-world data*, most of us immediately think of electronic health records, claims, and clinical registries as the most common sources of data. Many also include noninterventional studies, often referred to as *observational studies*. All of these studies are similar in that they typically focus on collecting patient demographics, conditions and diagnoses, medications, and other interventions.

However, as we continue to dive deeper into the world of data generated (and collected) for the purpose of caring for patients, we quickly venture into a whole new frontier. Whether it's an app that uses your typing speed to detect changes in mental health (*https://oreil.ly/6wxHo*), a phone that uses your gait to track movement disorders (*https://oreil.ly/jri8b*), or a baseball cap to detect seizures (*https://oreil.ly/8OIPt*), the possibilities are endless. However, it does mean that nearly anything can be considered real-world data if it can be used to detect, treat, or manage some sort of health condition.

Working with these data is quite complex, and compared to most types of data, we must adapt our processes, workflows, and methodologies when embarking on the RWD journey. The specific definition of "real-world data" varies, and there is no clear consensus. However, most seem to incorporate the following notions, some more implicit than others:

Reflects routine clinical practice
> In other words, the data reflects routine care and not highly controlled situations such as clinical trials.

Secondary analysis
> The data was collected during the delivery of healthcare and is now being used for scientific research, evidence generation, etc.

Retrospective
> The data was collected, and we are now going back to analyze historical data versus developing a study protocol and then collecting data over time on a specific cohort of patients.

Some broadly define RWD as any healthcare data collected outside the context of randomized clinical trials. Others define it as noninterventional studies (i.e., not collected to measure the difference in outcomes between those who do and do not receive a therapeutic intervention). We have yet to come to a consensus definition, though I'm not convinced that a singular definition of what is (or isn't) RWD would be helpful. When following one definition, clinical registries may be considered RWD while another definition may exclude it. Does this actually matter?

As data scientists, data engineers, analytics engineers, or key healthcare stakeholders, we want to use all of the data to which we have access so that we can improve the quality and efficiency of care for patients. So, instead of focusing on defining what is or isn't real-world data, let's focus on the key characteristics of such data and what we must do to effectively leverage the data.

First, we want to consider what is the source of the data. This helps us understand the context and meaning of the underlying data. We need to understand this context to know if we can adapt the data to our use case and what, if any, scientific considerations we need to make when interpreting the data and the results of analysis.

There are specific questions we would want to ask, depending on the type of the source data. It is not possible to list all of these questions ahead of time, so it is critical that you engage a suitable domain expert. For example, if working with EHR data, it is important to engage the chief medical informatics officer (CMIO), chief nursing information officer (CNIO), and specialists who understand the nuances of the clinical domain. Just as you wouldn't ask a neurologist for advice on breast cancer, it would be detrimental to your oncology project to rely on a physician who is not an oncologist. Similarly, if working with clinical registry data, engage a clinical registrar. While a CMIO is familiar with healthcare data, they are not experts in managing clinical registries and won't be able to speak to the nuances of the data within one.

That said, here are some example questions we would want to ask:

- Is it from an *electronic health record*? If so, what type of EHR? Is it a hospital-wide system or one tailored to a specific service line or disease area (e.g., an oncology-specific EHR such as OncoEMR from FlatIron).

- Is it from a *clinical registry*? How was this registry set up, and what was the intended purpose? Was it to track biospecimens, a specific cohort of patients, or a specific set of interventions?

- Is it from a *healthcare payer*? Is it a government payer or a private insurance company? What is the claims process? How much detail is required to process a claim?

- Is it from a *digital health device or app*? Was this device or app cleared by the FDA? If so, was it a 510(k), and what is it equivalent to?

Regardless of which type of data source I listed, there are some questions that we always want to ask so that we can better understand the context of the data:

- Who entered the data? What was their clinical background?

- What protocol or process guides the data entry/collection?

- What coding systems were used, if any? How were negatives handled (e.g., absence of a positive code or presence of a negative code)? When a concept was not well-aligned with an existing code, how was that handled? Did they omit a code and add a free-text note, choose the "best" code, or something else?

- Has the data been cleaned or processed? If so, how?

- Have any data quality assessments been performed on the data? By whom and what were the results?

This list is by no means exhaustive but highlights the types of questions you must ask. Making assumptions about the data is a great way to set yourself up for failure.

All of this highlights that healthcare RWD and how we work with it are constantly evolving. We must continue to learn, share our knowledge, and adapt how we ingest, clean, process, and analyze healthcare RWD. Part of this evolution also comes in the form of what data are being generated and integrated into the delivery of healthcare. Let's quickly look at how RWD might change over the next few years.

Other Types of Healthcare RWD

Let's shift gears a little bit. Instead of thinking about RWD from the perspective of use cases and the various types of data sources, let's look at data from the perspective of the data itself.

Up until now, we have spent a lot of time discussing data without highlighting that most of it is assumed to be structured or semistructured data, with the occasional mention of unstructured/free-text data. Structured data typically comes in the form of a relational database and reflects values chosen from a prespecified list. This is the easiest data for us to work with but is also the most restrictive for the person entering, generating, or collecting the data. Semistructured data is typically a text field that asks for a specific type of data and usually only a few words in length. Examples of this might be a field asking for the name of a medication. While the specific string is uncontrolled, we know that the value is intended to be a medication. Lastly, we have free text, which is generally unconstrained and the user can type anything they want.

Relational databases, document databases, and graph databases are great for storing these types of data; NLP is helpful at bringing some order and structure to the free text. But, what about all the types of data we haven't yet discussed?

We have not spent much time talking about all of these other types of data that could be considered RWD. At least in the pharma industry, most of the focus is currently on accessing EHR and -omics (*https://oreil.ly/MM1c0*) (e.g., genomics, proteomics, metabolomics, etc.) data. One increasingly common source of RWD are the results of molecular tests such as next-generation sequencing.

However, we also see increased research focused on time-series data, as highlighted in Figure 8-1.

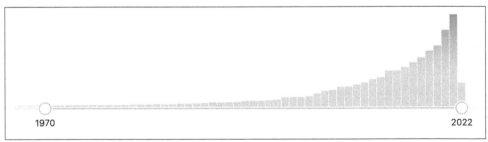

Figure 8-1. Time series papers in PubMed

As with many things in healthcare, "time series" is a very broad term and is used to describe everything from the periodic collection of data on the order of days/weeks/months to low-frequency physiologic sensors (e.g., continuous glucose monitoring) to high-frequency sensors (e.g., EEG). It also encompasses the use of sensors that are nonspecific to healthcare such as accelerometer data from a phone or watch.

Phenotypes

While *phenotype* is generally used in the context of genotypes, it is becoming more common when looking at other biomarkers, including digital biomarkers.

The term *phenotype* is used to describe the set of observable characteristics of an organism. For example, the shape of a leaf, the color of your eyes, or having Type 1 Diabetes are all phenotypes.

By themselves, time-series data can tell us only so much about a patient. We need to connect these data to the patient's clinical phenotype. This allows us to then correlate the time-series data with actual clinical changes. At a high level, this is the same approach that we follow with -omics data. In genomics, we are correlating genotypes with phenotypes. We look at what is common (or different) from one phenotype to the next, searching for correlations between mutations/variants and phenotypes. When we find a strong correlation, we often call the identified variant a *biomarker*— an objective measure or sign that tells us something about the underlying biological or disease process. When working with time-series data, we often call them *digital biomarkers* (though digital biomarkers includes much more than time-series data).

As we see more and more innovation around different types of RWD, needs around normalization and harmonization will only increase. Data harmonization has been one of the themes underlying the whole book, but the next section is a chance for us to review it with a slightly different perspective.

Data Normalization and Harmonization

Whether we are working with purely structured clinical data or we are incorporating the latest in time-series and multi-omics data, the heart of the healthcare RWD challenge is the normalization and harmonization problem.

The need to harmonize RWD is not specific to healthcare. For a moment, let's forget about healthcare; let's define *real-world data* as data that is generated during the routine delivery of any business where there is a need to integrate data from multiple sources, each servicing a different aspect of the broader industry, and each with a different way to describe its portion of the business.

While this is a bit of a contrived definition, it highlights the key issues we have with healthcare RWD. At the end of the day, those of us working with RWD need to bring together different sources of data in a meaningful way. Most of this book has been focused on the data wrangling needed for harmonization. There are two different perspectives we need to consider with respect to data harmonization.

Merging Datasets

The first perspective is often where our minds typically go—how do we combine data from multiple sources into a single data source? Most often, this is part of an effort to increase the effective size of a dataset. Large hospital systems are a common place for such efforts since they are typically composed of multiple different hospitals and clinics, all servicing overlapping patient populations. It can be quite valuable to bring all of these data into a single data warehouse or commons where administrators and researchers can query patient data across the entire system. However, in the pharma industry, this is rarely a use case because nearly all of the RWD we access comes from third parties. Data use agreements often prohibit us from merging or linking datasets.

When linking datasets, it is critical to define the level of linking involved. Something like entity resolution is much more straightforward. If we are linking a hospital dataset with an overlapping prescription of claims dataset, we would want to make sure we are identifying the same patient in each dataset. This is the first level and quite similar to entity resolution in banking/finance or advertising.

The second level of linking involves harmonizing the clinical data—making sure that the diagnoses, medications, etc., mean the same thing across the different datasets. This is often where many projects get overly creative and start to come up with techniques for merging datasets that may yield erroneous insights.

I have seen projects that attempt to take diagnosis data from one set of patients and combine them with treatment data from a different set of patients (with an unknown degree of overlap between the two patient populations). This is problematic because of the variation in the delivery of healthcare itself. Such linkages make the implicit assumption that the diagnosis data of the first dataset are comparable to the diagnosis data of the second dataset, which is most often not the case.

Figure 8-2 highlights an example comparison of two datasets—say we have detailed diagnostic data on a set of cancer patients, including cancer histology, morphology, staging, and molecular testing, but the treatment data are of poor quality. In the other dataset, we have some diagnostic data (cancer histology and morphology, limited staging, and no molecular testing). However, in this second dataset, we have great treatment data. The obvious next step would be to combine these two datasets by using the diagnostic data (e.g., histology, morphology, etc.).

By linking these two datasets based on the diagnosis information, we are essentially making the following assumptions (among others):

- The treatment data in the second dataset is based on molecular testing.

- The two datasets follow the same staging guidelines (and version of the guidelines).

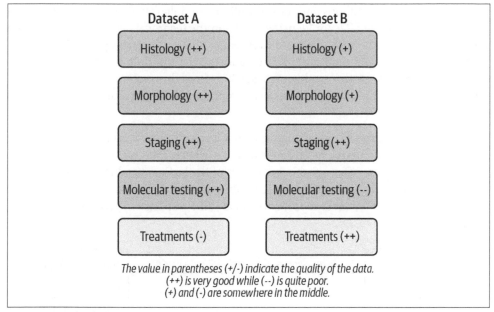

The value in parentheses (+/-) indicate the quality of the data.
(++) is very good while (--) is quite poor.
(+) and (-) are somewhere in the middle.

Figure 8-2. Example of linking two oncology datasets

Such attempts are fraught with risks—before embarking on such data journey, it is absolutely critical that you engage the appropriate clinicians (i.e., those specializing in the specific disease area or indication of interest) who are also data aware. This highlights one of the biggest gaps that I continue to see when it comes to data projects in healthcare—the need to bridge all of the various teams and stakeholders. In the next section, we look specifically at IT teams and "the business."

Bridging IT and the Business

This notion of bringing clinicians and other subject-matter experts closer to the technology teams is not nearly as common as it needs to be. Academic medical centers have done a better job than industry and have relied on trained informaticists and informaticians.[1] Though this started by integrating physicians and nurses who had a personal interest or prior training in computer science or IT, we are seeing more master's and PhD-trained people in these roles, in fields such as health informatics, medical informatics, and clinical informatics.

It is more important than ever to create truly cross-functional teams that are comprised of deep technical and deep healthcare expertise. I have seen project after

---

1 Speaking of terminology challenges, we still don't have consensus on whether to use *informaticist* or *informatician* to describe those who are informatics professionals.

project (many in the millions and tens of millions of dollars) fail because of the traditional approach of the IT team focusing solely on the technical details and asking "the business" to come up with clear requirements. This traditional approach (even if/when wrapped in agile methods) fails to address the multiple layers of complexity that exist throughout the healthcare "stack"—from how clinicians interact with patients, to how and why data is collected and processed, to the multitude of analytics use cases.

We need a new approach to organizing teams, projects, and products when tackling RWD projects, particularly in large companies where roles are often more clearly defined. Currently, we often see the separation of the business and IT teams (here, I'm using "IT" inclusively to include both infrastructural IT as well as software engineering/development). What ensues is a sort of call-and-response interaction, as illustrated in Figure 8-3.

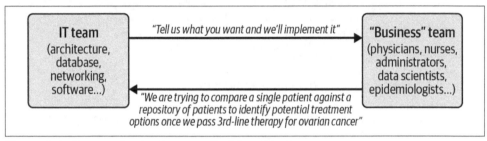

Figure 8-3. Communication between the IT and business teams

The dialogue between the two teams often goes something like (of course, simplified):

IT Team: Tell us what you need…

Business Team: We are trying to compare a single patient against a repository of patients to identify potential treatment options once we pass third-line therapy for ovarian cancer.

IT Team: Well, what sort of data are we going to get? CSV? JSON? Do we *need* to scan for viruses?

Business Team: What do you mean? We are getting a single patient at a time. We heard about FHIR—should we use it?

IT Team: Yes, FHIR is a JSON document, and we can load JSON into RedShift. We can set up a pipeline for malware scanning and data validation.

Business Team: What do you mean by "data validation"?

IT Team: We will check for null/missing values and validate the data types. For example, that there are no strings in numeric fields, or that dates are formatted correctly.

Business Team: How will we validate that we have captured the data correctly with respect to things like line of therapy?

IT Team: Yes, we have ICD-10 codes already loaded in RedShift.

Some of you might be wondering what's the point of this dialogue. Others are probably chuckling. Some might be crying. Unfortunately, this type of dialogue happens all too often and highlights one of the major disconnects between data/business teams and IT teams.

In the previous example, the business team is clearly stating what they want from a data/scientific perspective. On the other hand, the IT team is thinking about it from the perspective of the underlying technology infrastructure. While it would be great to find people who are well versed in both the technology stack as well as epidemiology, evidence generation, clinical practice, reimbursement, and other healthcare domain topics, very few such people exist.

The clean separation between IT and "the business" inevitably slows us down, especially as the use cases and underlying data become increasingly complex. We need to embed clinical and domain experts alongside their technical counterparts. Shortening this gap between "the business" and IT is critical to scaling our ability to leverage RWD for generating insights and ultimately improving the quality of care that patients receive.

Those who bridge this gap are often technologists who develop a good working knowledge of the business or domain experts who pick up technical skills and knowledge. One discipline that fits this perfectly is *medical informatics* (which may be evolving into *health informatics*).

Medical informatics

As I briefly mentioned earlier, medical centers and health systems (particularly academically affiliated ones) have been bridging this gap between the business and IT with a relatively "new" discipline called *medical informatics*. You may also hear the terms *health informatics* or *clinical informatics* often used. The main professional organization for medical informatics in the United States, the American Medical Informatics Association (AMIA), was formed in 1989 as a merger of several existing organizations. So, the field and discipline have been around for many decades, yet few still seem to know or appreciate its role when working with healthcare RWD.

As a field, medical informatics is not well understood, making it quite challenging to establish a clear value proposition. The field of medical informatics is quite broad and encompasses many skills and capabilities, many of which have no direct impact on working with data. However, in the context of this book and RWD, medical informatics plays a critical role bridging the gap between the generation/collection of data and scalable/effective analysis of the data.

Medical informatics professionals who work with data on a daily basis typically have a deep understanding of the following:

- How healthcare data is used in the practice of medicine and delivery of healthcare
- Healthcare data models and their trade-offs
- Clinical vocabularies, terminologies, and ontologies
- Interoperability standards
- Data visualization and analysis

Since medical informatics is not a primary field of study, most come with either a technical background (e.g., software engineering, IT) or a clinical one (e.g., physician, nurse, pharmacist). This is the source of the one of the biggest challenges facing the medical informatics community and profession—the field is so broad, and people come from such different backgrounds. Project and team leaders are constantly trying to find the best-fitting team members, but when everyone has the same title, this becomes quite difficult.

Let's go back to the sample dialogue from earlier—we know we need to build a system that helps match a patient against an existing database of patients. So, we know we need to build a database of patients of some sort, send/receive a single patient's worth of data, and ensure that the appropriate context/meaning of the data are preserved relative to ovarian cancer. But, does this mean we want more technically oriented people? Clinically oriented? Of course, the easiest answer is to say, "Yes! All of the above."

Most recently, I have been advocating a new role, the *medical informatics architect*. This person's main focus is to think through the high-level aspects of the solution from the perspective of the flow of data in the context of the clinical or scientific question. Though similar to a solution architect, this person is less focused on things such as identity management, networking, data storage, or security. Instead, they are focused on which interoperability standard to use, if a terminology service is necessary, or how to define "cancer line of therapy" in a computable way. This person is part solution architect, data architect, data engineer, data scientist, knowledge engineer and healthcare professional. This person needs to be able to ask the right questions, sketch out a high-level solution, and then identify and engage the appropriate subject-matter experts (SME) accordingly.

For the previous example, we would need to engage a traditional solution architect, a data engineer with experience in FHIR, a data scientist who has experience with ovarian cancer and the particular database of existing patients, an oncologist who was familiar with the specific patient population we are matching against our database, and a clinical terminologist with experience in cancer. As we dive deeper into the project, we may need even more specialized skills and knowledge, such as a clinical pharmacist who specializes in oncology. The architect must have enough knowledge and experience to develop the initial architecture, around which the appropriate experts are identified and engage.

The field of medical informatics encompasses much more than architecture and includes other key roles such as the clinical terminologist, clinical informaticist, and analytics engineer. As the healthcare industry continues to learn how best to integrate RWD throughout the value chain, we will see increased focus and utilization of people with backgrounds that naturally span technology, data science, and healthcare/medicine.

While we often look to technology to address many of our challenges, the reality is that technology is (at best) only part of the solution. At worst, it becomes a distraction. I truly believe that scalable impact of healthcare data and analytics requires three pillars—people, process, and technology. In the next section, we spend a bit of time discussing what this actually means for us when working with RWD.

It's a Human, Not Technical, Problem

When I first started attending medical informatics conferences, I remember a speaker who said, "Medical informatics is the application of technology to solve human problems." Unfortunately, I don't remember who this was or I'd buy them a drink!

This statement has stuck with me ever since. As a software engineer, I love thinking about the underlying technology—geeking out on the latest database technologies, machine learning algorithms, or orchestration tools. It is easy to lose sight of the fact that, within healthcare, our primary focus is improving the quality of care patients receive while being sensitive to cost. Clinicians and their patients don't care if we used the latest deep learning approach or if it was a simple bar chart.

The challenges that arise when working with healthcare data are not due to a lack of technology. Yes, the user experience for electronic health records is in the stone ages. Yes, we need to improve the quality of data at the point of collection. However, the answer isn't as simple as deploying a next-generation electronic health record built on bootstrap and angular/vue/react. Nor is it a function of changing the underlying database technology or data model.

The "real world" in RWD means the data reflects the complexities and intricacies of the delivery of healthcare. The reality is that the electronic health record collects data for several different purposes simultaneously—clinicians are trying to communicate with each other and themselves, and administrators are trying to fulfill reimbursement (in both single-payer/national health systems and privately insured systems) and reporting requirements.

In addition to these influencing factors, the practice of medicine itself is always evolving. The standard of care today may not be the standard tomorrow; the standard of care in one health system may not be the standard in another. How we diagnose a condition in a medical oncology practice may be different than in a gynecologic oncology practice. Until we understand the human body and its pathologies and interventions perfectly, there will always be ambiguity and nuances in the data that vary from provider to provider.

So, it then becomes a question of how can we leverage current, state-of-the-art technology in dealing with healthcare RWD? Knowing that these complexities will be there, how do we enable our data scientists and data analysts to operate at the top of their skillset? We know that most data scientists spend most of their time simply trying to access, clean, and process data—I suspect this number is even worse for those working within healthcare.

Though I'm not the first to say it, I'm happy to continue building upon the message: the solution is a combination of people, process, and technology (and, of course, data). Figure 8-4 shows my breakdown, with people being the core foundation (and most important!) part, followed by processes, and, lastly, technology.

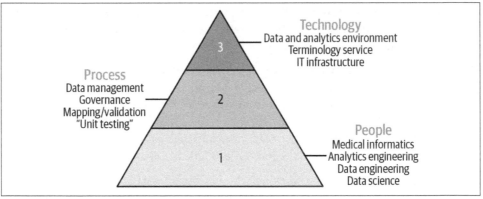

Figure 8-4. People, process, technology

People

We spent a bit of time discussing medical informaticists as a key resource when working with RWD. The key point here is that organizations rely too much on the broad role of "data scientist." It is important to remember that there are many different levels of people that we need to effectively leverage RWD at scale. In addition to clinical informaticists, clinical terminologists, and medical informatics architects, we need to rethink "data science" as a broad brush.

We need data engineers who are deeply familiar with engineering needs with respect to RWD. For example, if we are trying to move terabytes of genomic or imaging data, what is feasible given the functional and nonfunctional requirements? Given the use of terminologies, these data engineers also need to be familiar with semantic web technologies (and particularly, the pros/cons of different approaches, from performance to ease of deployment/management).

We need analytics engineers who have one foot in data engineering and one foot in data science. They are responsible for ensuring that we can effectively map between data models (especially "common" data models) while ensuring that the appropriate context of the data are preserved. So often, I see people assuming that once the data has been cleaned/processed for one use case, it is now usable for any use case. However, there is a good chance that, while cleaning the data for one use case, we've essentially made it impossible to reuse that data.

We all know that we need data analysts and data scientists to take that final step, but are they aware of the decades of best practices that the medical informatics community have discovered over the past several decades? We want to avoid the situation where a data scientist encounters a challenge (such as normalizing ICD-10 and SNOMED codes), only to reinvent a terminology service.

Process

Even with the right people, we need to ensure that our teams are working together effectively and efficiently. Much like software engineering, it is far too easy to let every data scientist go off and do their own data processing and feature engineering. While it's natural to think that this is the best approach (after all, we've hired the best and brightest data scientists, we should let them do what they do best!), it results in a hodgepodge of code and frequent reinvention of the wheel.

I really like the analogy of digging a well for water—some data scientists may want water to cook soup, while others are trying to make bread, yet every single one is digging their own well back to the same source of water. Bringing it back to healthcare data, I've seen multiple data scientists work from the same electronic health record data only to reimplement how they extract a cancer line of therapy. While there are situations where two data scientists need differing definitions of line of therapy, we should be promoting reuse when and where we can.

Whether we choose to follow DataOps, MLops, FAIR, or <insert other buzzword here> principles, the key is that we find a set that works for our teams and use cases. This is particularly important when we move away from biostatistics to machine/deep learning. If we have a model that we retrain when the source data are refreshed, will we be able to detect and differentiate between model drift, changes in the source data, or something else?

Technology

As much as I want to focus on people and processes, there are certainly some key opportunities for us to leverage the right technologies to help us tackle some of the most challenging problems.

Though many of these technologies have been around for a while, many started as academic projects and were often hammers searching for nails. However, I think that we still have ample opportunity to apply these technologies in the right places. For example, with the need to manage terminologies and ontologies, we are seeing increased activity around semantic web technologies, ranging from OWL to RDF triple stores. I continue to believe that rule engines and other inferencing methods are underutilized. Much of what we need to do to scale our ability to wrangle data can be classified as knowledge engineering.

In addition to applying these technologies in the right places, there is also the need to figure out how to scale these. For example, rule engines are quite slow relative to hard-coding some transformations directly in our code. From a data scientist's perspective, why build a more complex system (by including a rule engine) that is orders of magnitude slower when they can just hard-code everything? We know the benefits when it comes to reusability and perhaps reproducibility/replicability, but such benefits don't matter if it takes hours or days to process the data.

Of course, I am a huge proponent of graphs and graph databases. While SPARQL/RDF-based databases give us beautiful semantics and enable very elegant solutions, they may be overkill for our use case or simply beyond the skills/knowledge of our team. Property graphs are a bit more restrictive but can be much easier for developers and data scientists to learn.

Either way, I deeply believe that we are only at the beginning stages of experimenting with graphs (and knowledge graphs) when working with healthcare RWD. This is particularly true when we consider the possibilities in using graphs as part of the data engineering process. While many (most?) interesting uses of graphs involve some sort of analytics applied to the graph, what if we use the graphs as an intermediate representation of the data?

Graphs Can Be Part of the Solution

As we have seen throughout this book, graphs provide a new approach to interacting with RWD, one that embraces the inherently networked nature of healthcare data. While relational databases provide a simple interface to the data via SQL (thus allowing us to connect with an endless number of analytics and visualization tools), they also constrain us in what we can represent.

The nature of performing an extract, transform, load (ETL) of data into a relational database is lossy—this means that we made certain assumptions about the data and lost some information in the process of this transformation. There is also a lot of talk about extract, load, transform (ELT), an approach that I think is absolutely critical to the success of healthcare RWD. We need to be ready to (re)transform the data as our use cases change and evolve.

In this context, what I've essentially proposed throughout this book is a process that includes two transforms—extract, transform, load, transform (ETLT), as shown in Figure 8-5. Here, we have an explicit step where we transform the data into a graph-based structure that allows us to integrate with terminologies/ontologies while capturing and representing as much of the context as possible. Then, we can transform it back to a dataframe, relational database, or other suitable representation, depending on the specific analytics need.

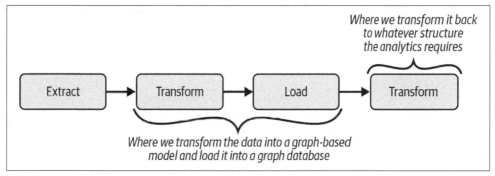

Figure 8-5. ETLT

Despite my own excitement about graphs and how we can integrate them into our data pipelines, the next section is a little bit of a reminder and reality check—that there is no one solution that is "best" or that will address all of our challenges.

Graphs Are Not a Silver Bullet

I am deeply passionate and excited about the potential for graphs across all of healthcare. Whether you are at a digital health company, hospital system, insurance company, or pharma, someone is probably thinking about how to incorporate graphs into the overall data stack.

However, it is also important to note that not every use case requires graphs. Like anything else, graphs are another tool for your toolbox—they are not a silver bullet. If your data are relatively flat and your use case is simple, a relational database or document store may be the appropriate solution. Databases such as ArangoDB try to blur these lines a bit by providing native functionalities that span both document stores as well as graph databases.

One of the main hurdles to the adoption of graphs is that we have so much invested in tabular structures. Whether you are building simple dashboards or applying the latest deep learning approaches, tables and dataframes sit at the heart of nearly every tool or library. Even if graphs are the perfect representation for your data, you need to determine if the mismatch among your existing tools, skills, and knowledge is worth the investment.

For many, the benefits of graphs are worth adding an additional process to the data pipeline that converts a subset of the graph back to a tabular form. Whether this is a viable option ultimately depends on the team, use case, culture, and other elements of your technology stack. While graph database performance is getting better with each release, they still often suffer from performance issues, especially as graphs get bigger.

That said, I'm a believer that new technologies are always worth trying because:

- You will learn something.
- You might discover a novel use case.
- It's just fun.

But, don't lose sight of the problem you're trying to solve and always ask yourself if you're trying to find a silver bullet and/or if you are trying to force a square peg into a round hole simply because it's cool technology.

Conclusion

Thank you for sticking with me this far! We have had quite the discussion around healthcare real-world data, starting with an overview of healthcare RWD and the many different ways this data can be captured. From electronic health records to digital health apps to clinical registries, the very definition of RWD means the possibilities are endless. As the way we care for patients evolves, the data that we generate and collect will also change.

However, regardless of the source of the data, we need to consider the nuances of data we are analyzing and whether it is suitable for the task at hand. We need to consider why the data were collected, who collected the data, the underlying study protocol (if any), and other biases that may be present in the data. If we are analyzing data collected prospectively using a clear study protocol, we may not have as much of a harmonization challenge, even if the data was collected across multiple organizations or institutions. On the other hand, if we are performing a retrospective analysis of EHR data that was collected by clinicians during routine patient care, we will have a lot of work ahead of us to harmonize the data.

You've probably heard me mention it so many times that you think I'm a broken record. The most common failure I have seen in projects involved RWD is the failure to appreciate the cost and complexity of harmonizing healthcare data. I often hear seasoned data scientists from other industries say something along the lines of "If healthcare would just do a better job of collecting data, we would be able to…." This is exactly the point—the complexities of the healthcare system and the practice of medicine are inherent to the field. Our understanding of the human body is constantly evolving, and each patient is a unique combination of genetics, pathophysiologies, lifestyle, diet, and other factors that contribute to the "dirtiness" of the data that we end up with.

Success with RWD requires that we embrace these differences and find techniques for mitigating the heterogeneity of the data. In my first startup, my co-founder and I came up with the phrase *mass customization*. It is certainly an oxymoron but also highlights the opportunity for innovative approaches. How do we balance the need to customize our data harmonization pipelines while also making the process scalable?

This is where graph databases have tremendous opportunity and so we spent a bit of time exploring a variety of different types of graph databases. Like most computer science tools/libraries, each has particular strengths and weaknesses. It is difficult to say that one is categorically better than another—it really is a matter of matching your functional and nonfunctional requirements to the databases.

Of course, graph databases shine when we start to incorporate elements such as controlled vocabularies, terminologies, and ontologies. Healthcare is ahead of many other fields when it comes to incorporating formalized semantic concepts. As with all human knowledge, the underlying semantics of these concepts vary from one use case to the next. So, we often see multiple different terminologies and ontologies that overlap with one another. Graph databases make it easy for us to store and manage these mappings in a natural way. More importantly, graph query languages allow us to traverse the graph in ways that SQL would not.

You have seen how we can use graph query languages to link data from both electronic health records and claims data. It is difficult to demonstrate all of the many possibilities on how we can integrate RWD, controlled vocabularies and then query the combined dataset. Ideally, the examples provided within this book have given you a starting point from which you can experiment and get creative!

Whether you're working with EHR data, claims data, or any other source of RWD, you will likely run into many other situations that we did not cover in this book. Natural language processing is still an active area of research and one that quickly intersects semantic computing and other aspects of knowledge engineering, both of which heavily leverage graph technologies. Consequently, I would expect increasing crossover between NLP and graphs, particularly the integration of graph embeddings.

Outside of NLP, trends such as federated analytics or federated learning also highlight the need for good data harmonization. This is one area where graphs may be an implementation detail—that is, a particular site may choose to use graphs to aid in the data harmonization process. Given the maturity needed across the federated learning libraries and platforms, and across the sites themselves, it might be difficult to directly link graph databases into the system. Regardless of the specific approach, federated setups absolutely require solid data harmonization across the entire network. It would otherwise be nearly impossible to discern between a poorly performing model because there is no signal or pattern to be found and a poorly performing model because the data has not been properly harmonized across the network.

Ultimately, success with RWD requires that we do a better job crossing the boundaries between what is traditionally "just IT" and what is "the business." The data is complex, and the approaches to harmonizing the data are also complex. What may be a beautiful solution from a semantic perspective may be intractable from a computational one, or vice versa. As an industry, we need more people who are well versed in the nuances of healthcare data, particularly RWD, as well as software engineering, data engineering, data science, semantic computing, terminologies and ontologies, and the practice of medicine itself. Medical informatics as a discipline begins to bridge this gap. However, even with an expert team of medical informaticists, we still need deeply technical people to learn more about healthcare data and clinicians to learn more about IT and data.

Only then will we be able to leverage the ever-increasing amounts of RWD to improve the quality and efficiency of care that healthcare systems can provide patients. Whether we are trying to make sure the right patient gets the right treatment at the right time, trying to predict high-risk patients, or simply improving hospital operations, RWD is the future of healthcare.

People often say "data is the new oil." I totally agree with this analogy but would extend it to say that many think we can take this oil and immediately use it to drive improved decision-making without first properly refining it. The refinery process is costly, cumbersome, and tedious but is absolutely necessary. It is also a tailored process to the desired end state. Whether we are making jet fuel or the plastic used in IV bags, we need to set up the refinery accordingly. Just as it is silly to think that we can set up a refinery for jet fuel and expect to use it for any other application, thinking that we can clean, process, and harmonize the data once for all use cases is just as silly.

Regardless of your background, company, or role, I hope this book has given you a deeper appreciation for the challenges and opportunities when working with healthcare real-world data. Most importantly, I hope it has given both talking points and concrete examples on how to approach RWD so that you can help your organizations and leadership build up teams with the appropriate people, processes, and technology to truly leverage RWD with the ultimate goal of helping patients.

Index

About the Author

Andrew Nguyen has been working at the intersection of healthcare data and AI for more than a decade. He quickly discovered graph databases and has been using them to harmonize disparate data sources for nearly as long. He has worked for a variety of organizations ranging from academia to startups. Andrew is currently a medical informatics architect and leads the Data Architecture and Informatics capability for real-world data at one of the largest biopharma companies in the world, where he is designing scalable solutions to harmonize healthcare RWD sources for all levels of analytics from statistics to machine learning. Prior to his current role, he served as chair of the Department of Health Professions, and director of the MS in Health Informatics program at the University of San Francisco. He also taught classes in medical informatics, semantic interoperability, machine learning, clinical natural language processing, and biosignal/time series data analysis. Andrew holds a PhD in biological and medical informatics from the University of California, San Francisco (UCSF) and a BS in electrical and computer engineering from the University of California, San Diego (UCSD). In his spare time, he enjoys photography, hiking/backpacking, and SCUBA diving, and serves as the technical rescue coordinator for his local Search and Rescue team.

Colophon

The animals on the cover of *Hands-On Healthcare Data* are hanging parrots, small birds in the genus *Loriculus* found in tropical southern Asia.

There are fourteen identified species of hanging parrot, all with striking bright green plumage and short tails. Often, a spot of color on a hanging parrot's head or throat can help classify an individual species; such is the case for the blue-crowned hanging parrot (*Loriculus galgulus*) and the Sri Lanka hanging parrot (*Loriculus beryllinus*)—which has an orange crown.

These parrots are unique among birds for their ability to sleep upside down by hanging from tree branches using both feet, or occasionally only a single foot, fluffing their feathers, and tucking their heads. This behavior is a protective measure against nighttime predators, disguising the inverted parrots as bright green leaves.

Certain species of hanging parrot are threatened by habitat loss. Many of the animals on O'Reilly covers are endangered; all of them are important to the world.

The cover illustration is by Karen Montgomery, based on an antique line engraving from Lydekker's *Royal Natural History*. The cover fonts are Gilroy Semibold and Guardian Sans. The text font is Adobe Minion Pro; the heading font is Adobe Myriad Condensed; and the code font is Dalton Maag's Ubuntu Mono.

Lightning Source UK Ltd.
Milton Keynes UK
UKHW052108290822
407898UK00013B/19